THE SURVIVORS

Lovely twenty-year-old Beth Wilmot survived to give graphic details of how she and her girl friend were forced to sexually submit to the handsome young man with adhesive tape over his nose, then were shot and left for dead by him.

Eighteen-year-old Jill Martin survived being robbed, sexually used, and locked up as her victimizer made his swift escape.

Attractive divorcée Arden Bates survived having the handsome young man living in her house and using his room as his sexual launching pad, yet she could not believe the truth about him.

Beautiful co-ed Shelly Janson survived falling in love with him and trying to make his most bizarre sexual fantasies come true.

But of the nearly fifty women who ranged from mothers of families to eleven-year-olds, few survived to help a police and prosecution team to free the Pacific coast from the one-man sexual scourge known as—

THE
I-5 KILLER

THE I-5 KILLER

ANN RULE
WRITING AS ANDY STACK

NEWLY UPDATED

A SIGNET BOOK

NEW AMERICAN LIBRARY

A DIVISION OF PENGUIN BOOKS USA INC.

Copyright © 1984, 1988 by Ann Rule

All rights reserved

SIGNET TRADEMARK REG. U.S. PAT. OFF. AND FOREIGN COUNTRIES
REGISTERED TRADEMARK—MARCA REGISTRADA
HECHO EN DRESDEN, TN, U.S.A.

SIGNET, SIGNET CLASSIC, MENTOR, ONYX, PLUME, MERIDIAN
and NAL BOOKS are published by New American Library, a division of
Penguin Books USA Inc., 1633 Broadway, New York, New York 10019

First Printing, March, 1984
Fourth Printing (*First Printing*, Revised Edition), December 1988

7 8 9 10 11 12 13 14 15

PRINTED IN THE UNITED STATES OF AMERICA

Dedication

This book is dedicated to Beth Wilmot for her courage in testifying against Randall Brent Woodfield, and to the memory of Shari Hull, Donna Lee Eckard, Janell Jarvis, and Julie Reitz.

With deep appreciation to the scores of lawmen who worked so many overtime hours to catch the "I-5 Killer":

In Oregon: Marion County Sheriff's Office, Salem Police Department, Marion County District Attorney's Office, Oregon State Attorney General's Office, Beaverton Police Department, Eugene Police Department, Springfield Police Department, Corvallis Police Department, Medford Police Department, Ashland Police Department, Grants Pass Police Department, Sutherlin Police Department, Linn County District Attorney's Office, Benton County District Attorney's Office, Lane County District Attorney's Office, Multnomah County Sheriff's Office, Oregon State Police.

In California: Shasta County Sheriff's Office, Redding Police Department, Yreka Police Department, Shasta County District Attorney's Office.

In Washington: King County Police Department, Clark County Sheriff's Office, Bellevue Police Department, Bothell Police Department, Olympia Police Department, Vancouver Police Department.

With the author's utmost respect for the efforts of Dave Kominek, Monty Holloway, Dave Bishop, Neal Loper, Ron Womack, Ron Griesel, Gene Farley, Rick Burnett, Rusty Brewer, Chris Van Dyke, and Lisa Cisneros.

For he that said, "Do not commit adultery" said also "Do not kill." Now, if thou commit no adultery, yet if thou kill, thou art become a transgressor of the law.

So speak ye, and so do, as they that shall be judged by the law of liberty.

For he shall have judgment without mercy that hath showed no mercy; and mercy rejoiceth against judgment.

What doth it profit, my brethren, though he say he had faith, and have not works? Can faith save him?

—James 2:11–14

For nothing is secret, that shall not be made manifest; neither any thing hid, that shall not be known.

—Luke 8:17

Prologue

The crimes began in a scatter pattern. One here. Another there. And another hundreds of miles and another state away. There was, in the beginning, no commonality. All of the victims were females, but then, females are often victims of violent crime. Some of the victims were teenagers, some were mature women, and two were only children. *He* had not yet achieved a nickname, and in the seventies and eighties, all "big-time" criminals had nicknames: Son of Sam, the Hillside Strangler, Ted, the Atlanta Killer, the Sunset Strip Killer, the Green River Killer.

He had no nickname, and he liked it that way.

As far as anyone knew, his crimes had been committed by a number of different men. As far as anyone knew, there was no pattern, only a series of isolated incidents.

One day soon, he would be deemed the "I-5 Bandit," and than the "I-5 Killer," the scourge of an eight-hundred-mile stretch of the freeway that follows the Pacific Coast from British Columbia to the Mexican border, and he would become the prime quarry for hundreds of frustrated detectives.

He did not mind his anonymity. Far from it, he reveled in it. As long as lawmen did not give him a name or a connection to the attacks, he was free to do as he liked.

The first incident occurred in Vancouver, Washington, at five-twenty in the evening on December 9, 1980. A twenty-two-year-old female cashier at Eddie's Arco station was robbed by a tall dark-haired man wearing an obviously fake beard. The spirit gum used to affix the beard had loosened so much that the beard was about to fall off.

"He showed me this small silver gun," the young woman told Clark County deputies, "and he said, 'It's for real.' "

She gave him the money in the till, and he told her to turn

around and "watch TV." He was referring to a surveillance camera that, unfortunately, was malfunctioning; the tape had stuck between the camera heads.

A composite picture drawn from the victim's recollection of her attacker showed a dark-eyed man with a beard, a young man.

On December 13, in Eugene, Oregon—108 miles south of Vancouver—a man with a fake beard and a Band-Aid across the bridge of his nose walked into the Baskin-Robbins ice-cream parlor on Villard Street at six P.M., brandished a silver pistol, and forced the clerk to give him the contents of the cash register.

"Now, turn around and walk into the back room and stay there, and don't do anything stupid," he ordered.

As she walked away from him, she fully expected to be shot in the back, but he left without harming her.

"It was so strange," she told the officer who took her report. "Fifteen minutes before he came in, there was a real grubby-looking kid in here who told me how easy this place would be to rob. *He* just bought an ice-cream cone and left, and then this clean-cut guy comes in and robs me."

The next evening two eighteen-year-old clerks at the Arctic Circle drive-in in Albany, Oregon, encountered a bearded man. He walked up to the drive-in window carrying a used Arctic Circle bag and a paper cup. He asked the girl on duty to fill the cup with water and throw the bag away. Then he asked for a clean sack. As he talked, he watched traffic on the street. When the street was empty of cars, he handed the sack back to her and barked, "Fill it up."

"I don't understand," she said.

And then she lowered her eyes and she did understand. She saw that the man was pointing a silver gun at her heart. She was so frightened that she forgot which buttons to push on the computer cash register and had to call her fellow worker to do it. The bag was filled with two hundred and eighty dollars in cash, and the big man turned and ran swiftly away.

Four days before Christmas, a man answering the same description popped up more than two hundred miles north of Albany—in Seattle. But this time the man wanted more than money.

Kim Meehan, twenty-five, worked as a waitress at Church's Fried Chicken in Lake Forest Park, north of Seattle. Feeling nauseated during the early evening, Kim called her father at nine to ask him to come and pick her up. In the women's restroom she bathed her face with cold water. Suddenly there was a loud knock on the door, and she looked up to see a man pushing his way in. He grinned at her and said "Excuse me." But he didn't leave. Instead, he turned and locked the door behind him.

He pulled a silver revolver from the pocket of his hooded coat and ordered her to take her blouse off. "Do what I say and you won't get hurt."

She was struck almost dumb with shock, and she thought that this couldn't be happening—not with the other employees just on the other side of the restroom wall. She couldn't move, and the man, who wore a peculiar ragged beard, moved toward her and pulled up her blouse and bra and started to fondle her breasts.

"Now," he said, "I want you to beat me off."

"I don't know how," she countered.

"I'll show you how," he said, and moved the gun closer to her head.

She had no choice. She did what he asked, and after about two minutes the man ejaculated on her breasts. "That was good," he said calmly. "Now, you stay in here for five minutes. Count to a hundred and nobody will get hurt."

And then he was gone as suddenly as he'd appeared. She wanted to scream, but she thought he might still be outside listening. She waited five minutes before she pounded on the wall and screamed for help.

The restaurant's fry cook called the police and told King County deputies that he could describe the man too.

"I can't believe it," he muttered. "That guy was in here; he ordered a number-five dinner, and paid for it. He must have seen Kim walk back to the restroom. He was wearing a hooded brown corduroy or suede jacket with a sheepskin lining."

Twenty minutes later, the man in the brown jacket—minus his fake beard—lingered over an ice-cream cone he'd ordered at the Baskin-Robbins store in Bothell, Washington. The two teenage girls working that night were ready to lock the doors at ten P.M., but the man hung around. They whispered to each other, joking: "Maybe he's planning to mug us or something." They giggled.

The big man asked them to throw away the last of his cone. Then he wanted some ice water. They could offer him only tap water. He took one sip and asked for a lid for his water cup. Then he asked for a straw and a paper sack. He had played out this script before, but the girls in Bothell didn't know that. They just thought the guy was pretty nervous and a little peculiar, and they wanted him out of there.

Savoring the moment, the tall dark man slowly pulled his

revolver from his pocket. "Now, put all the money in the bag."

"All the money" at closing time meant a good haul: over five hundred dollars. The gunman ordered the two girls to sit on the floor, count to fifty, and look the other way as he left. They obeyed, but they remembered a lot about him. He had not had a car, at least not in the Baskin-Robbins lot. He was probably in his mid-twenties, good-looking, with a full mustache, tan complexion, and a thick head of dark brown curly hair. He'd worn blue jeans, a maroon-and-blue rugby-type shirt with a V neck trimmed in white, the brown suede jacket with sheepskin lining. The gun was silver, and they'd seen a round cylinder.

They did not know how lucky they'd been; it had been only twenty minutes since Kim Meehan was abused in the Church's restroom a few miles away, and he did not sexually attack the girls in Baskin-Robbins.

There was a spate of calm between December 21, 1980, and January 8, 1981. The man with the silver gun was apparently celebrating Christmas and New Year's.

With the new year, it looked as if he was starting all over again. He hit Eddie's Arco in Vancouver at nine-eighteen P.M., the same service station he'd robbed on December 9. Only the cashier on duty was different. He had the same small silver gun. The frightened woman handed over something less than a hundred dollars.

"Sit down on the floor," he ordered, "and take off your shirt. Lift your bra."

She did as she was told, and he gazed at her intently for a minute, and smiled, as she described it later: "evilly. Then he said either 'okay' or 'ugly'—I'm not sure which and I didn't care—and told me to count to fifty slowly. He left on foot."

This time the surveillance camera had been in good working order. The gunman's image had been captured. He was tall with frizzing curly hair, a fake beard, and he wore a hooded velour sweat jacket and blue jeans. He also wore dark "ski-type" gloves with light-colored stripes on the thumbs and fingers.

On January 11 the Grocery Cart Market in Eugene was robbed at seven-twenty P.M. by the oddly bearded gunman who wore, always, a Band-Aid over his nose and a hooded jacket and blue jeans. This time, too, he'd had on ski gloves, dark blue with white palms. He asked for Vantage cigarettes, and then for the money in the till. His take was only thirty-five dollars.

Twenty-four hours later he was in Sutherlin, Oregon, fifty

miles south on the I-5. Susie Benet, twenty, worked that Tuesday night as a cook at the Central Market in Sutherlin. She was alone, and had been for about fifteen minutes, as she watched television on the set about ten feet from the cash register. A tall man wearing a red knit hat and a green windbreaker jacket walked in, and she turned to wait on him. His complexion was dark, what she could see of it; he wore two Band-Aids across the bridge of his nose.

"Give me the money from the till."

She started to laugh, thinking that he was kidding her. He had a funny look on his face, as if he were teasing.

"Sure," she kidded back.

And then she saw that it wasn't a joke. He drew a revolver from his jacket, a nickel-plated gun with a short barrel. "This is a real gun," he warned.

Susie Benet just stood there for a moment, and that angered the gunman. He reached across the counter and grabbed her by the blouse.

And then he let go and the gun boomed. She felt something hit her and bounce off. She didn't know that she had been shot. She walked slowly around the counter to the cash register, and the man followed her, still pointing the gun at her. She looked down at her right shoulder and saw bright red blood staining her blouse. She wondered hazily why she could still stand up and walk around. She thought bullets killed people.

"Now, get down on the floor and stay there," he ordered.

"No," she begged. "No, I'll get the money for you."

"Just stay on the floor."

She heard him open the cash drawer, but she didn't dare look; she thought if she could just hide behind the counter he couldn't shoot her again. Finally she heard him leave. There had been three hundred dollars in the cash register, but it was gone when she staggered over to the phone to call an ambulance.

Medics found that Susie Benet had been very lucky; she had a through-and-through gunshot wound with entry in the upper-right shoulder and the exit slightly higher in her back. A few inches lower and the bullet would have pierced her lung.

Sergeant Bill Caldwell of the Sutherlin Police Department responded to Susie's call for help. He did not question her, due to the seriousness of her injuries, but later in the hospital Susie Benet described the man who had shot her.

Caldwell was able to retrieve the bullet where it had bounced behind a shelf along the wall. He also lifted a single print from the back of a check in the till; the gunman had had to lift the check to get to the cash beneath it. But the print was useless; it had been left by someone wearing gloves made of nonporous cloth.

For the first time, a possible vehicle was mentioned. A jogger had seen a Volkswagen Bug parked near the Central Market just before the shooting. All he could remember was that there was something "unusual" about the car.

The robber took one night off, but the next night he was prowling again.

On January 14, 1981, in Corvallis, Oregon, Merrisue Green, ten, and her eight-year-old sister, Megan, had been left alone in their home for only forty-five minutes; their mother routinely went to work out at a health club right after supper on week nights. Mrs. Green left the girls at five-thirty; they were happily watching television, and she promised to be back at a quarter after six.

Ten minutes later the doorbell rang, and Merrisue went to answer it. Before she opened the door, she flipped on the porch light, but the bulb remained dark. There was a big man standing there, a stranger. He wore a brown suede jacket with a hood, blue jeans, blue-and-white ski gloves, and jogging shoes.

He smiled at Merrisue and brushed past her without being invited into the house. "My car broke down," he said. "I need to use the phone. Where is it?"

The child pointed toward the kitchen. The big man was already in the house, and she didn't know how to ask him to leave. She watched him dial, but she suspected he was just making up numbers. He hung up the phone and turned toward her. "The line's busy. Where's your mother?"

Her words popped out before she thought, and then it was too late. "She's at the gym. She'll be back in half an hour."

He smiled and looked at the two little girls. "Can I watch TV with you?"

"No," Merrisue said firmly. "You can call somebody, but then you have to go. We'll wait by the door until you're finished with the phone."

She heard him dial again and talk to somebody named "Jim," but she wasn't sure there was really anyone on the other end. She'd seen bad guys do that on television, just pretend to talk to someone. He was telling "Jim" that his car had broken down and he needed a ride. Jim was supposed to pick him up by Albertson's supermarket.

Merrisue hadn't heard a car outside, and she couldn't understand why he had picked their house to come to.

The man smiled at her again, but there was something about him that made her shiver. She wished she hadn't answered the door.

"Can I just stay in the house to keep warm?" he asked. "I could watch TV with you until my friend gets here."

"No. I told you no. We're not supposed to let strangers in."

"But I'm already in," he argued.

"I'm scared," Megan whispered. She ran into the master bathroom, leaving Merrisue alone with the tall dark man.

"I think I'll just watch some television with you," he coaxed.

"No," she faltered. "I told you you couldn't."

And then the man pulled a silver gun out of his pocket and grabbed her by the shoulder. "This is a real gun. You get into the bathroom where your sister is. You do what I say."

She did what he said. Grown women had been terrified by this man and his silver gun. Merrisue was so frightened she could barely walk. The man showed the gun to Megan too.

"Now, both of you, take off your clothes."

The gunman subjected the children to the same abuse that his adult victims had endured. The fact that they were only children didn't seem to bother him at all. He fondled Merrisue's barely discernible breasts and complained at their smallness. He touched eight-year-old Megan's genitals while she sobbed in terror. And then he revealed his erect penis and demanded that they fellate him, that they masturbate him. Terrorized, they obeyed. He ejaculated and forced his ten-year-old victim to swallow semen.

In shock over a bestial act she could not understand, and gagging, Merrisue wiped her face and mouth with a towel. She thought that the man was probably going to shoot them. He toyed with the gun while the little girls cringed against the tub. Merrisue prayed that it was only a toy gun. After a long time the man told them to get dressed and that they must stay in the bathroom. If they came out, something bad would happen to them. They clung together, afraid that he was still someplace in the house.

At ten minutes after six their mother came home. Despite the January chill, the front door was standing wide open. Alarmed, she walked into the kitchen and saw that the phone was off the hook. When she tried to replace the receiver, she couldn't find it. It wasn't anyplace in the room.

She called for her children, and heard Merrisue answer from the bathroom, "Can we come out now?"

Running toward the bathroom, she met her daughters.

"There's a burglar in the house," Merrisue gasped. "I think he's still here."

Mrs. Green didn't stop to look around; she grabbed her children and ran for a neighbor's house, where she called the Corvallis police.

Merrisue and Megan made excellent witnesses; they had memorized everything they could about their attacker. They'd seen the "San Francisco" label on his blue jeans, the white X's on the back.

"He had a beard—a funny beard," Merrisue told detectives. "I don't think it was real. I don't think the gun was real, either. I think it was a toy gun. He was going to shoot us, but he couldn't."

It had not been a toy gun, of course. It was a real gun.

The Corvallis attack outraged lawmen. Taboos as old as civilization had been broken. Initially the perversions against the Green children seemed to have no connection to the fast-food robberies. Even sexual psychopaths have "rules." It is rare indeed for men who attack mature females to violate children or for pedophiles to seek out adult women as victims. When a sexual criminal moves outside his victim pattern, it is an indication that he is in the grip of almost maniacal frenzy.

He was a murder looking for a place to happen.

And, still, the man with the silver gun retained his anonymity. He was very clever. He knew the value of moving on before investigators could link him to a series of crimes. He knew the limitations of their teletype networks.

1

Salem, Oregon, January 18, 1981, 21:45 hours.

The big man ran fluidly and easily, an athlete's effortless movement. Through the dark streets he ran, turning here, turning again, leaving the bleeding women behind him. The adrenaline he'd always felt on the playing field when the pressure was on coursed full strength through his blood, making him feel as though he could run ten miles, twenty miles, without stopping. He could do anything!

He *had* done it; he had orchestrated the whole scene to his own plan. He had found the girls there, just as if they were waiting for him, and he had made them do all the things he liked. He had humbled them, and toyed with them, and finally he had destroyed them. He felt as if he were the most powerful male who had ever lived; he was consumed with his own power. No woman would ever, *ever* control him again.

The streets were so quiet, as quiet as death itself. No one had seen him. No one would ever know that he had been the one.

It was cold, but he was perspiring, just the way he always did in sports. This *was* a kind of sport, if you looked at it from the proper perspective. Stalking the women, finding them, and then being so strong and confident that they obeyed his orders.

But this game had been the best game so far; this was the first time he had killed women simply because they were female. Strangers. Nobodies. If they weren't dead by now, they soon would be.

They wouldn't tell on him the way girls always tattled. They could only lie there in pools of their own blood, silenced . . . punished.

He allowed himself to stop running. He walked easily now,

pulling his hood closer around his face. He felt invisible. He didn't even need to look away from the headlights that were bearing down on him. He *was* invisible.

Salem, Oregon, January 18, 1981, 21:54 hours.

Salem Fire and Ambulance Dispatch Hot Line: 911.

Zena Harp and Dave Cameron were working the late-evening shift on this black, moonless Sunday. A quiet night; there was time to talk, time to complain desultorily about the weather—as if the threat of rain were not the expected, accepted condition for January in Oregon. And yet, they were not bored. No one is ever bored while manning an emergency hot line. The next call—or the one after that—may signal catastrophe.

Now, just six minutes before ten P.M., the phone *brrr*-ed, its red bubble light blinking frantically. Zena Harp reached for the receiver, and Dave Cameron picked up another to monitor the call.

And, instantly, each of them tensed. This was not a routine call; this was trouble. They heard a woman's voice, a faint voice, full of pain and terror.

"We've been shot . . . please help us!"

Zena Harp kept her own voice calm; she had to find out location, specifics, before she could send help. "Where are you?"

There was a long pause, so long that Ms. Harp thought the caller had gone off the line. And then the voice came again, more faint, if possible, than it had been before. ". . . River Road . . . or Commercial Street."

"What address?"

". . . near the Fun Machine."

Dave Cameron had heard enough; he knew where the Fun Machine was—on the outskirts of Salem near Keizer—and he could pinpoint the location enough to dial the telephone operator and ask for an emergency trace. Within moments the operator reported that the call was coming in from the TransAmerica Title Building.

Now Cameron reacted almost automatically, asking the operator to patch the call into the Salem Police Department's Communications Center. And then he dispatched paramedics from the Keizer Fire Department and an ambulance to the building where the woman waited.

While this was being done, Zena Harp talked to the terrified woman.

"Please hurry," the girl begged. "He's gonna come back and kill me. I think she's dead. . . ."

"Do you want me to stay on the line?" Ms. Harp soothed. "An ambulance is on the way."

The girl on the other end was drifting away. Her voice was thready, and her answers weren't responsive. "Oh . . . oh, I think she's dead."

The patch had been made within a matter of a few minutes. Zena Harp handed the caller over to the Salem police dispatcher.

Liz Cameron, the Com Center operator for the Salem Police Department, spoke to the woman in the TransAmerica Title Building. There was no time now to speculate on why anyone would be in the office building late on a Sunday evening. Liz knew that an ambulance and Marion County Sheriff's squad cars were on the way. She had to find out as much as she could. If the gunman was still in the building, the officers had to be warned.

"Ma'am," Liz Cameron began, "what is your name?"

"Beth Wilmot. I've been shot in the head. *Hurry!*"

"We have an ambulance on the way. Who shot you?"

"Some man . . . I don't know . . . with a gun."

"Okay."

"We were cleaning the office, and he came in."

"Okay. We have somebody on the way. Can you tell me what he looked like at all?"

"Ah . . . Oh, my God. He had dark brown hair."

"Dark brown hair."

"And he had . . . he had a Band-Aid on his nose."

"Okay. Was he a white man?"

"Yes."

"About how old would you say he is?"

"Oh, I don't know. Around twenty-seven."

"Okay, and how tall?"

"Oh, I . . . ah, five ah nine, six foot, I don't know. Something like that. Five-nine, a little over the average size of a—"

"Do you remember what he was wearing?"

To a layman, Cameron's questions might seem harsh, but she was sending policemen into an area where they might well be perfect targets. They had to know who their enemy was. The woman on the phone sounded weak but rational. Later, Liz Cameron would marvel at the victim's ability to respond—later, when she learned the extent of the girl's injuries.

"Do you remember what he was wearing?" Liz Cameron probed.

"Oh . . . ah . . . ah . . a coat . . . ah."

"A coat."

"Ah . . . leather coat, or something."

"A leather coat."

"And a pair of cheap jeans."

"And jeans. Okay, you stay right on this phone with me. We have several people on the way."

"I'll wait."

"And we have an ambulance coming too."

"Could I just give you a number so you . . . so I could call home, please, just call them . . ."

"I'd like to keep you on the line, if I could, until a deputy arrives and makes sure you are all right."

"Oh, my head . . . Hurry. It hurts."

There was another long pause. Liz wondered if Beth had lost consciousness, and then her voice came again, pleading for help.

"I hurt . . . I hear the ambulance."

"Just a minute more."

"Poor Shari is going to die."

"The lady who was shot?" The police dispatcher thought that Beth was talking about her own injuries. The whole conversation was garbled—the frantic girl on the phone, and Liz Cameron trying to keep a lid on the hysteria she could hear bubbling up.

"She is going to die. We didn't do anything."

"Okay. The ambulance should be there anytime."

"Talk to me," the girl pleaded. "So you'll make me feel better, please."

"Okay. I'll talk to you, Beth. How do you feel now? Any better?"

". . . ah . . . ah, a little better."

"Okay. You just calm down. There's going to be somebody there shortly. Is there anyone else there with—?"

"I should go home now, but I hurt."

"Is there anybody else there with you?"

"Yes, my girlfriend."

"Okay, what's your girlfriend's name?"

"Shari Hull."

"Is she waiting for the ambulance to let them in?"

"It's open. The door's open."

"Okay. Which way did the man go when he left? Did you see?"

"I don't know—my head was down. I was on the ground when he shot us. He told us to put our heads down."

"Okay. Well, we have somebody almost there. We are going to let them talk to you . . . and is your friend there? I could talk to her too."

"Oh," the girl cried, "I don't know what happened. She's on the ground. Please don't talk to her. She's . . . I think . . . almost dead."

"Did he shoot her?" Liz Cameron had thus far thought that Beth Wilmot was the only victim—that Beth's friend was waiting to signal in the deputies and the ambulance. Now the situation sounded even more desperate than it had first appeared.

"Yes."

"He shot—"

"He shot five times," the girl blurted.

"He shot her as well?"

"Yes. Yes, three times. I can hear her breathing really hard. I'm afraid he's going to come back. *Please hurry!*"

"Okay. We have people on the way. Okay, have you ever seen him before? Did he leave in a vehicle—you know—a car?"

"I don't know. Her truck is running though."

"Her truck is running?"

"Yes."

"Okay. What kind of a truck does she have?"

"She has a Bronco."

"A Bronco."

"A green Bronco 'cause we had it running 'cause we were about to leave."

"Okay. Which room are you in there? Is there . . . is it—?"

"It's just a little office."

"Okay, just a minute, Beth. Okay. We have somebody who will be there real shortly. You keep talking to me. Can you give me your home phone number in case we need that?"

"555-5411. It's an answering service, but nobody is home and they will . . . Oh! Somebody is here."

"Okay. Somebody there now?"

"The ambulance. Can I hang up now?"

"Okay. You *see* the ambulance?"

"Yes."

"Okay, you go over to the ambulance now."

"Bye-bye," the girl named Beth whispered.

2

The TransAmerica Title Building—from which the frantic call for help had come—was only one of several in the business complex on River Road, the area just beyond Salem's city limits. The complex was new construction, solid modern buildings and businesses separated by parking areas. On a weekday, the region would have been full of people, but on this gloomy black Sunday, the entire complex seemed hollow and deserted. Even the eating establishments nearby were closed; their customers were home for the weekend.

Indeed, aside from the two girls who were in the TransAmerica Building, only a handful of people were in the entire complex.

Two women worked in the back room of the Celebrations Designs bridal shop almost directly across the parking lot from the entrance to the TransAmerica offices. Dorothy Hall, the owner of the custom-bridal-gown shop, had had no choice that afternoon; she had promised to have a bridal gown and bridesmaids' dresses finished in time for a wedding. She had worked in the sewing room of her shop since late afternoon, stitching beading, lace, yards and yards of delicate wedding finery. One of her seamstresses, Bev Johnson, worked with her, and Mrs. Hall's daughter, Patrice Walters, had promised to come in later to help.

Mrs. Hall had felt a little uneasy all afternoon. She'd commented to Ms. Johnson how lonely and almost "spooky" the mall seemed when its weekday inhabitants were gone; it seemed a modern ghost town, all concrete and walls of black windows that only occasionally reflected headlights of the few cars that passed by. She regretted that she had asked her daughter to come down in the evening to work alone. Even though her shop locked up tightly, she worried.

Time had passed rapidly throughout the afternoon and into the evening, and Mrs. Hall was surprised when her daughter arrived and announced that it was a quarter after nine. The gowns were almost finished, and Patrice said she would stay and put on the finishing touches. The three women chatted for a few minutes, and Mrs. Hall heard the nine-thirty news broadcast come on the little radio in the back room. She looked at the clock then to confirm the time, and left with her seamstress, but only after warning Patrice again to be sure that she kept the doors locked and the lights out in the showroom facing the mall.

"Don't advertise that anybody's in here," she told her daughter. "Just stay back in the sewing room, and don't stay late."

Dorothy Hall was exhausted and anxious to get home for a hot bath and something to eat, but as she walked to her car, she saw that there was a reddish four-wheel-drive vehicle with its motor running, parked on the south side of the TransAmerica Building. Seeing the unfamiliar vehicle there, and knowing her daughter was alone, she was disturbed as she drove away from the area, disturbed enough that she turned her car around and came back.

She saw that the lights were on in the TransAmerica Building, and she drove slowly around the structure to see if anyone was inside. It was easy to see in; the building had window walls on all four sides, and the windows fronting the parking lot had only tie-back curtains. The windows on the River Road side were covered now by blinds. But even with the blinds, it was possible to see every part of the building from the outside, all of the rooms except for the employees' lunchroom.

The parked truck was empty. Odd that it should be sitting there empty with its motor running. But then Mrs. Hall looked into the TransAmerica Building and was suddenly relieved. She saw two young girls dressed in old clothes—obviously a janitorial crew. One of the girls was down on her hands and knees scrubbing the foyer of the building and the other stood beside her with a broom in her hands. The front door of the building was closed, and presumably locked. The bridal-shop owner concluded that the unfamiliar truck belonged to the girls who were cleaning.

Mrs. Hall eased her car slowly out of the mall. She saw no one else, no one walking, no other cars. The area north of the complex was deserted too, except for two boys she saw cleaning the floors of an ice-cream parlor.

One thought struck her; the boys were moving vigorously as they swabbed the ice creamery's floors, and the girls in the TransAmerica Building seemed like frozen statues in comparison.

And then Mrs. Hall drove on home.

It was nine-thirty-five P.M.

Patrice Walters sewed for an hour in the back room of the bridal shop. She had the radio turned down low, and she heard a loud bang somewhere between nine-thirty and ten P.M. It sounded as if someone had slammed the lid of the dumpster garbage bin outside. She wondered idly who else might be in the area, but it didn't really concern her; she was too involved in her work.

When Patrice walked out of the shop at ten-thirty, she heard sirens keening in the distance and then drawing closer. More startling, the parking lot in front of the TransAmerica Title Building was already alive with flashing blue and red lights. She saw aid cars, an ambulance, and county sheriff's cars, with more deputies' vehicles racing in.

She could not imagine what might have happened.

Over the last half hour, while Patrice sewed on, completely unaware of what was happening outside her mother's darkened shop, the police radio channels had been alive with communications going back and forth. Beth Wilmot's first call had been monitored at six minutes to ten. The patrol deputies' voices responding to Com Center's request for their locations began to cut in at three minutes to ten.

The operator's terse announcement: "Roger 9 and 112, we have a shooting at the TransAmerica Title at River Road and Cherry. It is unknown circumstances. The fire department called it in."

"112 copy." (Deputy acknowledges call.)

"145 to 112, do you want us to roll?" (Another deputy offers to help.)

"Roger 9. Copy. En route."

"112 to 145. That's affirmative."

Dispatcher: "112, this should be the cross street. It should be Hollyhock. Evidently the victim was cleaning the office when a male subject came in. Fire advises she was shot in the head. Suspect description is a white male, twenty-seven, five-feet-nine, with brown hair. He was wearing a leather coat and jeans. Has a Band-Aid on his nose."

Precious little information for officers going into an unknown situation where a suspect is armed with a gun. But that was all Liz Cameron had been able to elicit from Beth Wilmot. If the man was still in the building—a building with windows on all four sides—no deputy going in would have a chance.

With a wounded victim—probably *two* wounded victims—in the building, no deputy had a choice.

Roger 9, Reserve Deputy Greg Roach, was the first deputy to arrive at the TransAmerica Title Building. He made the River Road address in a minute and a half with blue lights revolving and siren screaming. The aid unit from the Keizer Fire Department had arrived thirty seconds earlier. One of the emergency medical technicians ran over to him.

"There's someone moving around in the building."

Roach looked into the glass-walled structure and saw a naked female in the main office portion; she was walking toward a smaller office located in the southwest corner of the building. When he looked in that direction, he saw a second young woman lying on the floor in a prone position. She too was nude. Her face was turned away from his view, but he could see a spreading pool of blood around her head. For just a moment he felt as if he were viewing a movie screen showing a horror film instead of seeing reality, shockingly true, in the well-lit building.

Roach instructed the fire personnel to wait outside, drew his service revolver, and entered the building. He dared not wait for backup from other deputies. The women inside might die if he did. He felt the hairs prickle at the back of his neck as he checked each room for a suspect who might be waiting with his own gun ready. The offices, the restrooms—all empty. Roach came to one locked door. He debated only a second. He kicked the door and the lock gave. The room was empty.

Roach signaled to the paramedics that it was safe to enter. There was no place else inside where the assailant might be hiding.

Sergeant Will Hingston in Unit 112 arrived sixty seconds after Deputy Roach, and within minutes the building was surrounded by every Marion County officer available in that section of the county: Deputies Bernie Papenfus, Frank Crandall, Don Dolan, John Braun, Detectives Dave Kominek and Jay Boutwell, Lieutenant Kilburn McCoy, Captain Richard Bay, and Undersheriff Robert Prinslow.

The Keizer fire chief, John Sanford, and his emergency medical technicians and paramedics advised the lawmen that there seemed to be two grievously wounded young women.

Beth Wilmot was in deep shock; she was unaware that she was nude, and the paramedics covered her with a blanket. One of her eyes was blackened and the right side of her face was oddly swollen and bruised. Blood oozed from a spot near her right ear.

When a medic examined her, he gasped and looked up in amazement.

"She's been shot in the head. We'll have to transport her at once."

Deputy Bernie Papenfus was assigned to ride in the ambulance with Beth as she was rushed to Salem Memorial Hospital.

The other victim, the girl Beth had said was Shari Hull, was in much worse shape. She was comatose, and the Keizer paramedics found that she had sustained three wounds to the head, wounds that appeared to have been caused by bullets. Shari's vital signs were almost too faint to be measured. The medics shook their heads as they attempted to find some indication that the slender girl might survive. They "bagged" her—forced oxygen into her lungs—as she was lifted onto a gurney and wheeled rapidly toward an ambulance.

Accompanied by Detective Boutwell and Deputy Dolan, Shari too was rushed to Salem Memorial.

Beth remained amazingly coherent as she rode in the ambulance. She was able to tell Deputy Papenfus that she and her best friend, Shari, cleaned the TransAmerica Building every Sunday.

"We were almost finished. Shari went outside to her car, and I had a little cleaning left to do. I was just rounding a corner, going toward the entrance, when I saw Shari and this man walking toward me. He had a long-barreled gun in his right hand. He took us to a room and told us to take off all our clothes—that he wouldn't hurt us. He made us lie down on the floor. We did that, and then he shot Shari in the head, and then he shot me. I pretended to be dead, and I could hear Shari moaning. Then I heard another shot, and heard him—the man—leave. When I was pretty sure he was gone, I crawled to the phone in the office and called the fire department."

"Had you ever seen the man before?" Papenfus asked.

"No."

"Did he molest—bother—either of you?" Papenfus asked gently. "Did he rape you?"

"No . . ." the girl whispered, and added somewhat obscurely, "No, I never touched him."

Perhaps the shock and her terrible wounds had temporarily blocked the ugliest memories for Beth Wilmot. Perhaps she could not yet bring herself to tell anyone what the man had done to them.

Papenfus sensed a rage in Beth. She was shaking from shock, but she was also livid with anger that a stranger could have shot her and Shari. She insisted on giving a description of their attacker again.

"He was a white man, in his mid-twenties, five-feet-eleven to six feet. Slender build. Dark brown hair. Hooded black leather waist-length jacket. Band-Aid . . . a Band-Aid on his nose."

Beth was not as sure about the gun; she wasn't familiar with guns. Papenfus made a move to show her his own service weapon for comparison purposes, but the sight of a gun—any gun—sent Beth into hysterics, and he quickly slipped the gun back into its holster.

Again and again Beth begged Papenfus, "Will I be all right? Am I going to die?"

Papenfus assured her that she would be all right, although looking at the blood, her blackened eye, and swollen face, he was not sure.

"Shari!" Beth kept asking. "Is she all right? Is she gonna die? She was breathing so funny, and moaning, and she wouldn't talk to me. Is Shari gonna die?"

The deputy didn't want to answer that question. Shari Hull had lain so quietly on the lunchroom carpet, and there had been so much blood, pints of it seemingly, seeping steadily from her head, and a slight protrusion of brain matter from the wounds. Papenfus knew that it would take a miracle for Shari Hull to survive.

There would be no miracle. Shari Hull, twenty years old, died in the emergency room of Salem Memorial Hospital at one-twenty A.M. without regaining consciousness.

While Bernie Papenfus waited outside the emergency room for Beth to be examined, a memory kept coming back to him—a recent memory. While he was racing to the TransAmerica Building on the Code 3 call, he had rounded the corner of Broadway and Pine Street at about four minutes after ten. He had just heard the description of the suspect given by the dispatcher, the same description that Beth would repeat to him later in the ambulance. At that moment, as he turned the corner, he had seen a man standing in a well-lit area only ten feet from his patrol car. The man had stared back at him boldly, almost challengingly. It was one of those moments that are over almost with the blinking of an eye but which etch themselves indelibly in the subconscious mind, only to be recalled later in perfect detail. The man had worn jeans and a fleece jacket—but Papenfus had had the impression that the jacket was turned inside out.

That corner had been 1.2 miles from the shooting scene. Only an athlete could have run so far in the short time since the first call for help had come in. But it *was* possible to cover a mile in that time, *if* the runner was young and in prime condition.

Papenfus had eased his foot onto the brake pedal and had radioed for a better description on the suspect, but then another deputy's voice had cut into the radio with the report that the gunman might still be in the building at the crime scene. Papenfus had hit the accelerator then and headed for the shooting scene. Now he remembered the man standing on the corner, the dark eyes that had stared back at him without flinching. He saw that face in his mind; he would never forget that face. What if he had stopped and questioned the guy? He berated himself that he had not, but hindsight is always clearer. Papenfus had assumed that he was needed to back up officers at the shooting scene. No, knowing what he knew at the time, he should not have stopped.

In his own mind the deputy was sure that he had stared into the eyes of the killer. And now the killer was long gone.

The physicians treating Beth Wilmot looked at the slender dark-haired young woman who seemed younger than the age she gave them—twenty—and marveled that she still lived, although her condition was clearly critical. When they had washed the blood from her face and hair, the doctors found a flattened slug, probably a .32-caliber bullet, nestled in the matted hair at the back of her head. It had not penetrated the skull, but the force from the bullet would have been powerful enough to knock her off her feet. The ammunition might have been old, or it might have been fired from a gun of the wrong caliber, or Beth Wilmot might be one of those rare individuals whose skull density is thicker than normal—thick enough to protect the brain even against a bullet.

Moreover, X rays indicated that there was a second bullet, a slug that had penetrated the scalp at the back of Beth's head, but, again, not the skull. This bullet had only plowed a furrow beneath the skin on the right side of her head and come finally to rest just in front of her ear. Beth Wilmot had beaten death. Twice.

Dr. Robert Buza removed this second bullet and turned it over to Detective Jay Boutwell, who entered it into evidence, along with the first bullet found in Beth's hair.

Beth had denied that the gunman had sexually attacked either her or Shari when she gave her first statement in the ambulance, but swabs were used to check for the possible presence of semen in the mouths, rectums, and vaginal vaults of the two victims.

These swabs were then saturated with acid phosphatase. The telltale bright pinkish-purple reaction that indicates the presence of male ejaculate appeared on the swab from Beth's throat.

The killer had ejaculated into her mouth.

Beth had not lied; Beth had only denied the memory of the nightmare she had endured. Later, she would remember . . . and wish that she had not.

Dave Kominek was one of the two detectives on call that dark night in January. He had already responded to one homicide scene earlier in the day, and now he'd been summoned to the shooting scene. Detective Jay Boutwell was at the hospital, and Kominek would remain at the TransAmerica Building to process the crime scene.

Kominek is a compactly muscled, intense man, still in his thirties, and he can seem deceptively easygoing *off* the job. But Dave Kominek was a detective who had already been involved in most of Marion County's most intricate homicide probes. And the county, situated in the idyllic Willamette Valley, had had several bizarre murders in the past half-dozen years—not easy to solve, but solved.

Married and the father of two sons, Kominek does not come from a family of lawmen, nor did he grow up with a burning ambition to be a cop; he looked upon law enforcement initially as just another job. It was to become a way of life for him.

Kominek speaks with the "Oregon drawl," a pattern of speech common to the area around Salem, an accent that sounds almost southern to the untrained ear. Like many Oregon detectives, Kominek wears cowboy boots, although the "Old West" lives in most of Oregon only in history books. The band of his hat is a real rattlesnake. He traps the snakes himself, and fashions the distinctive bands. He skis—both snow and water—in his spare time, plays tournament golf, and he built his family home from the ground up, but his true love is police work.

Born in Nebraska, Kominek moved to Salem with his family when he was ten years old. He grew up there, the middle son in a family of three boys. "We're one hundred percent Czechoslovakian on both sides—both my mom and dad," he comments.

After graduating from high school in 1964, Kominek married. "My friends told me I was crazy to get married so young." He laughs. "But that was the smartest decision I ever made."

He joined the Air Force and was sent to Vietnam on a flight

crew, where his job was "basically balancing airplanes. I was a load master on a four-engine turbo-prop C-130."

After Vietnam, Kominek was assigned to a base in South Carolina, where he served for two more years on a flight crew as a load master on C-141's. "It wasn't a difficult job; those are the most forgiving airplanes flying." The Komineks' son Eric was born while they were in South Carolina.

Back in Oregon after his service stint, Kominek attended Oregon State University for three years, taking engineering and business courses. Police work was the farthest thing from his mind.

But by now, Kominek and his wife, Gail, had a second son, Chad, and family responsibilities demanded that Dave take a full-time job before he could graduate from Oregon State. He bought a truck, but the man he worked for went bankrupt. He applied for several jobs, including that of deputy with the Marion County Sheriff's Office. "I had halfway decent qualifications. I'd never been in trouble—and that was the main qualification. They hired me."

That was in February 1973. In March 1974 Kominek went undercover, working narcotics investigations. He grew a beard and long hair and wore the garb of the "doper." His own mother wouldn't have recognized him on the street. He was a member of MINT (Marion Interagency Narcotics Team). After some tense experiences during his year as a narc, Kominek moved into the Detective Unit.

He had scarcely had time to become oriented to his new assignment when he and Detective Sergeant Jim Byrnes were plunged into the macabre investigation of the murder of a woman whose mutilated body was found—literally in sections—floating in a river outside Salem. They identified the victim as a woman visiting relatives in the Salem area. The last time anyone had seen her alive, she had been having a drink at a popular restaurant. The only physical evidence Byrnes and Kominek had was a receipt from a local dump, but the two detectives used that—and a lot of legwork—to trace the killer, a recent parolee from the Oregon State Penitentiary. The man had been sent up a dozen years before for an almost identical crime. His victims were all strangled and then dismembered.

"Jim and I worked the same way—all-out. That usually meant thirty-six to forty-eight hours at a stretch, without sleep, until we found our killer. You can always catch up on sleep, but you can't afford to give murderers the luxury of time."

Kominek and Byrnes worked together for two years, a period of epidemic violent crime in Marion County, and Kominek learned rapidly. When Byrnes left the sheriff's office to become an investigator for the Oregon State Attorney General's Office, Kominek found himself the lead investigator of homicides in the Marion County Sheriff's Office. He was not quite thirty years old.

Kominek took advantage of every seminar and school available in homicide investigation on subjects ranging from blood-pattern evaluation to hypnosis of victims and witnesses. He was particularly fascinated with hypnosis as a tool in police work, and rapidly became adept at the sometimes controversial art that some experts feel can unlock the subconscious memory of those who have endured severe trauma. When he attended the homicide school at the Southern Police Institute at the University of Louisville—*the* homicide school in America—Dave Kominek ended up teaching the techniques of hypnotizing eyewitnesses.

As a homicide investigator, Dave Kominek proved to have that ability that all good detectives have, the innate sixth sense that makes him doubt the obvious, that compels him to dig beneath the surface of what seems to be the truth. One of his earliest cases involved the "suicide" of an older man, a boarder in a private home. "His landlady said he was depressed, that he'd just picked up her gun and shot himself in the neck. But something bothered me when I viewed the body at autopsy. For one thing, male suicides don't shoot themselves in the neck—they aim at their temples or into their mouths. Number two: there were no powder burns—none. We checked ballistics and we found that old man would have had to have had arms forty-two inches long—minimum—in order to shoot himself and leave no debris from the barrel around the wound. We went back and found there *had* been an eyewitness, another old guy who had been terrified to talk for fear he'd get shot too. He finally told us that the landlady had shot our victim—because he wouldn't run an errand for her! We didn't think she should go to prison, because she was clearly off the track, but we wanted to find out the truth. She was committed to the state mental hospital.''

Throughout the next years, Kominek worked dozens of murder cases, many of them taking him to distant parts of the United States before they were successfully concluded. He admits that he can be a stubborn bulldozer when he's working a homicide, although he is quick to give credit to other detectives and forensic science experts who have worked beside him.

On this gloomy Sunday night in January 1981, the term "I-5 Killer" had not yet been coined. None of the investigators knew that a Pandora's box of sexually motivated murders had been opened wide. What they did have was bad enough.

Kominek had already notified the office manager for Trans-America, who came to the scene and viewed the offices. The manager found nothing missing. Obviously theft had been neither the primary nor the secondary motivation for the carnage.

Shari Hull's father, rendered almost speechless by the news of the shootings, had finally been able to explain that his janitorial service had no set hours for cleaning the TransAmerica Building, but that the building was the girls' assignment.

"Shari and Beth must have got there late; they had other buildings to clean this weekend—they should have been finished with the TransAm Building well before nine. But they were dependable—they would have worked past midnight if they had to to get it done."

The immediate concern in the aftermath of the first call for help had been, of course, the survival of the victims. That is always the first priority for police officers. If the victim is alive, or might possibly be alive, they must strive to preserve life at all costs. And so there had been paramedics walking through the crime scene, and many deputies helping to search and secure the building. It was only after Beth and Shari had been rushed to Salem Memorial Hospital that Dave Kominek had time to stand back and observe the shambles murder had left behind, and only then could he attempt to find something that the killer might have inadvertently left.

A call for assistance from the Oregon State Police Crime Lab had gone out shorly after ten P.M., and Kominek was joined in the eerily empty building at twelve-thirty A.M. by his lieutenant, Kilburn McCoy, and Lieutenant William Zeller and Trooper Ray Grimsbo from the state crime lab in Portland. The need for haste was gone. There was time now for hours and hours of painstaking work to retrieve physical evidence.

The red Ford Bronco (mistakenly described as "green" by Beth in her terror) was still parked outside the building, keys in the ignition, engine still running. There were two women's purses inside, and the rear window was rolled down, revealing cleaning equipment.

The lunchroom—where the attack had taken place—was at the end of a short hall leading from the front door of the TransAmerica Building. The floor of the room was strewn with clothing and paraphernalia left behind by the fire-department medics. Two pools of blood, their perimeters already beginning to dry in darker segments like mud around a pond in deep summer, were at the end of the counter—mute testimony marking where the victims had lain.

Small-size clothing lay where the garments had been dropped at the gunman's order: two pairs of blue jeans; a brown-and-white sweater; a blue-and-white sweatshirt; a pair of lavender panties; a pair of green-and-pink bikini panties; a size 32D brassiere—heavily bloodstained; a woman's white imitation sheepskin jacket; a woman's brown leather jacket; a pair of brown shoes, their laces still tied; and a pair of blue-and-yellow running shoes, their laces also firmly tied. All of this clothing clearly had belonged to Shari and Beth.

There were no clothes left behind by the gunman.

A ring of keys rested in the middle of the carpet. But when Kominek tried them in the TransAmerica Building's front door, they proved to be, as he had feared, only keys to the building.

There were bullets—one .32-caliber slug caught in the folds of the white coat, and a second, similar bullet nestling on the carpet where the rug abutted the sink counter. The path of this second bullet could be traced. There was an indentation in the cabinet door below the sink, and strands of Shari Hull's light brown hair were embedded in the spot where the bullet had struck the door and ricocheted. There was a hole five inches below the indentation in the cabinet door. Inside the cabinet, a plastic cleanser can showed damage where the bullet had bounced off it.

Blood had sprayed over the walls as well as the carpet, and there were smears of red on the phone Beth had used to call for help. Grimsbo's report noted "white viscous material" (which would prove disappointingly *not* to be semen when tested) that had seeped into the carpet. The clothing was bagged and labeled, and the bullets placed carefully in containers that would preserve them just as they had been found. Slides were taken of the blood that seemed to be everywhere in the room.

Finally the room was vacuumed carefully, so that all the gunpowder particles, all the hairs, and whatever other debris might have been left could be saved.

That was all the investigators had as the dawn of January 19, 1981, slowly broke. *If* they did not find a gun to match the bullets to, *if* Beth Wilmot did not survive, or *if* she could not identify some suspect they might come up with, *if* his semen should prove to have come from a man who was not—like 85 percent of the population—a "secretor" of blood type in his bodily fluids, there was every chance the crime might never be solved. All detectives agree that the hardest kind of murder case to solve is one in which the victim and killer are strangers to one another; there are no prior threads of confrontation to weave into a meaningful pattern.

The big man who had wrought such havoc on Shari Hull and Beth Wilmot was out there somewhere, but Dave Kominek had no idea who he might be.

3

Dave Kominek attended the autopsy of Shari Hull's body at the Howell Edwards Doerksen Funeral Home in Salem, and took the pictures that are a necessary part of a homicide case file.

Dr. Ray Patton did the postmortem exam. There were no surprises. Shari's skull had been fractured on the right side; bullets had plowed into the left side of her neck, the right side of her skull three inches above her right ear, and the back of her head. A fourth wound appeared to be an exit wound. Fragments had entered the right temple area and virtually obliterated the center of her brain. Shari's hair—like Beth's—was blackened with the debris of the gun barrel, a barrel held so close to her head that the killer could not possibly have missed. The wounds were "execution-style" wounds; the gunman had fired at point-blank range into the back and right side of the helpless girl's head. There were no defensive wounds on Shari's hands. She had gone down without a fight. Seeing the damage to Shari, Kominek marveled that Beth could have taken the same bullets and lived.

While Beth Wilmot continued her almost miraculous recovery, detectives from the Marion County Sheriff's Office considered the problem of tracking the man who had irrevocably changed his victims' lives in a twenty-minute spate of mindless violence. The case was a natural-born "loser." The killer was a stranger to both girls; Beth was still positive she had never seen him before, and she had sensed that Shari didn't know him either.

The physical evidence the investigators from Marion County had gleaned was pathetically sparse: the most important items were the bullets. Criminalist Ray Grimsbo reported that tests had isolated certain characteristics in the slugs. The bullet retrieved from the sink in the lunchroom at the TransAmerica Building was in fairly good shape. It was a .32-caliber lead bullet fired from a weapon with a right-hand twist, and with five lands and grooves etched into its surface by the gun's barrel. The gun they were looking for had a barrel land measuring 0.083 inch, and a barrel groove width of 0.103 inch. The other whole bullets had been removed from the victims' bodies and were badly flattened and damaged, as well as stained by the girls' blood. Still, several of them were intact enough so that Grimsbo could determine that they fit into the same class and characteristic parameters of the first bullet. At this point they were useless, but if and when a suspect gun was located, Grimsbo would be able to tell if that gun had fired the fatal bullets.

Feeding the specifications into a computer linked to the FBI's National Crime Information Center, Grimsbo received the information that the bullets had "most likely" come from the following revolvers or nonsemiautomatic weapons: a Smith and Wesson Double Action-Third Model, a Harrington and Richardson Model 1905 or Young America–Bull Dog, a Meriden Fire Arms Company pocket revolver, or a Thames Arms Company pocket revolver. Guns of these makes were available to Grimsbo, and test-firing had elicited the same right-hand twist, with five lands and grooves. It was possible, however, that there might be other weapons which would fire in the same pattern.

Where the death gun was, however, was anybody's guess. The killer might still have it with him, or he might have thrown it away—possibly in one of the many rivers that abound in Oregon. If he still possessed the gun, he might use it again, and if he did, there was a chance that some other police agency would impound it.

If . . .

Beyond isolating the weapon the killer had carried, the Oregon State Police Crime Detection Lab criminalists had been able to determine the blood type of the killer by testing the semen-soaked swab taken from Beth's throat. The material was positive for viable spermatazoa, and—most important—the semen had come from a man who was a "secretor." The killer had either Type A or Type B blood. More than half of all people are A and/or B secretors, although B secretors are far less common, less than 9 percent of the population. This information might serve to build a preponderance of evidence against a suspect.

The smallest piece of possible physical evidence they had picked up was listed on the evidence manifest sheet. At the time, it did not seem that it would be particularly vital to the probe. Grimsbo, Zeller, and Kominek had found one coarse, almost black pubic hair on the rug of the lunchroom. It would not match either of the victims' pubic hairs in class and characteristics under a scanning electron microscope. It might have come from the killer, and it was of Caucasian origin. But, like the blood-type classification, hair is only probable physical evidence—not absolute. Although it was not likely that the unknown pubic hair had come from one of the officers or medics at the crime scene, since they had all been fully clothed, they had to be positively eliminated as sources. Dave Kominek contacted all of the paramedics and all of the police personnel and asked them to submit a sample of their pubic hair.

Kominek would later recall with a grin, "I went out to the fire station and handed everyone a comb and a small plastic bag. They looked at me at first as if I was nuts, and asked if I'd given up police work and become a Fuller Brush man giving away free samples."

None of the hairs gathered matched the dark pubic hair retrieved from the crime scene.

The vicious attacks on Beth and Shari appeared to be a tragedy born of opportunity. This killer had to be a random, senseless murderer, one of the new breed of killers who began to rove America in increasing numbers during the seventies. The profile of murder had changed, so subtly at first that lawmen didn't pick up on it, but the dramatic increase in random murder can no longer be ignored.

Always before, there were rules of thumb detectives could trust when it came to homicide suspects: look with suspicion first upon relatives and friends of the victim. Familiarity sometimes breeds murder. Look next for someone with a motive that makes sense: jealousy, greed, revenge.

But by 1981 the rules had changed. In 1966, only 5.9 percent of all homicides could have been considered "random and senseless" by the researchers for the FBI's Uniform Crime Report—644 victims killed in the entire United States for no apparent reason. That meant that more than ten thousand murder victims had been killed by someone who had a motive that, while hardly condoned, could be explained. Explainable motive makes for a high incidence of successful case closures, and nationwide the statistics looked good on the charts. Eighty-eight percent of all murders in America were solved in 1966; 1,310 murders went unavenged.

Shari Hull would become a statistic in the Uniform Crime

Report for 1981, and those figures, when compared to 1966, would be horrendous. By the end of 1981, 17.8 percent of all murders were deemed random and senseless, perpetrated for reasons no rational mind could understand: 22,519 murder victims in 1981—more than double the number fifteen years earlier in 1966; 4,007 of those victims killed in 1981 had died for no discernible reason.

Not surprisingly, the successful closure rate on homicides dropped dramatically in 1981, when only 72 percent of killers were brought to justice, and that meant that 6,304 murder cases would end up in the loser files.

In late January 1981, the murder investigation in Shari Hull's case seemed almost hopeless. The responsibility for solving her murder would fall most heavily on the shoulders of Detective Dave Kominek and Corporal Monty Holloway. They knew their chances of finding the dark-eyed man in the hooded jacket were almost nil. Beth and Shari would have made attractive targets as they worked alone in the building whose lighted windows made it a fishbowl. The killer had seized the opportunity and then vanished into the night—perhaps forever.

The task of eliciting an in-depth statement from Beth Wilmot fell to Dave Kominek. When he talks with other detectives, Kominek can be brusque and businesslike, so caught up is he in trying to work through a case to a successful conclusion. But with victims Kominek is a different man. His sympathy for their losses is apparent; his kindness allows them to tell him things that might seem unspeakable.

Beth Wilmot would come to think of Dave Kominek as a big-brother figure, someone she could talk to through the months ahead. And the months that lay ahead would not be easy.

As Beth lay recovering from surgery in Salem Memorial on January 19, her room was under heavy guard. Shari Hull's killer had left the TransAmerica Building confidently, sure that he had silenced all witnesses. Beth Wilmot's survival had made headlines in Portland and Salem papers, and when the killer heard the news that one of his victims still lived, there was a chance that he might come back and attempt to silence her.

Dave Kominek met Beth for the first time on the day after the shootings. He had seen accident and assault victims before, of course, but it was still appalling to see Beth's puffy, bruised face. Her blackened eyes made it impossible to tell what she had looked like before the attack.

Despite her injuries, Beth Wilmot was anxious to give a

statement. Whatever she might have forgotten immediately after the incident, she remembered everything now.

Beth explained that she had known Shari Hull for a long time, that they had been best friends. Shari's family had welcomed Beth into their home when she moved to Salem from Spokane, Washington, to find a job, and both young women had been doing some work for Shari's father's janitorial service. The TransAmerica job was their Sunday assignment. It usually hadn't taken them very long, as the building was basically kept very clean and it was new.

Explaining how she and Shari had come to be in the building was the easy part. Beth's voice dropped, and she looked away from Kominek, staring at the window, where raindrops spattered and then melted into each other.

"Tell me what you can remember, Beth," Kominek began. "Just take your time. Tell me about going to work that night."

Beth sighed and nodded. "We went out there about nine-ten or nine-fifteen, and we were all done cleaning in about twenty minutes . . . but then I noticed that a window was dirty, and I went to the back room to get a spray bottle.

"The man must of saw us cleaning alone, 'cause Shari went to empty the garbage alone. She did that without telling me. We usually empty it together. I got done vacuuming and she just got done cleaning and emptying the garbage. I went to the back room to get the spray bottle. She was near the door or something, and when I got to her, he was there pointing the gun at both of us. I guess he just walked in."

Beth paused, and tears came into her eyes. "He killed my best friend."

"Try to tell me about it, Beth. Tell me the words he said, and tell me what you and Shari said," Kominek prompted softly.

Beth explained that the only place in the whole building blocked off from view of anyone in the parking lot or on River Road was the lunchroom—that that was the room where the intruder herded them.

"He said, 'In the back room—both of you. Both of you take off your clothes. Strip. All of them. Get down, and stay down. He told Shari to take it all off, and I said, 'My dad will be here pretty soon.' ''

It had been a pathetic lie; Beth said that she knew there was no chance that anyone would come to save them. She had hoped that she could frighten the big man off, but he wasn't buying her story.

"Shari was hesitating. She didn't want to take her bra off. "He said, 'Come on, now, take it all off.' He made us kneel on the floor and he was standing up."

Beth closed her eyes and asked if she had to tell everything that the man had done to them. Kominek told her that it wouldn't be her own words speaking—that she would only be repeating what the killer had said.

She explained that the man had unzipped his jeans and exposed himself, and then he had demanded that the girls fellate him.

"What did he say to you? Remember, what you tell me will be his words—not yours."

Beth closed her eyes and took a deep breath.

"Okay. He was talking to Shari, and he said . . . he said, 'Suck on me. Come on, make me come.' And then he said to me, 'You suck on my balls.' He told both of us, 'You make me come. Both of you suck on me.'

"He told Shari, 'Play with yourself,' and she said no, and then he told me to suck on Shari's breast. I did, but I faked it.

"He told me to stand up and spread my legs apart so he could have intercourse with me. His penis wouldn't go in, and he said, 'Shit, you've got a tight cunt.' "

Beth Wilmot talked very softly, spilling out the details of the savage attack she and her friend had endured for some twenty minutes. Twenty minutes that had seemed like hours. Beth had thought only of placating him, feeling that that was the one way they might survive. But, Beth said, Shari had reacted with something close to hysteria, crying uncontrollably as the dark-complexioned man gave his orders. Shari's bubbling panic had seemed to set the man off, making him edgy and angry. He had changed for the worse when Shari had given in to hysteria.

"Eat me," he'd commanded, standing triumphantly over the kneeling, naked girls. "Which one of you wants to eat me?"

"He made Shari go first, and then me, and then both of us at the same time."

Beth turned her face away. "He came . . . finally. We thought he was done with us. He told us to lie down on the ground—facedown on the floor. He was asking us for rope. He said, 'I need some rope. Do you guys have any rope? Do you know where any is?'

"We both said no. And then Shari said, 'Don't hurt us. Please don't hurt us. We won't tell anyone. Just let us go.' Shari was crying and begging, and I was saying, 'Please, please, don't hurt us. We won't tell anyone.' ''

Beth had wanted to tell Shari that she should be quiet, that her crying and screaming were making the man crazier—but she was afraid to speak out loud.

"He was quiet for about five seconds, standing over us. We could hear him breathing, and it was like he was trying to decide."

Dave Kominek noted that Beth had begun to tremble, almost imperceptibly at first, and then more violently. She caught her hands together, trying to maintain some kind of composure.

"And then . . . ?" he asked quietly. "And then what happened, Beth?"

"Then a shot goes off. I think that he shot Shari first, and then he shot me . . . and then he shot Shari again . . . and then me. And then a final shot to Shari. After the first shot, I just lay as still as I could and pretended to be dead. Shari kept moaning, and maybe that's why he shot her the last time. I was praying and hoping that she was pretending to be dead too. After he shot me the second time, I couldn't hear anything but ringing in my ears. I was afraid to get up because I couldn't hear if he was still there or not.

"After about five minutes I got up and I could walk and I went to the restroom and I looked in the mirror. There was something wrong with the whole right side of my face; it was all swollen out, and there was blood. I was so frightened; I thought he might be outside watching me, so I got down on my hands and knees and I crawled to one of the phones in the office, and I pushed a button and called the operator."

Kominek waited, saying nothing. The story was pouring out from Beth unbidden now.

"Shari was dying then, and I'm scared half to death, afraid I'm going to die too, and that he's going to come back and shoot me again. Then I could see the ambulance lights and the police driving up, and I run to Shari, and I say, 'Shari, talk to me!' Only Shari couldn't say anything. It was too late."

Tears were coursing down Beth Wilmot's cheeks. She turned to Kominek and said. "Do you know what my last words were to Shari? The *very* last words? I said, 'Oh, shit, Shari—we forgot to clean the door,' and her last words to me were, 'Oh, shit. Let's do 'em.' ''

The same thought occurred to the detective and to the sobbing girl at that moment, and it hung in the air of the hospital room. If

Beth and Shari had left a few smudges on the front door of the TransAmerica Building, if they had not been so anxious to do a good job of cleaning, they would have been safely in Shari's Bronco and driving away from the parking lot before the killer could get to them.

4

He was to have been the perfect child, the son his parents had longed for. He was most assuredly *not* one of the "throwaway" children who are initially unwanted and then buffeted from foster home to foster home. No criminologist could ever call Randall deprived. He was born into a loving home to educated upper-middle-class parents. That he might one day become a criminal, a violent, sadistic killer, seemed patently impossible. And yet, he was to find—and lose—success far beyond any boy's dreams, and finally, instead of fame, he would wallow in infamy.

His father, Walter "Jack" Woodfield, and his mother, Donna Jean, were products of an era when one fell in love, got married, and settled down to raise a small family of perfect children. That was the dream of the forties and fifties. Daughters would grow up, go to college, and marry professional men. Sons would become star athletes, excel in their studies, and make their parents proud.

For many of those young couples who married just after the end of the Second World War, the dreams came true. For others, like the Woodfields, something would go terribly wrong, and they would never understand why. If, indeed, the Woodfields' approach to child rearing was somehow flawed, it was with no thought to harm; from the very beginning, they wanted only the best for their children. By some curious but unwritten rule, families of that time three decades ago invariably wanted to have a boy baby first. Thus the father would have a small image of himself to mold and to present with all the advantages that he himself had missed when he grew up during the Great Depression. Although Donna Jean had had two years of college, the war had intervened, and Jack Woodfield had only a high-school diploma. He had joined Pacific Northwest Bell when he was twenty-one, and he was very successful. He would stay with the phone company for more than thirty years.

Donna Jean Woodfield gave birth first to two daughters in a row: Susan and Nancy, pretty, smart, good little girls. Both parents adored their daughters, but they still longed for a boy, and Donna Jean was certain that her third pregnancy in 1950 would bring the son that would make their family complete.

Friends remember that she selected and then rejected many names for the baby boy she confidently expected, explaining that a name was so important for a boy. The wrong name could make all the difference. Good solid boys' names like John and Charles and Joseph had gone out of vogue by 1950; a profusion of Brians and Kevins and Marks appeared in the "Births" columns in newspapers. The new idea was to give a boy baby a special name, something that he could wear proudly throughout his life. It was no longer popular to name boys after progenitors. Grandfathers might merit a middle name in tribute, but rarely a first name.

Donna Jean finally settled on what she thought was a wonderful name: Randall Brent Woodfield. She would call him Randy.

When Donna Jean Woodfield went into labor late on Christmas Day 1950, it seemed that she was, indeed, about to give birth to a special child. She did give birth to a boy, but not until after midnight; Randall Brent Woodfield was born on December 26 in Salem, Oregon. His mother was twenty-four years old; his father was twenty-seven.

Randy was a beautiful baby, born with a thick head of almost black hair. Within months his slate-blue eyes turned dark too, and his hair became a dense mass of curls. A woman who baby-sat for the Woodfields recalls that Randy was a very placid baby to care for. "He was very quiet. I remember that I worried sometimes because he was almost *too good . . . too quiet.*"

Randy turned over and crawled earlier than other babies, and he walked earlier too. Jack Woodfield was sure that he had a blossoming athlete on his hands, and he was delighted.

Donna Jean breast-fed her son—that too just coming back into vogue after years of rigidly scheduled bottle-feeding. Randy's older sisters doted on him, treating him like a big doll.

The Woodfields remained in Salem for about a year after Randy's birth, and then moved to Corvallis for two or three years. Jack Woodfield was then transferred to Otter Rock, Oregon, where the family would remain for many years.

The Woodfields felt that it had all turned out perfectly. The girls were a pleasure to raise, and Randy would be the "all-American boy." His father would tutor him in sports, and his mother would see to it that he would have social grace, manners, and popularity. He was such a handsome, smart little boy that it could not be any other way.

There were minor problems; it wasn't long before Randy began to chafe against a household heavily weighted with females, with a father who worked long hours as he rose rapidly through the hierarchy of management in the Pacific Northwest Bell Telephone Company. Randy began to resent his sisters mightily; he complained that they were always allowed to do things that he couldn't. The explanation that they "were older" only enraged him.

Randy concluded that girls got to do what was fun and that girls were free. His sisters could go places by themselves and he had to stay home. Worst of all, he had to have a baby-sitter, and they didn't. As a schoolboy he rebelled against baby-sitters, demanding to be left alone. The few times he was left alone with his sisters, however, his jealousy at them exploded, and there were fights. He felt that he was the one who always got blamed, even if it wasn't his fault. He fumed because Susan and Nancy teased him, and tattled on him, and he was punished.

His mother was usually the one to mete out the discipline—not physically painful, but humiliating to Randy because he felt that he had disappointed her. He was torn early on between his desire to please his mother, to be a "good boy," and his anger at her because it seemed impossible to meet what he considered to be her expansive and unrealistic goals for him. Still, as an adult, he would recall that his relationship with his mother was "real good. I'm closer to my mother than I am to my father."

For the rest of his life, Randy Woodfield would misperceive women, overvaluing *them* and denigrating himself. In the end, his self-esteem would become totally dependent on how women viewed him.

And yet, for all of his grade-school years, Randy Woodfield would seem to be exactly the child his parents wanted. He was good in school, made excellent grades, and he was exceptional in sports. He and his father participated in what Randy describes as "a lot of father-son activities." He was a boy that any family would be proud of—handsomer than ever as the years passed, and popular with his fellow students. If he was occasionally given to temper tantrums at home over conflicts with his sisters, well . . . all little brothers acted that way.

Father Knows Best was what people watched on their television sets in the fifties, the kind of family every family wanted to be. The mother never got angry, and the father never made a mistake, and, sure, Bud sometimes became furious with Betty, his big sister, but that's the way things were supposed to be. In the final scenes, everybody made up and laughed about the problems.

Nobody talked about sex in situation comedies in the fifties. Nobody talked about sex *period*. And no one, certainly, talked about sex in the Woodfield home. That was something that could wait until high school. This didn't make them different from any other family of that period. Not at all; they were mirroring the image of the times.

Randy soon came to hate his nickname. It was a "baby" name, something his mother called him. His name was Randall, but as much as he fumed, "Randy" stuck to him like glue.

As their family grew, the Woodfields lived in Otter Rock, a town with only a few thousand citizens, located on the Oregon coast. Situated just north of the spot where Yaquina Bay empties into the Pacific Ocean, Otter Rock could vie with any town in America for sheer physical beauty. There seemed to be a "safeness" for children there; the closest "big" town was Corvallis, fifty-four miles to the east, and even Corvallis had only thirty-five thousand residents. Salem and Portland were a goodly stretch up the I-5 freeway, and fears that Otter Rock teenagers might be exposed to drugs was minimal when compared to problems parents faced in Portland.

Otter Rock was a town full of good neighbors, and the Woodfields were considered "pillars of the community," an exceptionally nice family. Jack continued moving up in the telephone company, and after Randy was ten, Donna Jean took a job at a drugstore in Newport as a clerk. A pretty woman who always dressed with style and flair, she looked several years younger than her actual age. People responded to Donna Jean, but then, people liked the whole Woodfield family.

Randy Woodfield reached puberty early, and his confusion about sexual matters grew, as did his misperception of the female. He was still trying to please his mother, but it was much more difficult now to be the perfect son. He continued to validate his own worth by how well he met Donna Jean's expectations. She was not aware of it; no one was aware of it. Randy resented his sisters because they were in high school and he was only in junior high. They could still go places forbidden to him, and they could take driver training and obtain driver's licenses.

His frustration level reached the danger point. He was a male, and males should be paid attention to. But females were running his life. He felt powerful sexual feelings, and then consuming guilt because he felt that way.

At the same time, the teenage Randy Woodfield was becoming known as the outstanding young athlete in Newport, where he attended school. His coordination marked him a prodigy on the playing field. It didn't seem to matter which sports he tried. He was a star in all of them: track, baseball, basketball, football. The towns of Otter Rock and Newport were proud of him. His father began a scrapbook of pictures and clippings extolling Randy's success. Eventually he would have three scrapbooks thick with Randy's honors. It isn't often that a town as small as Newport, Oregon, can claim an athlete with as much promise as Randy Woodfield showed.

It wasn't enough. The roar of the crowds, his father's pride, and the fact that he seemed slated for greatness could not counter-balance the doubts Randy had about his competence, and, indeed, about his masculinity.

His first overt demonstration of sexual deviance can be traced back to his days in junior high school. When the pressure and conflicts became too great for him to deal with in accepted channels, he began to expose himself. He knew that this was not something a "good boy" would do, but the obsession was all-consuming. Through exhibitionism he could not only demonstrate that he was a male but also subconsciously get back at his mother, who seemed to demand perfection that he could not deliver. Even more gratifying than this subtle revenge was the sight of a woman's or girl's frightened reaction to the shock of seeing his genitals.

The instances of exposure were seldom isolated. Randy would expose his erect organ to a woman on one side of Newport, revel in her reaction, and then sprint to other areas and find still more victims. He reasoned that he was not actually hurting anyone, and that made it, if not all right, at least acceptable. His own fear of discovery concurrently excited him and filled him with dread.

Eventually, of course, he was caught. And he was recognized. Newport wasn't big enough to allow anonymity, and Randy was well known in Newport.

Tragically, he drew no real punishment and was not referred for treatment. The teenage exposer is a somewhat rare phenomenon, and when an exposer is still only in junior high school, bright red warning flags should have been raised. But police officials looked the other way. This was the kid that was going to make the rest of Oregon and perhaps the rest of the country look to Newport when he reached his peak as an athlete. To charge him, to perhaps send him away to reform school, would mean the end of the glory of Randy Woodfield.

The exposing incidents were whitewashed. Randy stayed in school, and he stayed at home. Years later, when he was a man and in profound trouble with the law, Randy Woodfield's parents would deny that they were aware of any sexual problems he might have had. It is possible that the officers who encountered Randy in his first acting out of sexual deviance did not tell his parents; it is possible that the suggestion that their son might be sexually abnormal in some way was repressed so thoroughly that the Woodfields do not, indeed, remember.

As far as Jack Woodfield can now recall, Randy did not become sexually active until he was in high school. He remembers that Randy mentioned to him once that the girls in high school were "loose." This could have been construed as "man talk," and Jack Woodfield did not pursue it.

Randall Woodfield's father states adamantly that his son had no problems while growing up. He was not involved with alcohol or with drugs; Randy had participated in none of the forbidden activities that many teenagers dabbled in in the sixties. His father recalls that Randy was extremely close to his mother, both as a child and as a young man.

One of Randy's closest friends was Mike Schaeffer, now a teacher at a Newport school. Schaeffer even now cannot comprehend that Randy would ever hurt anyone, much less kill someone. When Schaeffer and Woodfield were close, Schaeffer recalls that Randy was not a "kiss-and-tell" dater, so Schaeffer never knew what sexual contacts Randy might have had. He would date one girl almost exclusively for a few months at a time—but never longer.

"He had a good relationship with his parents, but whenever he did anything wrong, his mother always knew," Schaeffer remembers. "He threw a party once when his folks were out of town. He was really careful, and he put throw rugs and plastic over the carpets so there wouldn't be any damage done, and then he rounded up a crew of girls to stay around after the party to clean up. That place was just immaculate afterward, but when his mother got home, she *knew*. She just seemed to know everything he was doing."

Randy Woodfield was a very important member of the class of 1969 at Newport High School. He is well remembered.

"He was a beautiful kid, the star football player," one of his classmates recalls. "He was a relatively popular kid."

Some members of his graduating class recall Randy as a quiet, almost shy young man. Others say that Randy was given to pranks—things like teasing animals.

The girls Randy had dated for a while—all of them long married now—were the most popular, the most desirable girls. Interviewed by detectives in 1981, some of them were in tears over Randy's arrest. At least one of them could not bear to watch the television news and see Randy in handcuffs. Her husband, one of Randy's friends who stayed supportive for years, comments that she ran from the room whenever Randy's image flashed onto the screen.

Randy always seemed to prefer younger girls. Perhaps he found them less threatening, less controlling. As he grew older, he would continue to be attracted to girls a half-dozen or more years younger than he. He liked to have his girlfriends wear jeans, and he was disturbed when they wore sexy or what he called "flashy" clothes. He liked slender girls, but he was invariably attracted to big-breasted girls.

He was a good student at Newport High School, excelling particularly in mathematics, and he was moved into advanced math classes. Teachers would later praise his intellectual ability and the way he seemed to get along with everyone. The Newport Rotary Club once selected Randy as Boy of the Month. He belonged to the German club; he was much more than "just a dumb jock."

But it was in sports, of course, that Randy Woodfield made the most lasting impression. He made the all-state first team in football when he was still only a junior, and again when he was a senior. He received an honorable mention in all-state basketball when he was a senior, he played varsity baseball, and he was a sprinter and field-event specialist on the track team. His ambition—his obsession—was to play professional football, and few who knew him doubted that he would achieve that goal. He was a wide receiver without peer, and you could confidently put him up against any end from high schools in Portland or Seattle—or Houston, for that matter. According to Randy, in his senior year he was recruited for sports scholarships by "all the major colleges in the Northwest," and there is no evidence to dispute that.

Randy was very handsome, despite a stubborn case of teenage acne, and he was big—almost six feet, two inches tall, a hundred and seventy pounds.

The world should have been his oyster.

The summer after graduating from high school, Randy Woodfield worked for Pacific Northwest Bell in Newport, driving trucks and cleaning and repairing telephone booths. In the fall of 1969 he enrolled in Treasure Valley Community College in Ontario, Oregon. Ontario is a town only slightly larger than Otter Rock, all the way across Oregon and hard by the Idaho border. His good friend from high school, Mike Schaeffer, was his roommate at Treasure Valley.

For the year he was at Treasure Valley, Randy made a GPA of 2.5—roughly a C+ average. He was co-captain of the varsity football team and was on the varsity basketball and weight-lifting squads. In track, he held the freshman record for the long jump: twenty-two feet, six and a half inches.

Schaeffer considered that Randy was talented, gifted, and he had never seen him be spiteful or cruel to anyone. But he had glimpsed a dark side to his best friend on occasion.

"Randy stole some cassette tapes from some guy in the dorm. I knew he had those tapes, but when the guy asked about them, Randy lied and said he didn't have them. I told him it was his story to tell, and I wouldn't say anything, but that when it came down to his getting into trouble over taking them, he'd have to tell the truth. Later he confessed to the dorm proctor that he'd had them all along, and he gave them back."

Randy Woodfield dated one girl at Treasure Valley Community College, Sharon McNeill. He seemed to be more attached to her than any girl he'd known before.

"Sharon did her share of catting around," Schaeffer recalls, "and they were having troubles. Anyway, they broke up."

Apparently Randy couldn't handle Sharon's rejection, and there were allegations that he had broken into the McNeill home on August 3, 1970, and completely "trashed" Sharon's room in reprisal. Entry had been made through a bathroom window. The only thing stolen was, oddly, a stuffed animal—a small bull, a present given to Sharon by Randy.

He was arrested by Ontario, Oregon, police and charged with vandalizing his ex-girl's room. He was later found not guilty in a jury trial; there was no physical evidence linking Randy to the vandalism and theft.

But there had allegedly been incidents of exposing in Ontario too, and it seemed prudent for Randy to move on. He arranged to transfer to Mount Hood Community College for one term. He went alone; Mike Schaeffer enrolled in Southern Oregon College.

Sharon McNeill's parents were adamant that she have nothing further to do with Randy Woodfield, and she agreed with them. Even though he left Treasure Valley, he continued to bombard the young woman with letters and phone calls. Sharon would eventually be forced to obtain an unlisted phone number. Almost ten years after she had last seen him in Ontario, Sharon received a letter from Randy containing a nude photograph of himself. The final message was a Christmas card in December 1980. She had never given him any encouragement during the decade that intervened between the vandalism incident and his final Christmas card. She often wondered why he would not just let her go and forget her, but his peculiar attentions didn't really frighten her.

"After we left Treasure Valley," Mike Schaeffer remembers, "Randy never visited me at SOC. A long time later, I got letters from him where he sounded quite religious and was quoting the Bible. It just wasn't him . . . not the Randy I knew."

For the next two summers Randy Woodfield returned to the Oregon coast to work—this time for the Georgia-Pacific plywood and stud mill in Toledo.

Randy had another "girlfriend" during that time—a Newport eighth-grader named Traci Connors.

"He was home for the summer from Treasure Valley," she remembers. "I met him at the Newport High School football field, where he and his friends were playing football. I used to go and watch them, and I got to know Randy pretty well. It was just friendly; he was sort of the big brother that I never had. He was always nice to me, and we didn't really have dates—but I spent a lot of time with him. He'd drive me home from the football field in the black Volkswagen Bug he had then. It had a sun roof, and Randy always had rakes sticking out of it. He took the rakes along to smooth out the long-jump pits."

For Traci it had been a case of platonic hero worship. She was only in the eighth grade, and he was a college man, a football star, who was being nice to her and spending time with her.

On one occasion, however, Randy had surprised her and frightened her a little. Traci was no more than fourteen or fifteen, and Randy was about twenty. His parents were out of town, and he invited her to spend the night in his house with him. She drank two beers with him, and was thrilled when he kissed her a few times.

The encounter escalated to petting that resulted in climax for Randy, but she had refused actual intercourse, saying, "No, I don't do things like that."

"He just said, 'Okay,' and went to sleep in his own bed. I slept all night in another bed, and that was all there was to it."

Traci would have done almost anything for Randy Woodfield— short of sex. She even intervened and attempted to help him reconcile with the lost Sharon from Treasure Valley.

"One time Randy had me call up this girl over by Treasure Valley. He couldn't do it because her parents wouldn't let her date him anymore. He said they'd accused him of breaking and entering their house. He said he'd just taken back all the things he'd given her. Except for that girl, he never seemed to have a steady girlfriend.

"At the end of the first summer I knew him, he went back to college and I didn't see him for a long time. He sent me a couple of letters from school, but I didn't hear from him again until after I'd graduated, and I was married."

As a grown woman, Traci Connors still remembered Randy Woodfield as "a happy, funny, good person. He stayed in shape, and he was real clean and fun to be with. He had a great memory and he was sincere—not a phony. If you needed help, Randy would help you. He was always macho, and his father always wanted Randy to be something big. It seemed like he tried really hard to be what his parents wanted, but he always thought that his sisters were 'neat' and could do no wrong in his folks' eyes."

Traci did acknowledge that Randy was a "little sneaky" at times, and particularly good at "planning things out."

"One time he was going to make money by getting ten cases of Coors beer in Idaho and bringing them back to sell to the kids at Newport High at a profit. He brought the beer and hid it behind some church in town. He sold me a case, but before he could sell the rest of it, somebody found it and stole it. He asked me about that—as if I might know who'd done it, but I didn't know. He wasn't really mad, but he lost money on that deal."

According to Traci, Randy Woodfield had been very concerned about what other people thought of him—particularly his high-school friends. "After he went to prison that first time, he asked me if Mike Schaeffer was really ashamed of him because he'd been in prison.''

Traci Connors was to continue for years an off-and-on friendship with the man she'd idolized when she was a young teenager. And like so many of the friends who had known Randy in his glory years, she could never really visualize his doing the terrible things he was accused of.

5

By the spring of 1971 Randy Woodfield had passed his twentieth birthday and was far behind the carefully programmed schedule he had set for himself to play big-league ball. He should have been playing first-string varsity by now on a Pac-Eight team: the University of Washington Huskies or the University of Oregon Ducks. The life cycle of an athlete is short. Beyond Y. A. Tittle and a few other "old men" who have lasted in the pros after forty, there aren't many football players who are not over the hill by the time they reach thirty-five.

Treasure Valley had not proved to be a college where big-league scouts trolled. Randy thought he never should have gone there in the first place. He had repetitive nightmares of waking up at thirty without ever having made it. He'd been a big fish in a little pond, and the world of athletics was full of minnows who got swallowed up when they ventured out of their safe waters.

Sports was the one area in which Randy felt whole and competent, and he had kept his underlying compulsions quelled, if not completely under control, by working out and keeping his body in prime condition. He was not perfect socially, he was not perfect scholastically, but he was still pretty damn good on a football field and in the 100- and 220-yard dashes. And when he was home in Otter Rock and Newport during vacations and summers, he was still a hero to the kids of the area who hung around the field and watched him catch passes.

That wasn't enough; that was nowhere near enough. He had made mistakes at Treasure Valley, and his image was tarnished. The theft in the dorm that he'd had to confess. The look in the proctor's eyes when he did, and the ignominy of having to return a lousy bunch of tapes, burned in his memory. The trial over the breaking and entering at the McNeills' house had been worse.

And Sharon. Sharon had dumped him. He'd never been sure

that he was masculine enough, a good enough lover, or as well endowed as other men. She'd taken everything he had to give her, and then she'd gone out with other guys behind his back. She as much as told him he didn't measure up.

He'd thought he might feel better after taking his presents back and leaving her room a mess. But that had only gotten him in more trouble, and then she *really* wanted nothing to do with him.

He'd concluded finally that Sharon was treacherous, like most of the women he'd known in his life. She'd run tattling to her folks, and she'd made him look like a fool. That was the whole thing about females. They acted soft and pretty, but they demanded more than any man could be expected to give. He'd kept thinking that if he could just talk to her, it would be all right, but it wasn't, and every time she'd told him to go away, he'd felt worse.

He had tried to tell himself that he and Sharon were through. The hell with her. There were other women. But the memory of Sharon's betrayal would sneak up and confront him when he least expected it. It was almost impossible for him to really let go of her. Indeed, he would come to blame his "bad luck" at losing her for his growing sexual obsessions.

In the spring of 1971 Randy registered for classes at Portland State University. Portland State seemed to him to be a far better choice than Treasure Valley in his quest for eventual football fame. And Portland State's coaches were certainly pleased to have Randy.

Portland State wasn't in the Pac-Eight, of course. They played other small universities in Oregon and Washington, some of them very good, considering their size: Willamette (where his mother had gone to college), Linfield, Whitman, George Fox, the University of Puget Sound. The pros didn't draft many players from small colleges, but there were always some scouts keeping an eye out—just in case. Jim Zorn had come out of Cal-Poly-Pomona, and Eddie LeBaron had come from the College of the Pacific. There were scouts who still called Randy from time to time. If he could make a good showing at Portland State, he still had a chance to achieve his dream.

After the spring term at Portland State, where he participated enthusiastically in spring practice, Randy once again worked for Georgia-Pacific, this time for the entire summer. He did not earn much during his employment there, and he applied for and was granted food stamps from the Multnomah County Public Welfare Commission in September 1971.

Randy attended Portland State on a full-time basis from 1971 to the winter semester of 1973. He majored there in health education and physical education, and made average grades. He was a valuable member of the Portland State football team's line, a wide receiver who could be counted on to perform. He somehow managed to combine spring training for football with track, in which he once again competed and won in events that demanded speed. He also took courses in handball, wrestling, weight lifting, and gymnastics.

He worked part-time as a cook and waiter at the Burger Chef restaurant near Portland State.

But there had been a distinct personality change in the young football star by the time he arrived in Portland. He had been quiet, but something of a prankster, occasionally a thief, sporadically gripped by rage at rejection. He had, of course, been an exhibitionist, but that was still a side of him that no one claims to have known about—no one but the police in his hometown. He had never been a show-off, and he was not in 1971.

Randy turned, at Portland State, to religion. His teammates of that era describe Randy Woodfield as "soft-spoken and mild-mannered . . . very, very religious." He was a member of the Portland State University Campus Crusade for Christ and of the Fellowship of Christian Athletes. He was known to date only "Christian girls." Indeed, he embraced religion with the same fervor he had hitherto shown only for athletics, as if combining the two pursuits could cleanse him of whatever demons waited inside, scratching and clawing to get out.

And there were demons.

No matter that Randy Woodfield's football career had picked up appreciably when he moved to Portland State, no matter that he was once again being wooed seriously by football scouts from the pros, and no matter that he could date almost any coed he chose. He was still an exhibitionist; the sexual rush he got when he exposed himself to horrified women was so much stronger than any other gratification.

There is little doubt that there were many, many episodes of exhibitionism for which he was not caught. He had the whole of Portland to rove in, and he had only to drive across the bridge over the Columbia River in his old Volkswagen to be in Vancouver, Washington. The majority of women don't bother to report exposers; the fallacy remains that exposers are not inherently dangerous, just as voyeurs are thought to be basically harmless. Certainly the experience can be momentarily shocking, but if women are not actually touched or abused, they tend to put the incident out of their minds.

Still, Randy Woodfield, the tall-dark-and-handsome football star, the Christian athlete, was playing Russian roulette with his genitals. There had to come a time when he *was* reported, when his speed at running from the scene was not swift enough.

His first adult arrest occurred in Vancouver, Washington, on August 7, 1972. He was charged with indecent exposure and he was convicted. He received only a suspended sentence. There is no record of probation. There is no indication that authorities at Portland State were aware of either his arrest or conviction.

He maintained his "Mr. Clean" image on campus, attending religious meetings and doing well in class and better on the playing field. He traveled to Lake Tahoe, California, in 1972 and 1973 to participate in conferences for the Campus Crusade for Christ, taking a janitor's job at the Driftwood Lodge there to support himself.

An almost compulsive saver of records and minutiae, Randy Woodfield carried souvenirs, notes, old checks, letters, cards, and miscellaneous papers wherever he went. He filled several notebooks with memoranda on religion, and one contained his "personal testimony" as a born-again Christian. In it he deplored his constant seeking after three goals in his life: "to be successful in school (grades); to reach the highest honors I could in my range of athletics; and to be popular with all the girls."

He testified that he had turned away from religion because he thought his life was more exciting without the rules and regulations that constrained his friends. He wrote that he had come to see that his former achievements were "actually only trophies or memories I could hang on the wall. I suddenly found myself going nowhere in school and just wandering around."

The Campus Crusade for Christ and the summers in Lake Tahoe estranged him somewhat from his father. Jack Woodfield was concerned that Randy was plunging into religion with almost maniacal fervor. There were arguments between son and father that seemed to have no resolution. Had Jack Woodfield known of the struggles within his son, he might have welcomed *anything* that could divert Randy from the path he was treading.

Randy Woodfield was, then, in the early 1970's, an avowed Christian, but it did not seem to help with his sexual obsessions. It did not stop his prowling to find women to whom he could reveal that he was a male, and a male with genitals he now considered exceptionally large.

Some of his victims were more puzzled than frightened. They saw a handsome, well-built young man—a man they might have been eager to date, given other circumstances—who stood in the shadows with unzipped fly, whispering softly: "Look at me. Look at *this*." This wasn't the standard creepy little man or some senile old fool forcing them to look at his pitiful penis. This man just didn't fit the stereotype they had come to expect.

But of course there are no valid stereotypes for sexual criminals.

Randy Woodfield was caught and arrested again on June 22, 1973, in the Portland area, and charged with indecent exposure, resisting an officer, and attempting to elude arrest. He appeared chastened and repentant in court. He was sentenced to five months and twenty-five days in jail (which he did not serve), and one year's probation. The resisting-an-officer charge was dropped.

On February 22, 1974, he was arrested for public indecency and received five years' probation. Counseling was a mandatory part of his probation—but he never followed up on it. And no one forced him to.

Records did not indicate that he had ever actually *hurt* any woman, and he seemed to the sentencing judges to be a good risk. He was a student, a star athlete, and he had goals. He was working to support himself at the Tektronix Company in Beaverton, Oregon. Beyond that, there was—and is—the continuing problem of overcrowding in prisons. If every exposer arrested were sent to "the walls," the walls would burst. Twice more, then, Randy Woodfield was given a suspended sentence and placed on probation. His promises sounded sincere; he always promised he would seek therapy if he thought he could not control his impulses to expose himself. He reported regularly—although grudgingly—to his probation officer.

After the 1973 football season at Portland State, Randy Woodfield's dreams came true. He was drafted in the seventeenth "out" by the Green Bay Packers! The small-town football hero had seemingly achieved the impossible.

Vince Lombardi had been dead for three years, but the Packers' glory still lingered: five NFL championships and two Super Bowl victories. This was the team that the boy Randy had watched avidly on his family's television set through his growing-up years. This was the top, not some "loser" team, but the best. The very best. The Green Bay Packers wanted *him*.

Randy signed his contract on February 20, 1974. The Packers therein promised to pay him—a "skilled football player"—sixteen thousand dollars for the period extending from the date of signing until the first of May following the close of the 1974 season. In addition, he would receive board and room and traveling expenses during preseason training, as well as during the regular season. To sweeten the pot, there were bonuses to be had. For Randy Woodfield there was a three-thousand-dollar bonus going in. If Randy should survive the cuts and become a member of the forty-seven-man roster for the first league game of the 1974 season, he would receive an additional twenty-five hundred dollars. If he should catch twenty-five passes in the regular NFL season, he would receive two thousand dollars, and if he should catch *thirty* passes, he would be rewarded with a three-thousand-dollar bonus.

In return for all this, the contract stipulated that Randy was obligated to keep himself in excellent physical condition, avoid any drinking of intoxicants, stay away from gamblers and gambling resorts, and wear a coat and necktie in hotel lobbies, public eating places, and all public conveyances. He had to promise that he would not write or sponsor magazine or newspaper articles or endorse any product or service or participate in any radio or television programs without permission of the Green Bay Packers.

There was not—at least in the official contract—any clause regarding moral turpitude, conviction of crime, and the like. It apparently was a given that players screened carefully by the Packer scouts would have no such skeletons in their closets.

The Green Bay Packer segment of Randy Woodfield's life was probably the most memorable, although it was soon to be blighted. He saved all communiqués from 1265 Lombardi Avenue, Green Bay, Wisconsin; he would carry the stack of personal letters and mimeographed sheets with him throughout his myriad changes of residence over the coming years.

They were akin to messages from Hollywood to a would-be starlet. *They were magic.*

Immediately upon his signing the contract, letters came with instructions about early training camp to be held in Scottsdale, Arizona. An airline ticket arrived by certified mail. The early training session would be a "get-acquainted period so that in July we can all begin together toward our common goal, 'The Championship,' " wrote Hank Kuhlman, an assistant coach. A dinner would be held in Phoenix on Apirl 4, and the Packers would pay all travel, lodging, and meals plus fifty dollars for pin money. Randy saved even the airline-ticket carbon, carrying it with him for the next eight years.

Everything was being provided for him, everything but running shoes and football shoes.

The Sporting News wrote from Missouri, asking for information for their Football Register so that Randy's name could be added to the new edition. Randy Woodfield was suddenly "somebody" again.

His life was all football that spring and summer of 1974. Things went well for Randy in Scottsdale, and he returned to his Portland apartment to await further flurries of mail from Wisconsin. Each envelope bearing the logo of the Packers' helmet gave him more proof that, by God, he had been chosen.

Trainer Domenic Gentile sent diagrams for building muscles. John Polonchek, another assistant coach, suggested that Randy try to combine Gentile's stretching exercises with pass receiving. "I would suggest that you catch as many balls as possible each week, both standing and moving catches."

In June there was another certified letter with a first-class airline ticket—this time to Green Bay. A limo would be waiting to take Randy directly to the residence hall at St. Norbert College in West De Pere, Wisconsin. Rather than flying, however, Randy chose to drive his own car to the Midwest; it would give him added mobility.

There were rumors that the NFL players' union was threatening to strike training camps in July if no prior settlement was made, but letters to Randy assured him he was under no compunction to join the NFL Players' Association or to participate in the strike.

Randy didn't worry about it; he was too busy exercising, catching passes, planning for his career in the pros. When he received two letters from head coach and general manager Dan Devine himself, sending warm personal regards, it was the frosting on the cake, the stamp of approval. He would survive all the cuts; he would be on the forty-seven-man traveling squad—he was sure of it.

But Randy Woodfield didn't make it with the Green Bay Packers. He was cut from the traveling squad. He would later say that they treated him "more as a tackling dummy than anything else." His forte was in catching passes, and the Packers were, according to Randy, working with a preponderance of running plays.

After he was cut, Randy stayed on in Green Bay for a while—

but on the farm team, playing for the Manitowac Chiefs from September 1974 until December, and working for the Oshkosh Truck Corporation as a press-brake operator in the manufacture of fire trucks.

Even though he had been cut from the 1974 traveling squad, Randy still thought he might work his way back up. He was content for the moment to play for the Chiefs. He would always remember that the roar of the crowds at the rookie games—forty-thousand voices strong—was music to his ears. He loved every-thing about being with the Packers, even if it was only on the farm team. For the second half of 1974 Randy Woodfield lived his dreams, as happy as he had ever been in his life. He hated only the weather in Wisconsin. He had been raised with rain and roaring surf in the wintertime; he could not deal with endless snow.

The question of why Randy Woodfield was dropped by the Green Bay Packers has different answers—depending upon who is giving those answers. Randy himself says that he tensed up when he should have been playing confidently, went out too wide for passes that just tippled on his fingers and then dropped to the ground. Oddly, for an athlete whose best skill was in catching passes, Randy Woodfield has incongruously small hands. The rest of his body nears perfection; in photographs he usually poses casually with his hands behind his back. Given his prob-lem with catching passes, and the fact that the Packers were stressing ground offense, he was the wrong man at the wrong time.

He was, indeed, the wrong man.

The Green Bay Packers will not comment on why he was cut. The Green Bay Police Department declines to release any re-cords they might have on Randall Brent Woodfield—at least officially. But rumors would come back seven years later to Detective Dave Kominek that there had been between ten and twenty incidents of indecent exposure in Wisconsin involving Randy Woodfield.

One Wisconsin detective commented off the record: "He couldn't keep the thing in his pants."

Randy Woodfield would not be the first—or the last—athlete to see his blossoming career turn to ashes because of his sexual behavior. It is almost expected that pro players will be cocksmen who seduce willing female fans, the pretty little groupies who are there for the picking. That is the macho thing to do, and if it doesn't interfere with the player's performance on the field, who's going to blow the whistle? But when Lance Rentzel was arrested for exposing himself to young girls, he was, for all intents and purposes, through with the Dallas Cowboys. When Randy Woodfield's nocturnal exhibitionism got back to Packer management, he was finished too.

Randy packed up and returned to Portland. He had sought one goal for most of his twenty-three years. He had had it within his grasp, and then he had lost it. The parade had passed him by. He was destroyed. He felt that he had failed himself, and, worst of all, he had disappointed his mother, who had always predicted and urged greatness for her only son.

There was depression, and then there was rage.

Randy returned to Portland, but there was no reason to go back to Portland State, even though he was within three terms of a college degree. He'd really gone there to play football, and he was no longer eligible to play amateur ball.

Randy worked desultorily at an electronics firm in a Portland suburb, he worked part-time tending bar, and he dated many women, never staying with one very long. He shared a two-bedroom apartment with Tim Rossi, a friend who had graduated from Portland State University. Tim was his best friend and was currently an assistant professor at Reed College in Portland.

Randy still saw old friends from high school from time to time. He talked fondly of the glory days at Newport High School and complained about the raw deal he'd received from the Packers. He told friends he'd been cut from the Wisconsin team for "flinching on the line." He promised that he would show his old friends footage that showed him playing with the Packers, explaining that Dan Devine himself had promised to send him films. But the films never arrived.

Randy was almost twenty-five years old now. Most of his friends were married and parents, moving ahead in the adult world. Mike Schaeffer was a schoolteacher. Some members of the class of '69 were architects, medical students, dental students. But Randy Woodfield was going no place fast. . . .

In the first months of 1975, the Portland police were dealing with an inherently explosive situation. Several women had been accosted at knifepoint by a man who prowled Duniway Park at S.W. Barbur Boulevard and Sheridan. Their attacker had exposed himself and then forced his victims to fellate him to ejaculation. After he had been satisfied sexually, he had stolen their purses. The man was described as "big" and "dark" by the victims. A few of them remarked that he was young and good-looking. He had sneaked up behind them so quietly in the lonely park that they had had no chance at all to scream for help.

When stakeouts by male police officers at Duniway Park did not turn up the attacker with the knife, it was decided that a decoy was needed to lure him from the woods. The decoy would have to be a female.

Policewoman Annette Jolin volunteered for the assignment, aware that her safety could not be guaranteed. Jolin would have to walk down the deserted pathways alone while backup officers watched from some distance.

Jolin was given eight dollar bills whose serial numbers had been recorded. She walked through the quiet park on several occasions, but nothing happened. Perhaps the park prowler had sensed that the police were watching; perhaps he had moved his operations to another of Portland's many parks.

Shortly after noon on Wednesday, March 5, 1975, Jolin's neck crawled with the feeling that someone *was* padding behind her through fir thickets that shut out light, their feathered branches so dense that she could no longer see even the sun. She forced herself to walk slowly, to mimic the movements of the natural victim—the woman who is unaware of her surroundings, who appears to be distracted. She told herself that the officers who were backing her up weren't really far away, that she wasn't alone. She had a signaling device to call for help if she needed it.

Shortly before, one of the surveillance officers had observed a Pontiac GTO as it pulled into the Terwilliger Plaza and parked. The driver, a tall male, strolled into Duniway Park and started up a trail. The officer waited; this was the sticky part—he had to wait for Jolin to signal if she needed help.

Suddenly, deep in the park, there was a sound behind the policewoman, a soft footfall on the dirt path, an intake of breath. She half-turned, and felt the blade of a knife pressing against the flesh of her neck.

Although Jolin could neither see nor hear her backups, they could see her signal, and they tensed. The man was demanding her money as he held the knife against her throat. She handed the eight marked dollar bills over and saw her assailant staring back at her boldly, apparently weighing something in his mind. His hands darted out and stroked her breasts, and then he turned and headed back down the trail.

The officers who had staked out the park perimeters were waiting for her assailant as he emerged from the park.

The suspect was big and muscular, but he was so surprised to find that he had attacked a policewoman, and a policewoman accompanied by several other officers, that he did not offer any resistance. He handed over the knife. It was a paring knife.

"What's your name?" the Portland officers asked.

"Randall Woodfield. I go to Portland State U."

6

This time, there would be no probation for Randy Woodfield. In addition to the paring knife he'd used to threaten Officer Jolin with, arresting officers had confiscated a gun he'd carried with him that March day. It was an Italian-made starter pistol. Randy Woodfield's attacks against women had escalated far beyond the incidents of exhibitionism. First charged with first-degree robbery, Randy entered a plea of guilty to a reduced charge of second-degree robbery on April 29, 1975. The oral-sodomy charges involving previous victims were dropped. He was set for sentencing on June 4—but first his case was assigned to the Diagnostic Center of the Oregon State Department of Human Resources. He discussed his "problem" with a state psychologist in the Rocky Butte Jail.

Randy admitted that he was "totally guilty" of the crime against policewoman Jolin and said that he was "very sorry and deeply hurt" that he had caused so many problems. He seemed almost relieved to have been caught, and suggested that he possibly had a problem that would require hospitalization.

According to Randy, his life had "collapsed" three years before because of "sexual problems." (That would have been at the time of his first arrest for indecent exposure.)

Randy related that he had discovered in college that he could not cope with his sexuality, and he felt he had had much "bad luck." He had lost a cherished girlfriend, had had his car stolen, and had withdrawn from college. Then, he said, he had met two religious friends who had introduced him to the Christian faith. He blamed his current troubles with the law on his own inability to follow his faith. But as far as sex was concerned, he insisted that the impulses that had driven him obsessively were out of his control.

He was not sure why he could not control himself with

women; he did not take drugs, and he had not drunk alcohol since becoming a Christian in 1972. He said he had taken steroids to help build his body. He thought that perhaps the steroids had magnified his sexual urges.

As far as his leisure activity, he listed only music—playing the accordion—sports, and reading religious literature. He mentioned that he had tried to curtail his dating activity, as he thought removing himself from sexual opportunity might help him contain his lust for women.

Financially, he had nothing. He had had $57.50 in a bank account before his arrest, but he'd turned that over to his attorney. He owed almost three thousand dollars to the telephone company's credit union for a school loan, and three hundred dollars to his parents for gas needed to drive to Green Bay.

Randy Woodfield talked in a soft, well-modulated tone in speaking with the state psychologist. He appeared resigned, and depressed. He opted for jail forever—or even death—if that would mean that he could not continue his sexual prowlings. He wanted treatment now, even though he had never followed through on counseling before, although it had been a mandatory stipulation of his probation. He insisted that he had robbed the women only because he needed money and had been "too proud" to borrow from his family. And yet all of the robberies combined had netted him less than twenty-five dollars.

Randy Woodfield was given a brief intelligence test, and scored surprisingly low. This test indicated his IQ was around 100. If it was accurate, he would have had considerable difficulty in college, and could not have hoped to meet grandiose expectations others had for him.

The aspects of Woodfield's personality that alarmed the examiner were his detachment from his crimes and the fact that he had used a knife and had actually touched his victims. These factors separated him from the typical exposer. It was possible that there was an underlying psychotic thought process which was not easy to detect. Randy's near-fanatic preoccupation with religion might be a danger sign.

The final evaluation read, "It would be my opinion that Mr. Woodfield's problem is so severe as to be a very serious threat to the community, and although treating him as an outpatient might actually present him with a greater opportunity to be treated, I think this would present too great a risk to the community. For the safety of the community, he needs to be in an institutional setting. However, chances of being successfully treated in such a setting are rather dim.''

Catch 22. Randy Woodfield might be successfully treated while he was free, but he was too dangerous. Locked up, treatment didn't look hopeful. He had shown that he would not seek treatment unless he was compelled to do so. No one—*no one*—had any idea just how dangerous Randy was.

On June 10, 1975, Randy heard himself sentenced to ten years in the Oregon State Penitentiary for armed robbery. The Multnomah County judge who sentenced him decried the fact that the charges resulting from the sexual offenses in the other park cases had been dropped. He opined that Randy Woodfield should be placed in a program for sexually dangerous offenders in the Oregon State Hospital's psychiatric unit instead of the state prison.

Instead, Randy joined the general population at the state penitentiary in Salem. A year earlier, the world had been his; he had been on his way to join the Green Bay Packers. Now he was only a convict with ten years hanging over his head.

Where had it all gone?

Randall Woodfield had another number now, not a two-digit number emblazoned on a football jersey, but a longer number: OSP 37376. He was not a compliant prisoner; he received several disciplinary "tickets" during his first months in prison. He did not believe that he deserved to be in the penitentiary in Salem, and he was not about to obey the rules. Guards warned one another that Woodfield had a "bad attitude."

There was one thing that really angered Randy about the Oregon State Prison. He resented the fact that some of the guards were females, feeling that it wasn't fair that women could guard male prisoners, although male guards never were assigned to the female prisoners' sections. He was particularly annoyed when women guards seemed to have free access to shower rooms and toilet facilities. "I was in there for being an exhibitionist, and here's this female guard watching me take a piss. It was ironic, and it made me angry," he would tell detectives years later.

In a group-therapy session sponsored by the Oregon State Hospital, Randy bristled when a nurse asked the group to share their sexual fantasies with her. He stared back at her and said, "You share your sexual fantasies with us, and then I might share mine with you."

She declined, and wrote him up as antagonistic in group therapy.

Some of his other infractions were more trivial. He grew a

beard—mostly to annoy the prison administration. And he had
high-top Nike basketball shoes smuggled in to him in prison. His
knees were going bad after football, and his ankles were failing
on him too; he needed the support of high-top shoes. He laughed
when someone cited him for an infraction because of the shoes.
"You get dope smuggled in all the time—so why get bent out of
shape over a pair of basketball shoes?"

By 1976 Randy had acclimated somewhat to prison. Since he
had been sentenced only on the robbery charge, he did not carry
the stigma of "sex pervert" which alienates other prison inmates.
He made friends, some relationships that would continue after he
had served his sentence.

Randy was assigned to work in the dining room and kitchen,
where he was paid fifty cents a day. He took college extension
courses through a program furnished by Chemeketa Community
College in Salem, earning A's and B's in courses in typing,
accounting, computer programming, economics, and . . . human
sexuality. He did not participate at first in institutional therapy
programs, but he did involve himself in a group-therapy program
run by the Reverend Simon Beach. Randy joined the Masters
Men's Bible Club, the Freedom in Christ group, as well as a
Bible-study group that met informally in the "yard" whenever
the weather was nice.

He was far from abandoned by his family; his approved
visitors' list included his grandmother, his sisters, his parents,
three of his closest friends, and women listed only as two
"Christian girls."

In his leisure time he played basketball, ran track, and lifted
weights until his body developed into a mass of muscles. He
soon looked like a candidate for the Mr. America contest.

All in all, Randy Woodfield considered himself several rungs
above the average prison inmate. But he enjoyed the other cons'
adulation when he told them about his days playing with the
Green Bay Packers. Mostly, however, he concentrated on building up a huge network of correspondents *outside* the joint.

Randy wrote to friends from prison, reaching far back into the
past. He found the address of Traci Connors, the little girl who
had had such a crush on him years before. Traci was surprised to
hear from him, and even more surprised to learn that he was
writing from prison.

"I was married when I heard from him. It must have been
1976 or 1977. His letters were kind of off-the-wall. He wanted

me to sell some wallets he was making in prison so he'd have some spending money.

"He never told me why he was in prison, and I never asked him about it."

Traci Connors wrote back to Randy Woodfield. Although she was a grown woman, she still remembered how she'd felt about Randy when she was only a girl, and she couldn't turn her back on him just because he was in prison. She didn't have much luck selling the wallets he'd made, but he seemed glad to have a correspondent anyway.

Randy sent Traci a picture of himself and a pretty girl, and she thinks he wrote that the girl was from California. His letter explained that he had been engaged to the girl in the picture at one time, but he said something had happened and they'd broken up. Still, he asked Traci to send the picture back after she'd looked at it. She did send it back, and enclosed a picture of herself that he'd requested. Their correspondence while Randy was in the state penitentiary was platonic.

Randy had always been a letter writer, and he kept up voluminous correspondence with old friends while he was in prison. He wrote to Mike Schaeffer, but Schaeffer answered only rarely. They had stayed in tenuous touch until Randy's conviction, but the chasm between them now widened irrevocably. Schaeffer felt guilty about abandoning Randy, and would wonder later if he shouldn't have done more to help his old friend—if it would have made any difference at all.

Randy Woodfield continued to theorize about what it might have been that precipitated his attacks on women. He speculated to prison psychologists that it might be his ex-girlfriend's fault—because she had rejected him. "I wanted to get back at a girl for something." He thought that his animosity toward Sharon had generalized until he felt vindictive toward *all* women. Asked if he felt inadequate around females, he said no. He felt that he was attractive to women and that he was quite capable of maintaining a good relationship with a woman.

His insight into his problems was seriously flawed; his exhibitionism had preceded the breakup with Sharon at Treasure Valley by a half-dozen years. His outward vanity and self-confidence warred with his suggestion that one rejection was enough to spark violence toward all women. No, he had been aggressive toward females for a long, long time—but he could not acknowledge any inadequacy as a male. He was big and strong; he looked like an Adonis. His facade was all perfection.

As far as sex was concerned, Randy explained to prison psychologists in 1976 that he thought he had found a way to forestall any trouble once he got out of prison. "What's going to help me is not getting involved with a girl physically. I always felt kind of guilty about sex. There's more to life than sex."

It was, of course, a most unrealistic and patently impossible path for him to follow; sublimation of his burgeoning sexual drive was a simplistic and flawed solution to his problems.

Randy stated confidently that his life's new goals were to help others, to seek a woman for spiritual reasons, to find a wife and settle down and raise a family when he was free.

He insisted that he had never hurt anyone. "I am not a violent person."

Psychologists felt differently, and recommended against his release in the foreseeable future.

Randy Woodfield did not serve ten years in prison. He soon became con-wise. Being a smart-ass wasn't getting him out, and out was where he wanted to be. He learned that there were approved responses when dealing with prison counselors. He told prison psychologists that he had accepted his guilt, that he realized he needed help. If he got out, the first thing he would do, he promised, would be to seek psychiatric help. He pointed out that he had solid support from his family and friends and that his former employer was willing to give him back his job at the electronics firm.

"I've come to the point where I am beginning to accept myself and stop being a phony," he told a staff psychologist. "I know I have a problem, and I want to keep on top of it at all times. I've learned to accept rejection from others, especially females. I don't take it personally anymore. It's taken me twenty-seven years to grow up, but I'm making it now. I have excellent family support. I used to be too ashamed to admit that I had a problem. But I found out in Reverend Beach's group that other guys have problems, and if they can overcome them, I can do it too. I am not the same immature fellow that I used to be. I used to just want to play football and have fun. But now I know that work is important. . . . I've got to stop running and face myself for what I am. I have now got the courage and confidence to meet my problems directly. I no longer feel a need to hide from them."

This time, Randy convinced the psychologist that he had gotten his life together, and the counselor would write in his evaluation: "Woodfield's attitude is excellent. This interviewer has met with him many times and has come to know of Woodfield's *sincere* desire to change. Given Woodfield's good intelligence and abilities, his sound support from others in the community, his insights into himself, his remorse for what he has done, and his sincere desire to change, his long-term prognosis is favorable. He is a fitting candidate for Work Release, and it would be a good transitional move for him to make. It would help to bolster his self-confidence and give him time to readjust to being free again in society. He is not an escape risk, nor is he a violence risk.''

Randy's file was full of letters from friends and business associates, all of them extolling his basic good character, all of them reassuring that he would never get in trouble again.

After less than four years of a ten-year sentence, Randy learned he was to be paroled in July 1979. It occurred to him that it had been ten years since his high-school class had graduated from Newport High School and that it was time for a reunion. Since he was still constrained by his incarceration, Randy wrote to another old friend—Alex Carter—and suggested that Alex set up a reunion. Since Alex was happily married to one of Randy's old girlfriends, perhaps he felt he owed something to his former classmate.

Alex did all the work contacting the class of '69 and organized a celebration for August 25, 1979. With Randy urging him on through letters, Carter managed to draw quite a turnout.

Randy walked out of the Oregon State Penitentiary in Salem two days after the Fourth of July holiday. The state of Oregon had furnished him with $86.35 and he had $13.65 in his prison trust account. He was not concerned; he had a job waiting for him.

He did not expect to return to the walls.

The official program for the reunion of the Newport Cubs of 1969 listed Randy Woodfield at the head of the reunion committee.

There was a picnic and a volleyball game on the beach during the day, and that evening, a banquet at the Inn at Otter Crest. Randy Woodfield, out of prison since July 6, was an enthusiastic participant in the reunion. He sported his prison-grown beard and he had a pretty girl on his arm. He posed with the rest of the class of '69 for a tenth-anniversary picture. He joked with Mike Schaeffer and seemed not to bear a grudge because Schaeffer had not written to him during his last few years in prison.

Randy's classmates were tactful, and no one asked why he had been in prison. Indeed, many of them may not have known that he had been. He talked about playing with the Green Bay Packers, and seemed his old self, quiet but assured. Privately he explained to Alex Carter that he had gone to prison for robbing some Fotomat booths and that he'd been captured after police set up surveillance teams to trap him.

Half of that story was true—the part about the surveillance teams. Randy had simply omitted some of the more bizarre details of his encounters with the police.

Randy stayed with his parents during his visit to Newport for the reunion, and then he returned to the Portland area, where he was temporarily living with his sister Nancy until he got on his feet financially.

He recouped rapidly; his job at Tektronix paid him six hundred dollars a month, plus overtime. He became eligible to borrow from the company's credit union, and he took out a loan.

Randy had been assigned to the Clackamas County parole office, and to a female parole officer: Judy Pulliam. Again, he had to report to a woman, and meet with her approval in order to stay free. Still, he had a good chance to make it—if he could just stay within the restrictions of his parole.

Pulliam's supervisor, Terry Gassaway, acknowledges that Randy did report regularly to his parole officer at first. "He was basically hostile to authority. Sure, he would come in and he would report, but he was kind of an ego-macho type. He was evidently a football player and he fancied himself to be a man's man."

Randy was hard to keep track of because he moved from place to place so frequently, and he was resistant to any direction from other people—either the employees at the Clackamas County Community Corrections Center or his family—but he broke no serious rules that were detectable. There were no incidents between Randy and Judy Pulliam that betrayed his resentment of women.

"A lot of these guys are hostile toward their parole officers," Gassaway commented, "but there was nothing to show he had hostility toward her [Pulliam] because she was a woman."

Randy had a lot of girlfriends; he was rarely seen with the same woman twice. Soon his little black book contained 255 names and phone numbers—and all but a handful were women's.

He abandoned his job at Tektronix for bartending jobs, and that opened up a whole world of women to him. He was handsome and sympathetic and charming to the girls who came into the lounges where he worked. If some of them were underage—and many of them were—he was not a stickler for ID.

He was so dedicated to making up for the four years of forced celibacy in prison that he would later admit, "I screwed up. I was in too much of a hurry, and I got herpes from one of them."

Traci Connors saw Randy for the first time in years in September 1980. She was in the hospital in Raleigh Hills outside Portland and she phoned Randy and asked him to come and visit her.

"He came to the hospital on September 4 or 5, and he brought me a kitten. He was the same old Randy—at least he seemed the same. He was working at a bar near the hospital, and he seemed quite happy. He told me that he was going to get into management where he worked. He was driving his mother's gold VW with a sun roof."

Just as always, Traci found that Randy seemed genuinely interested in what she was doing, and he told her about his life. He explained that he was living with a seventeen-year-old girl named Lucy and that Lucy worked as a cocktail waitress, using ID that said she was twenty-one.

Randy explained the ground rules of his relationship with Lucy. "I love her, and she loves me, and we don't sleep with anyone else, but we each have other friends. The only thing that bothers me is that I come home from work ready to go to bed, and Lucy comes home later, and then all of her guy friends are out partying in the living room when I try to sleep."

Traci saw Randy Woodfield once more—on September 7, 1980—when she visited the bar where he worked. She talked with him for about half an hour and then got up to leave.

"I told him I was going to hitchhike home, and Randy got real upset. He offered to pay for a taxi for me. He told me that I didn't know what kind of people might be out there, and he asked me what I would do if a crazy person got hold of me. I finally took the bus home so he wouldn't worry."

7

Beth Wilmot remained in the hospital on January 22, 1981, recovering from both her wounds and the shock of the attack that had taken the life of her best friend. She was still under guard. Until the night of January 18, Beth's life had been uneventful. Born on May 30, 1960, she had grown up in California, attending Castroville Elementary School in Castroville, and graduating from North Salinas High School in Salinas. In the short résumé she'd mailed to Salem businesses in early January, 1981, Beth had attached a sheet listing her work experience. She was only twenty, and the list was short; she'd worked as a cashier at the Giant Artichoke Restaurant in Castroville and as hostess and bus girl at the Apple Tree Restaurant in Spokane. She had had a semester of typing and two years of home economics. She described herself as being five feet, five inches tall and weighing one hundred and fifteen pounds, and noted that she had never learned to drive.

Of the three personal references she'd given, Shari Hull was now dead, and the other two were from out of state. Beth was virtually alone now in Salem, and Dave Kominek and his wife, Gail, "adopted" Beth, letting her know that there were people in Salem who cared about her.

As Beth recovered, she received another blow. Physicians at Salem Memorial Hospital discovered that she had contracted herpes; the killer-rapist had infected her with the venereal disease for which there is no cure.

Dave Kominek sent out the first of what were to be a flurry of bulletins seeking information on the killer he sought. Using an Identi-Kit, technicians had come up with a composite picture of the suspect. Later it would prove to be incredibly similar to the actual killer. In that first flier, the line-drawing image stares back

74

at the viewer through cold eyes set in a rather handsome mustached face. The hair is covered by a hood-cap garment.

Suspect: WHITE MALE, 25 to 30 years, 5'10'' to 6', 140 to 160, sandy color hair, i.e.: brn to dishwater color, collar-length. Ruddy complex (possibly pockmarked). Deep voice. Clothing: blue jeans, tennis shoes, hooded tan-colored jacket (vinyl, leather, or polyester). Waist-length. Wearing driving type gloves.

Weapon: Dark blue revolver, with four- to six-inch barrel. .32 cal. 6-shot.

Any avail. info. contact Det. Kominek or Det. Boutwell, Marion County SO. Ph. 588-5113. Refer to our case CR81-3152.

When that first bulletin went out, Dave Kominek had no warning of the deluge of calls that would follow. There were scores of departments working unsolved assault cases against young women. At this point, no connections had been made. When the pieces finally fell together, a hundred detectives would realize that they were all looking for the same man. But in the first days of February 1981, they were looking for a phantom who seemed to rove at will up and down the I-5 freeway.

Kominek conferred with the new district attorney for Marion County, Oregon, Chris Van Dyke. Van Dyke would be catapulted into the public eye as he worked constantly with the detectives who sought the man called the I-5 Killer. And, like the lawmen, he would find that all personal considerations would be put on hold until the killer was caught. Seven months of his life would be totally taken up with the I-5 Killer.

Van Dyke had lived with celebrity all of his thirty years, but a different kind of celebrity. Chris Van Dyke is the son of comedian Dick Van Dyke, and he resembles his famous father a great deal. He too is tall and lanky, and the grin that spreads over his long-jawed face is his father's grin. He moves with the same awkward grace. By 1981 Chris had traveled far from Hollywood—both in distance and in life-style.

Chris Van Dyke attended college first at Occidental University in Los Angeles. He took a year off to travel before graduating, a year in which he covered twenty thousand miles seeing the United States. Months of that period were spent in the Northwest, and he found the region much to his liking. He attended Whitworth University in Spokane for a while, but he returned to Occidental to receive his undergraduate degree. He obtained his law degree at Arizona State University, graduating near the top of his class.

The Northwest still beckoned to Van Dyke, and, as fate would have it, one of his professors at Arizona State was Oregon Supreme Court Justice Arno Denecke, on sabbatical to teach there. When Van Dyke had his law degree, he knew that the place he wanted to be was Oregon, and he applied for positions there. Justice Denecke remembered the young lawyer and the brilliance he had shown in grasping the law. He hired Chris Van Dyke as his legal assistant and Van Dyke moved to Salem in 1975.

After two years with the chief justice, Van Dyke served as a deputy district attorney in Benton County in Corvallis, Oregon, for two and a half years, and then he returned to Salem to work in the appellate division of the Oregon Attorney General's office.

In May 1980 Chris Van Dyke took a gamble. He ran for Marion County district attorney—and won. He was only twenty-nine years old, and he had yet to prosecute a murder case.

Chris Van Dyke is as dedicated to the law as his father is to the theater, and as punctilious about the detail and hard work that go with career success. Van Dyke worked closely with Kominek and Holloway to track Shari Hull's killer. Van Dyke agreed that Beth Wilmot might remember more about her attacker if she were to undergo hypnosis. Beth trusted Dave Kominek, and on February 3 she agreed to be hypnotized in the presence of police artist Dave Barrios, in the hope that a more precise image of the hooded killer might emerge.

Kominek asked Beth to pick a place where she felt safe and happy, and she chose to picture herself in the room of a boyfriend whom she cared about. She would be safe, Kominek assured her continually; she would view what had happened on a "television set," removed from all danger. She would not have to relive the attack; she would only be an observer—as if she were only watching a television show.

"Now, Beth," Kominek's voice droned, "while you're in this very, very comfortable place, you just really feel good. You can hear everything that's going on and you just want to remain like you are. You're very, very relaxed, very, very comfortable. I want you to just think now, imagine that you're at the top of a stairs, and the stairway is about ten steps . . . real gradual steps. I want you to imagine that you're going down. Each step you take, you're going further and further into relaxation. You start with the top step, and that's number ten, and then down to nine . . . down to eight . . . down to seven . . . six. Five. Four. Three. Down to two . . . one.''

Beth was in a beautiful garden. An imaginary balloon was tied to her wrist and her arm was light as a feather as it floated upward with the balloon's delicate tug. Kominek asked her to imagine a calendar, and then the pages were ripped off until she found herself once again back to the eighteenth of January.

"You remember that you are not really there; you can just watch this. You are watching this on TV. You can take this TV and bring it up close or you can push it further away.''

Beth smiled and nodded. She was not afraid.

"You and Shari are going to get the gas. Now you are going to have to go to work. You can see that Shari has to take a shower. Now you are getting ready to go to work. It is just you and Shari, and you go to work.''

Again Kominek reminded Beth that she was only watching the scene on a television set—that she was in no danger, that no one could hurt her.

"Now, this man is going to enter. You can see this on the TV. He comes through the door. You can see him coming through the door. He's got a gun in his hand. Now, Beth, I want you to watch him. I want you to concentrate on what he is wearing.''

The tape recorder spun on as Kominek left the room. There was no sound but Beth Wilmot's relaxed breathing. Then Kominek ushered Dave Barrios in to listen to Beth's responses and sketch a face as she talked. Even in Beth's hypnotic state, the tape recorder would pick up some tension in her voice, fear that surfaced despite Kominek's repeated assurances that no one could hurt her.

Slowly Beth described the killer again.

Beth: "I can't see his hair.''

Barrios: "You can't see his hair. Did he have a hat on?''

Beth: "He had a hood.''

Barrios: "He had a hood on? Did he keep that hood on all the time?''

Beth: "Uh-huh.''

Barrios: "Like a sweatshirt hood . . . or a jacket hood?''

Beth: "Jacket.''

They worked on. Beth's eyes teared and her mascara melted into smudgy streams down her cheeks. She did not notice. For an hour she answered Barrios' questions. At length his sketchpad was filled with a ghostlike face. The killer looked at him from lidded eyes, his mouth drawn into a cruel, tight line. The hood had emerged almost like a monk's hood.

Gently Dave Kominek led Beth back through the days of the calendar until it was once again February 3. She sat up and looked around.

"How long do you think you were in here?" he asked her.

"A half hour."

"Okay. What time did we come in?"

"I don't know."

"It was about two-thirty. It's five after four now."

Beth was amazed. "Really! How long have I been in here?"

"An hour and a half."

Kominek handed Beth a tissue and suggested that she wipe the smeared mascara from her cheeks. She couldn't remember that she had cried. Embarrassed, she was a typical teenager again, worried that her makeup looked "awful."

"I didn't remember enough," she apologized. "I saw his eyes. I kept seeing his eyes."

Beth looked directly at Kominek. "I want you to take me to TransAmerica. We'll go back there and I'll remember more. I'm afraid to go back there, but I will if it will help."

Kominek agreed to drive Beth to the building where she had come close to death. But even when they walked through the lunchroom at the TransAmerica Building, she remembered no more. The man was young, tall, and cruel. He had worn a Band-Aid on his nose, dark red and white sports shoes, and a hooded jacket. The memory of his face still terrified her, frightening her so much that her mind shut down whenever she tried to recreate it in detail.

"Catch him," Beth said. "If you catch him, I'll know him. I'll never, ever forget that face."

8

After the death of Shari Hull, citizens in Salem, Oregon, had flooded the Marion County Sheriff's Office with tips on possible suspects in the murder. Detectives were receiving over two hundred phone calls a day. Marion County had only four detectives, and Lieutenant McCoy and Jay Boutwell were working on another, unrelated homicide. That left Dave Kominek and Monty Holloway to find Shari's killer. The pair followed each new thread of information to its end, finding nothing that would help in the investigation.

They obtained computer listings of all parolees released in the previous two years from the Oregon State Penitentiary after serving time for rape, other sex offenses, or murder. They ran down the location of each parolee, and found not one who physically resembled Shari Hull's killer.

The only conclusion Kominek and Holloway could reach was that the killer with the Band-Aid on his nose was not local, that he had to be a drifter who had seized the moment when he chanced to glimpse the two girls cleaning the TransAmerica office. If he was not local, he might well be anywhere, long gone.

Deputy Bernie Papenfus had told them that he'd seen a man just after the first call for help came in, and that man had been on foot. That did not mean that he hadn't stashed his vehicle somewhere safely away from the crime scene and walked back to confront the girls. But no one could know what that vehicle looked like. No one but Beth Wilmot knew what the man *really* looked like.

On February 3 Dave Kominek sent out a teletype request for information on similar crimes to the seven western states. The M.O. (modus operandi) of murder and sexual assault was new to

79

Salem; Kominek hoped that it might sound familiar to detectives in other jurisdictions.

"We got a call the next day," Kominek recalls. "From all the way down in California, Shasta County to be exact. Captain Jim Carter and Detective Gene Farley called. They had had a double murder down there the very day I sent the teletype—a terrible crime—and they thought that the death weapon might have been a .32-caliber gun, just as ours was. They were waiting for autopsy results to be sure."

On February 3 Steve Eckard, a Redding, California, firefighter had drawn a twenty-four hour shift at the Mountain Gate Station. It is ironic that policemen and firefighters, who protect other men's families, often have to leave their own families unprotected during the dark, dangerous hours of the night. Eckard's wife, Donna Lee, thirty-seven, and his fourteen-year-old stepdaughter, Janell Jarvis, were home alone on that Tuesday evening. A young stepdaughter, Kristin Jarvis, twelve, was away from home during the early part of the evening. The Eckard family lived at the end of Holiday Road in a development in Mountain Gate, California, some eight miles north of Redding, just south of the Lake Shasta Caverns and directly on the I-5 freeway.

Donna Lee Eckard worked as a registered nurse at Mercy Hospital on the day shift, and when Steve worked nights at the fire department, it seemed that they were like ships passing in the night—but they both were devoted to their professions, jobs that saved lives.

Steve Eckard talked to his wife for the last time at threethirty in the afternoon. Donna Lee had been to a doctor that afternoon for a minor surgical procedure, and she told her husband that she wasn't feeling well and that she was going to lie down.

Twelve-year-old Kristin Jarvis stayed late at the Bass school to watch a basketball game, and called her mother at six P.M. to ask permission to go to a friend's house. Donna Lee sounded sleepy to Kristin, as if she had just been wakened from a nap. She told Kristin that it would be all right for her to visit her friend if she was home by nine o'clock.

The seventh-grader arrived home promptly, and checked the downstairs clock, noting that it was eight minutes to nine. She called out to her mother and sister . . . but no one answered. Not really alarmed, she walked through the neat home, still calling to Donna Lee and Janell.

When she came to her parents' bedroom, Kristin Jarvis stumbled on a frozen tableau of horror—a sight that no twelve-year-old should ever have to see. Both her mother and her sister were in the house, but they could no longer respond.

They lay side by side on the bed. Donna Lee lay on her back; she wore only a nightgown that had been pulled down, exposing her breasts. Her glasses were still in place, but her ankles were crossed and bound with white surgical tape; her arms had been twisted beneath her and her wrists were bound with the same tape. A wide swath of tape covered her mouth and nose.

Fourteen-year-old Janell was completely nude, her face covered with blood.

Kristin accepted with dull shock that her sister was dead, but she thought her mother might be alive. She wrenched the tape gag from Donna Lee's face and begged her to answer. Her mother didn't respond.

And then Kristin was afraid that they were both dead. As a firefighter's daughter, Kristin had been taught what to do in an emergency. She had been told that you must never assume the worst, that sometimes accident or drowning victims could be brought back if medical help was called in time. She picked up the phone and dialed the emergency number that fed into lines at Mercy Hospital.

"My mother . . . my sister . . . send help quickly. Holiday Road. The Eckards."

The call came in at one minute after nine. Sergeant Boatner and Corporal Dan Cunningham of the Shasta County sheriff's patrol responded to the call, along with officers Coe and Wooden. Personnel at Mercy Hospital called the Mountain Gate fire station to ask that emergency medical technicians respond. For Steve Eckard, it was the nightmare that all peace and fire officers dread. This time, it was his own home where help was needed.

Chief Dave Selby, Assistant Chief Leroy Porteous, and Captain Dan Selby raced with Eckard to his home. It wasn't very far to Holiday Road; Mountain Gate is a small town. The fire-department personnel arrived at the Eckard home in five minutes. Two minutes later, the sheriff's men pulled up.

The deputies could see Steve Eckard comforting Kristin in the living room, and Dan Selby and Porteous advised them that there were two bodies in the upstairs bedroom. Steve Eckard told them that he had viewed the bodies, that they were those of his wife and elder stepdaughter.

Cunningham and Boatner could see what appeared to be a bullet wound in Janell Jarvis' neck, and the tape bonds on her mother. They immediately secured the scene and notified detectives Gene Farley and Rick Burnett.

Farley and Burnett recognized the "execution-style" method of murder. They saw that Donna had been shot too, possibly twice. Janell had suffered many wounds, at least a half-dozen, all in the back of her head. What they could not fathom was why this peaceful residence at the dead end of a residential street should be the scene of such carnage.

The two detectives had to ask the most onerous question, to get it out of the way, although they felt they already knew the answer. Detectives always look first at those closely related to murder victims, since statistics bear out the fact that most victims are killed by relatives and close associates. They signaled to the fire chief and drew him aside.

Where had Steve Eckard been during the previous three or four hours? The answer came immediately from his fellow firefighter. Eckard had been on duty at the station.

Kristin volunteered that she had talked to her mother at six and that she'd been fine then. A little sleepy, but she hadn't sounded frightened or alarmed about anything.

"Did she say anything, Kristin—anything about what she planned to do this evening?" Farley asked gently.

The girl shook her head, and then remembered. "She said she had to go down to Jake's Market to get a couple of things."

Farley and Burnett knew Jake's; everyone who regularly traveled the I-5 probably knew Jake's—a little store located just off the freeway at the end of the street where the Eckards lived. Vacationers traveling into the resort area around Lake Shasta could count on Jake's for a supply of cold beer, beans, hot dogs—the standard camping provender.

Janell's jeans lay on the floor next to the bed, and Burnett carefully fished a check from the back pocket. It was dated February 3, made out to Jake's, and signed by Donna Eckard. Something had stopped Janell from going into the store and cashing it.

No one but the killer could know exactly what had happened to Donna Eckard and her daughter, but reconstruction of the crime suggested that the two had left their home to make a quick trip down to Jake's to purchase breakfast supplies. Donna Eckard had apparently thrown on a coat over her nightgown and driven Janell down to the store. The coat was in the bedroom too, carelessly thrown over the end of the bed. All things being equal, Janell would have taken the check and gone in to buy bread, milk, and cereal.

The detectives checked at Jake's Market and found that Donna and Janell had not been in to shop earlier in the evening. They hadn't made it that far. Someone had intercepted them.

The motive for murder? Clearly sexual. The bodies were nude and half-nude. It would take an autopsy to determine if rape had actually occurred. Steve Eckard checked through the house and said that all the items a burglar or robber might look for were there: the stereo, television sets, jewelry. The only thing missing was his handgun: a .38 Special Model 60 Smith and Wesson. It was a unique gun with a stainless-steel three-inch barrel and walnut grips. Eckard was able to give the Shasta detectives the serial number of the missing weapon.

The bodies of the victims were removed to await postmortem examination.

When the results of those autopsies came in a day later, Gene Farley and Rick Burnett were back on the phone to Kominek in Salem. Donna Lee Eckard and Janell Jarvis had been shot in the head: seven bullets for the teenager and two for her mother. The bullets retrieved had come from a .32-caliber handgun, just as had the bullets in the shooting of Shari Hull and Beth Wilmot. Even though Mountain Gate, California, was more than four hundred miles south of Salem, a commonality was developing between the cases: female victims; two victims at a time; .32 caliber bullets; execution-style wounds to the back of the head; location of crime scenes hard by the I-5 freeway.

And there was more. Beth and Shari had been subjected to oral sodomy. Fourteen-year-old Janell Jarvis had been sodomized anally, after death. There was no evidence that Donna Lee Eckard had been sexually abused, although her nightgown had been disarranged. The victims had died only an hour before they were discovered by Kristin Jarvis; rigor mortis had not even begun when they were found, nor had there been any lividity patterns in the lower portions of the bodies. (Lividity is the purplish-red striation that results when blood settles after the heart stops pumping.)

Kristin's arrival home had surely come almost on the heels of the killer's departure. A few minutes earlier, and Kristin Jarvis too might have become a murder victim.

"And the Mountain Gate case isn't the only one that seems to fit," Burnett continued. "A subject wearing a green jacket, jeans, gloves, and tennis shoes, with tape over the bridge of his nose, is wanted down here for questioning in a rape, kidnap, and sodomy case in Redding on February 3. We've got one the next day in Yreka, and I've found a Winchell's Donut robbery in Grants Pass on January 29, a grocery-store robbery in Medford—same day—a motel robbery in Ashland on February 4.''

"I think we're looking for the same man," Kominek said. "It looks as though a whole lot of jurisdictions are looking for the same man."

They promised to stay in touch; the Shasta County sheriff's detectives would look through reports for more "Band-Aid" cases in northern California and southern Oregon. Kominek would check north from Eugene.

Shasta County was not the only department responding to Kominek's teletypes asking for similar cases. The response was far greater than he had expected. Indeed, he had begun to receive a virtual storm of replies.

9

Randy Woodfield had so many jobs and so many addresses between July 1979 and March 1981, it was hard for his parole officer, Judy Pulliam, to keep track of him.

He usually doctored his employment application forms so that the four-year gap left by his stint in the penitentiary didn't have to be explained. Basically, all he had to do was subtract those years from his age; he didn't like to admit even to himself that he was thirty years old. He was in good shape; he looked younger, and he could easily pass for a man in his mid-twenties.

Randy jumped from woman to woman, even more frequently than he changed jobs, trying to find someone who might remain completely entranced with him. While it might be expected that a man who had been without female sex partners for four years would be "hungry" for sex, Randy Woodfield was "starving."

Randy looked for likely female candidates everywhere, and he was very resourceful. Just after his release from prison in July 1979, he followed two pretty young women down the I-5 freeway, passing them, pulling back, and signaling until they stopped, rolled down their car window, and asked him if he wanted to go swimming. He nodded and followed them to their apartment.

The afternoon went well, and he called one of the girls, Moira Bandon, two days later. By mid-August they were living together. Shortly thereafter, Moira was chagrined to find that she had contracted herpes. She forgave Randy, and their relationship lasted until November, when they had a fight and Randy moved out. Beyond the herpes, she had a memento; Randy had gifted Moira with one of his nude photos. He continued to call her for the next year and a half, and they maintained a friendship, even though the romance had gone out of their relationship.

After Randy quit his job at Tektronix, he was hired by the Cheerful Tortoise lounge, where he worked at a bartender. Fellow employees at the Cheerful Tortoise were puzzled that Randy seemed fixated on young girls of sixteen or seventeen. Although his co-workers found him easygoing and a "pretty nice guy," they wondered why all of his close friends were women. One of the other bartenders describes Randy as "having an eighteen-year-old level of conversation. He was kind of a dumb-blond type—except that he was a man."

During his Cheerful Tortoise era, Randy did date one woman who was only five years younger than he was, a pretty woman who worked at a bank. She had met him on the street when he was riding his motorcycle. At first she'd found him attractive, but later she saw sides to him that troubled her. He was obsessed with female breasts, so much so that he seemed "kinky" to her. But what really broke them up was their almost complete lack of communication.

"He just wasn't very smart," she explained to detectives who questioned her years later. "I'm ashamed to think that I dated Randy at all. He wore thin pretty quickly."

Randy was incensed when the bank teller broke up with him, and he told co-workers at the Cheerful Tortoise that he wanted revenge. But after two days of blind rage, he stopped talking about the breakup.

Randy wasn't officially fired from the Cheerful Tortoise, but his employment there was terminated by mutual consent with the owners.

After he left the Cheerful Tortoise, he went to work at the Faucet Tavern on S.W. Beaverton-Hillsdale Highway in Beaverton, Oregon. He had answered an ad in the paper placed by the Faucet management in late March 1980. He was hired on April 9 to be a relief bartender and assistant manager. He worked the night shift from six P.M. to two-thirty A.M. His salary was two hundred and fifty dollars a week, plus tips. The money was good, and the women were plentiful. He liked the Faucet job, but he was let go on the first of October. His employer recalls that Randy was very soft-spoken and that he was simply unable to assert the authority that the job demanded. Randy was certainly big enough, but he didn't seem to have what it took to muscle pugnacious drunks out of the place, nor did he command much respect from the younger employees.

Within a week or two of Randy's dismissal, three thousand dollars was taken from the Faucet Tavern's cash register. Entry had not been forced, and Randy was the only person other than the owners who had a key to the place. The tavern owners went to Randy's home in Lake Oswego to confront him, and they finally found him hiding in the attic. He denied the theft, but he was furious that he had been accused. He wrote a thinly veiled threat letter to his former employers. Later, with some glee, he admitted to one of his few platonic female friends, Dixie Palliter, that he was the one who had ripped off the Faucet Tavern.

After the Faucet burglary, word got around, and Randy couldn't find another bartending job. He worked thereafter in jobs that didn't suit him nearly as well as the Faucet had. He was employed for a while at one of the Shakey's pizza outlets, and then as a clerk for a 7-11 store. He was fired from the 7-11 job too, although there were no overt reasons given.

Randy moved from his sister's home to Park Street in Portland, then to Oleson Road, and then to a rental house on Pilkington in Lake Grove, Oregon. Almost all of his mail bore at least one forwarding address.

It took a while for some of his correspondents to catch up with him. One letter was forwarded to him—a letter that he would save carefully in his memorabilia file. Randy had made it a practice in the past to send pictures of himself—in the nude or in bathing trunks—to women friends. In late 1979 he had decided to enlarge his circle of admirers. He sent one of the shots of himself with muscles glistening and bulging to *Playgirl* magazine in Santa Monica, California. *Playgirl* had had enthusiastic response from readers on its "beefcake" centerfolds aping *Playboy*'s gorgeous female shots. Randy figured he looked as good as any of the macho males he'd seen featured.

In May 1980 he received a letter in response from *Playgirl*:

Congratulations! You have been selected for possible publication in *Playgirl*'s Guy Next Door feature.

Please return the enclosed model release and information sheet *as soon as possible*.

Don't be discouraged if you do not hear from us right away. We reconsider all submissions each month.

Playgirl will notify you when we determine the issue for which you have been selected.

Thank you for your time and patience. *Playgirl* looks forward to seeing more of you soon.

Sincerely,

Alison Morley
Photo Editor

The letter came addressed to R. B. Wood. Randy was willing to bare his muscular body to the readers of *Playgirl*, but had apparently planned to do it with a pseudonym. He thumbed through *Playgirl* eagerly each month to see if his picture had been selected. It was never there, and, given his later notoriety, the magazine had been prudent in choosing not to feature him.

By the late spring of 1980 Randy had set up housekeeping with still another woman: Lucy Grant—the girl he had described to Traci Connors when he visited her in the hospital. They signed a lease together on June 10, 1980, for the house on Pilkington Road in Lake Grove, Oregon, on a month-to-month basis. Randy and Lucy promised to pay three hundred dollars a month. His cohabitation with Lucy was the longest stretch of domesticity he had ever enjoyed with a woman, and he'd been expansive when he described his love affair to Traci Connors, sure that Lucy was faithful to him despite her penchant for inviting young men home to listen to her stereo and party while he tried to sleep after working all night.

Randy himself operated under his own moral guidelines; he kept an eye out for new conquests. While he was living with Lucy, he met a seventeen-year-old girl named Julie Reitz at the Faucet Tavern. That meeting took place in August 1980. He'd graciously looked the other way and allowed the underage girl into the tavern. Julie, like most teenage girls, found him "cute" and she flirted with him. Later she met him for lunch. He told Julie that he'd been hurt by a lot of girls and that he couldn't risk seeing her anymore. This was, of course, a challenge to the teenager, who thought that she could make it up to him. That he was an older man only made him seem more desirable. Julie went out with him one night a few weeks later. She wasn't used to hard liquor, and she became intoxicated. They returned to the town house where Julie lived with her mother. Her mother was not home that night, but they were chaperoned by one of Julie's girlfriends.

To Randy's disappointment, the girls slept together, and he had to sleep in Julie's mother's room. In the morning he pranced into the girls' bedroom wearing only his bikini underpants and crawled into bed with them. He fondled Julie a little, but he left when she told him he had to.

The pretty teenager continued to be fascinated with Randy—until she found out that he was a liar. Julie, naively believing she was comforting a man who'd been hurt badly by women, had been furious when she ran into him in a bar named Euphoria.

Randy, of course, hadn't been bereft of female companionship; he was living with Lucy Grant. And Lucy was with him when Julie spied him at the Euphoria.

Julie became almost hysterical and called him an "asshole" for lying to her. And then she started to cry and ran out of the bar.

But after that Julie thought about Randy Woodfield, this handsome man thirteen years older than she was. When she saw him again, she apologized for screaming at him at the Euphoria. She told a friend later that she expected him to call her, saying that they had worked out all the misunderstandings they'd had. "We've agreed just to be friends."

Randy and Lucy Grant broke up in the fall of 1980, but not because of Julie Reitz; Lucy didn't even know about Julie. It may have been that Randy finally had enough of Lucy's young male friends; it may have been something else. Whatever caused the rift, his relationship with Lucy Grant disintegrated into petty quarrels. When Lucy explained to him that she thought she should date other men, Randy was devastated. She had turned out to be just like Sharon, his love at Treasure Valley, who had betrayed him, just like Moira, just like the woman who worked at the bank. None of them really cared about him.

Lucy was so anxious to move out that, as she laughingly told friends, she had forgotten to unplug the water-bed heater. The water bed melted, and Randy threatened to sue her. Lucy responded by telling Randy she was going to bring *him* into court to demand her share of the rental deposit. He countered with a scrupulously polite letter saying that she would get her money— minus any utilities owed. He told her he had gone to a lawyer over the matter.

Whereas Randy had shown overt anger when Sharon and the other women had rejected him, he had now learned to mask his anguish; he would not let Lucy see what she had done to him. But her defection only solidified his feeling that women were not to be trusted, that they would only pretend to love him and then betray him with other men.

Tim Rossi, Randy's best friend and former roommate, had suffered a similar blow. When Tim had moved from Portland up to Tacoma to accept an assistant professorship at Pacific Lutheran University, it had strained his relationship with his steady woman, Darci Fix. Darci had told Tim that she had found someone else. The young professor took the breakup well, and he had remained on friendly terms with Darci.

Tim told Randy that he and Darci had broken up when Randy visited him in Tacoma on October 11, 1980. It was not a propitious visit; Tim found that Randy had changed radically since they'd known each other at Portland State, since they'd shared an apartment after they left college. The pious, gentle young athlete had disappeared, and in his place Tim saw a swinger, a man who talked incessantly about women and bars. Randy was furious with Darci Fix for breaking up with his longtime friend, almost as angry as if she had left *him*.

Darci had only weeks to enjoy her new love; on November 27, 1980—Thanksgiving Day—the bodies of Darci and her new boyfriend, Doug Altie, were found in Darci's Portland apartment. They had been shot, execution style. Tim learned about Darci's death the day after the double murder in a phone call from Randy.

Tim was shocked speechless; he had visited Darci and Doug on November 25, the Tuesday before Thanksgiving, and everything had been normal then. In talking with Portland police detectives, Tim asked if Darci had had a chance to use her gun to protect herself.

The response was, "What gun?"

Tim said that Darci had had a small handgun when he lived with her. Her father, a physician, had given it to her for protection. In fact, Tim had seen the gun on November 25.

"It was lying on the floor next to her bed, a silver gun with a white handle. It had a short barrel. I don't know much about guns, so I couldn't tell you the caliber."

Darci's father told detectives that it had been an old .32 chrome revolver, so old that it had never been registered. He would not be able to identify it if it were found—except by appearance.

The gun was missing from the apartment when Portland detectives inventoried the contents, although nothing else was missing. They turned the place upside down trying to find it, but it simply wasn't there.

The murder of Darci Fix and Doug Altic has never been solved, nor has the missing gun ever surfaced.

Moira Bandon (Randy's first live-in lover, whom he had met on the freeway) saw the newspaper articles about Darci's murder and called Randy to tell him that Darci had been killed. She located him at his sister's home in Portland, where he had moved after breaking up with Lucy Grant. Moira was puzzled at the flatness of Randy's response to the shocking news. He seemed to accept it without any emotion at all. She might have been giving him a weather report for all the shock he showed at the news.

Darci was not the first among Randy's female acquaintances to be murdered in the fall of 1980. Cherie Ayers, who had graduated from Newport High with Randy in the class of 1969, was raped and killed in Portland on October 10 sometime before midnight. Cherie had worked with Randy on the class reunion held right after his release from the Oregon State Penitentiary. A brilliant, pretty woman, she had attended Oregon State University in Corvallis and then the University of Oregon Medical School. She was working in Portland as a radiologic technologist at the time of her death.

Portland Police Detective Bob Dornay investigated the murder of Cherie Ayers. It was a particularly ugly homicide; Cherie had been bludgeoned on the head and then stabbed repeatedly in the neck. In checking through a list of Cherie's friends, Dornay discovered that Randy Woodfield had visited Cherie many times at her home on S.W. 9th Place in Portland when he moved to Portland after being paroled. Given Randy's prison record, he was questioned closely during the murder probe. Dornay found Randy's answers about his whereabouts during the vital time period evasive and deceptive. He asked Randy to take a polygraph examination, but Randy refused to submit to a lie detector.

The Ayers crime scene had given up little physical evidence. There *were* secretions found in the young radiologist's vaginal vault, but no alien pubic hairs were detected. Dornay obtained Randy Woodfield's blood type from records at the state penitentiary: B negative. Analysis of the secretions in the victim's vagina indicated that they had not come from a B-negative secretor. Although Dornay was not entirely convinced that Randy had no connection with Cherie's murder, he was eliminated as a suspect. Still, there was always the possibility that the secretions might have come from an earlier sex act with another male, or might even have been the victim's own vaginal moisture.

At any rate, despite Dornay's gut feelings about Randy's involvement, there was not enough physical evidence to charge him with Cherie Ayers' murder. Her murder has not been solved at this writing.

It seemed odd that Randy had been closely associated with two women who had been murdered in the space of six weeks, so close that detectives had questioned him intensively in each case. Possible within the parameters of the law of averages . . . but odd.

Randy continued to be consumed with his pursuit of women. Although he complained that women had done him wrong, it did not occur to him that *he* had been far from a constant lover. In his mind, the fault always fell on the female's shoulders.

After a spate of recriminations and bitterness, Randy adjusted to losing Lucy Grant. He plunged into promiscuity. His hobby, his avocation, his passion, was women. He ''hit on'' almost every young woman he encountered. He was clumsy and transparent in his approaches, but by the sheer law of averages he scored with a lot of them.

Randy Woodfield had a grossly distorted view of the male-female relationship. When it came to women, his greediness verged on obsession. He was like a starving man let loose in a bakery, a man who snatched at everything he saw, taking one bite of every delicacy and then throwing it away before he could savor it. If one woman was good, two were better. If two made him feel safe, then three . . . or five . . . or a dozen might possibly fill his yawning need for feminine acceptance. Once he had made some contact with a woman, however tentative, he wanted to keep her in his stable. He bombarded her with calls and clever cards and drop-in visits to be sure that she remembered him and considered him important. He used the telephone compulsively, running up huge long-distance bills. That was necessary to ensure that all of his women remembered him. He often called late at night to remind them that he was thinking of them.

His frenetic campaigns didn't always work. Randy approached three kinds of women. Women near his own age saw through him immediately; they found him a shallow, odd phony and refused even to give him their phone numbers. Women a bit younger and less worldly found him, initially, rather attractive, but on closer inspection there was something about him that frightened them, and they refused his further attentions. Only the younger girls, like Julie Reitz, or the truly naive fell for his line of patter and professions of undying love.

Randy stalked most of his quarries in bars, the kind of bars where young singles gather, where both sexes are looking for that one true love. He was a handsome man; no one would argue that. His hair was permed to a thicket of dark curls, his mustache was neat and luxuriant, his eyelashes were so long that they just missed seeming feminine, and his muscles rippled. His only flaw was the scarring that remained from his teenage acne.

Randy dressed for his prowls in designer jeans and plaid shirts open almost to the waist to reveal his broad hairy chest. He wore the *de rigueur* gold chain and pendant, and boots with heels that made him even taller than his six-feet-two. His voice was deep and soft, and he never was disrespectful. He asked women to dance, and he bought them drinks. He referred to his "sad childhood" and suggested that his life had been one of tragedy.

He "fell in love" instantly, fixing all his attentions on each woman he approached. If he was rejected, he moved quickly to the woman sitting on the next bar stool. But he pushed too hard for intimacy. He held their hands at the bar, and he tried to kiss them. He moved from "What's your name?" to "I think we could fall in love" in a matter of minutes. He begged to be allowed to go home with his choices that very night. He would only sleep on their couches, he promised.

Randy's approach to women was so frenzied that he turned most of them off, and they rolled their eyes at each other when he wasn't looking and called him a "weirdo" in giggling whispers. He skipped vital steps in forming relationships; his greediness showed. Just as men, even in the sexual revolution of the eighties, find little value in a woman who is too easy, even marginally sophisticated females found Randy as transparent as a male dog in rut. And they turned their backs on him. Sure, he was a handsome hunk, but they were looking for something more than that.

Randy failed to see why women rejected him. He blamed the women. He felt that they were always standing him up. It never occurred to him that he had hounded the "no-shows" until they had agreed to "dates" that were not really dates, but half-promises born out of desperation.

Still, enough of them did accept dates with him, and he gathered his successes into his life and into his address book as if he were picking up diamonds with both hands. He had no ethics at all, no compunction about lying to women. He was only treating them as they deserved to be treated. When they refused him, he never let his anxiety show. He held it in. His anger grew, but he somehow knew that he would ultimately have his vengeance.

Randy Woodfield, for all of his outward glamour, was terrified of women. Behind the brash facade there was a shadow man, and he dared not let that man show. Despite his protestations otherwise, he saw himself as a wimp; the muscled man he saw in the mirror warred with the image he held inwardly.

As 1980 wound down, Randy thought seriously about leaving Portland. He had many reasons to feel uneasy about staying in the Portland area. He had been questioned about Cherie Ayers' murder, and even though nothing had come of it, the fact that the Portland police had homed in on him made him edgy.

Randy was far from the innocent lamb. He *had* been engaged in criminal activities. He liked to operate from a strong financial base, and he couldn't seem to find a job that paid more than the minimum wages offered at convenience markets and fast-food outlets. The solution was simple. He had contacted one of his old prison buddies, Tony Niri. The two joined up for some robberies. The Faucet Tavern first, and then a Safeway store in Vancouver, Washington, among others.

Niri was con-wise, and he'd instructed Randy on a simple but effective disguise. All one had to do was to plaster several strips of tape across the bridge of the nose, and no witness would be able to describe him afterward. Randy improved on that by gluing on a fake beard he'd bought at a novelty shop. Niri carried a .357 magnum during the robberies, but Randy made do with a toy gun. After the heists, Randy unpeeled the tape and the beard and hid them in his backpack or in his sports gloves. Sometimes they used Randy's car, a "Champagne Edition" gold Volkswagen Bug—but that was a fairly memorable car, so they usually used Niri's.

Nobody beyond Niri had any idea that Randy was involved in thefts.

Still, Portland hadn't been very lucky for him. There were all of his blighted liaisons with women, and all of the jobs he'd lost. He planned to move south, seventy miles south, to Eugene. He did not plan to inform his parole officer until the move was made. And perhaps not even then.

Randy had another friend from his days in the penitentiary: Ralph Wansee. Ralph had moved to Los Angeles after his parole, but he had family in Medford, Oregon, and the two men made plans to meet in Medford for the 1980 Christmas holiday.

Randy flew into Medford Christmas morning, and the two men spent Christmas Day with Ralph's mother and stepfather. The next day Randy suggested that they go out bar-hopping and looking for women. Ralph agreed, although he was far from the ladies' man Randy purported to be; Ralph had a harelip, which made him shy around women, fearful of rejection. Randy assured him that he had charisma enough for the two of them.

   And indeed he did. On December 26, Randy's thirtieth birthday, he managed to pick up not two women for them, but four. They were in the Bonanza Room of the Sandpiper when Randy brought the first set of women over to the table. Denise LeNoir was a pretty divorcée from Ashland, Oregon, out for the evening after hiring a baby-sitter for her youngsters. Denise found Randy very attractive, although her friend was not as taken with Ralph. The men wanted to party throughout the night, and Denise explained that she had to get home. She did give Randy her phone number, and he promised to call.

   Randy told Ralph not to worry. A short time later, he hit on a pair of beautiful sisters. Lynette Lacey lived right there in Medford, and her sister, Rose, had come up from North Hollywood to visit over Christmas. Ralph and Rose found common ground, since they both lived in the Los Angeles area, and Lynette initially thought Randy Woodfield was something special. They spent the rest of the evening together and made a date for the next night: Saturday, December 27.

   They met again at the Sandpiper and then Lynette and Randy had drinks at her house. Later they drove to Maxi's at the Red Lion to meet Rose and Ralph.

   During their second evening together, Lynette began to think she'd made an error in judgment. For one thing, her date had announced loudly to the cocktail lounge that he was looking for cocaine to buy. For another, Randy did not wear well; he was as insistent and pushy as an oversexed teenage boy. He suggested that he stay overnight with her. When she demurred, he argued that that was the only way they could really get to know each other.

   "I don't think so," she said.

   "You should want that. There's got to be something the matter with you not to," Randy argued.

   She looked at the dark man and thought that she'd been a fool; she was sorry she'd even kissed him. He was coming on so strong, with no encouragement at all from her. As far as she was concerned, the relationship was over before it began. Despite his protestations that she must be frigid or neurotic, she sent him away.

   Before dawn on Sunday morning, both Denise and Lynette heard from Randy Woodfield. Denise was surprised to hear from him at five A.M., and more than a little annoyed because he expected her to drive from Ashland to the Medford airport and pick him up. His plane was fogged in, and he needed a ride to Portland. She explained that her babies were sleeping and she didn't want to wake them.

"Leave them there," he said.

Naturally, her answer was no. She wondered that a man she'd met so briefly would expect so much from her.

Randy called Lynette next to say he was burned out from partying for three straight days and now he'd just missed his plane to boot. He was at the bus station, and he hinted that he'd like to spend the day with her. Lynette wasn't interested. She made small talk and hung up.

But both women's phone numbers went into Randy's thick little black book. He was particularly interested in Lynette. He wrote to her several times, apparently oblivious of the brush-off she'd given him.

"If we are meant to be together, it will happen," he wrote. "The stars just weren't right the night we were together."

She was a little bemused at his bland assumption that she was still interested in him. She did not know, of course, that Randy sent letters like that to dozens of women, that he might just as, well have had them run off by the gross on a copy machine.

He kept writing to her, and after a while she responded. He was very expressive in his letters. She thought maybe she'd misjudged him, and even toyed with the idea that she might visit him some weekend in Portland.

Neither Denise nor Lynette really expected to date Randy Woodfield again, but they had not seen the last of him, and his contacts with them would one day soon prove to be most un- lucky for him.

Randy Woodfield had claimed to want just one woman, a devoted woman who could be loyal to him. He had told his prison counselors that he longed only to find a good woman, marry her, raise a family, and that together they would work to help others. He had bemoaned the loss of several "special women," wondering why he was initially or ultimately rejected.

Two days after he struck out with the women in Medford, Randy was trolling again. He was staying temporarily at the New Oregon Motel in Eugene on December 30, 1980, while he scouted out housing possibilities in that city.

Shelley Janson was spending the Christmas holidays at her father's house in Eugene, home from college in New Mexico. On December 30, Shelley was four days away from her twenty-second birthday. She was a highly intelligent young woman; she maintained a four-point GPA at the University of New Mexico in Albuquerque. She was also very, very beautiful. But Shelley Janson approached life and the possibility of romance with surprising naiveté. Despite several disappointing love affairs, Shelley still believed in the "knight on a white horse." At some point, the perfect man would come along, and she knew she would recognize him the moment she saw him. He would be tall and dark and soft-spoken, sensitive just as she was. They would touch hands, and talk, and fall in love, to live happily ever after. Fate or karma would take care of that.

Shelley's karma led her on the night of December 30, 1980, to O'Callahan's in Eugene. She went there with a girlfriend to check out the possibilities of New Year's Eve parties the next night.

Shelley and her friend had stood on the edge of the dance floor for only five or ten minutes when a handsome man with curly dark hair approached them. "Excuse me." He smiled. "I think I left my drink on the ledge behind you."

Shelley turned and saw a man who fit her specifications for the "white knight" exactly. She was afraid he would go away, so she initiated a conversation to keep him at her side. He seemed to respond to her, and she was thrilled.

His name was Randall, he said, and he was from Portland, but he was planning to move to Eugene. He said he'd just celebrated his thirtieth birthday, and she laughed; he looked only about twenty-five. She demanded to see his driver's license, and saw that he *had* been born in 1950.

"I'm a Capricorn too," she said. "I'll be twenty-two this Saturday."

She was happy that they had something in common. Randall explained that he planned to attend the University of Oregon in the spring and that he'd be taking courses at Lane Community College in the interim. He was going to complete two degrees, one in business and one in health and physical education. She was impressed when he said he planned to find a job bartending and save all his money for his education. The man was clearly going places, and prepared to work hard to finish his education.

They danced only two dances that first evening; they were too busy talking. And the conversation was heavy, not the usual singles-bar stuff. Randall talked to her about his desires for the future, family, goals, morals. His voice was deep but soft, and he looked right into her eyes with his burning gaze. He told her about a woman in Medford who had refused him, and said he'd just "walked away." He would not force himself on a woman who didn't want him. She felt a little jealous, even though that had happened before she'd met him. But he assured her he cared nothing for the other woman.

Shelley felt like pinching herself to see if it was all real.

She regretted only that she had to go back to Albuquerque in three days. They were obviously so right for each other, and Randall was already suggesting that they might want to get seriously involved. Shelley had no way of knowing, of course, that Randall *always* came on this strong, that he suggested solid commitment to almost every woman he met. She was already falling in love. The hours flew by, and she was amazed when two A.M. came and the bar closed. Her friend tugged on her sleeve and whispered, "It's nice to see you so happy again. I'm going to leave you here with him."

Randall walked Shelley to his car and they stood in the winter chill in the parking lot until it was almost empty. "We were shocked," Shelley recalled to detectives later, "to have those incredible feelings so quickly. We just stood there talking about our feelings."

Finally they got into Randall's car, his Champagne Edition gold Volkswagen. When he kissed her, it felt right, and it didn't seem to matter that she'd known him only a few hours. They talked and kissed, and she finally asked him to take her to her friend's house because she'd left her purse in her friend's car. The plan was that he would then take her home to her father's house.

Shelley never went home that first night. Halfway to her dad's house, they mutually agreed that they would go, instead, to Randall's room at the New Oregon Motel. She stayed with him all night. He was very considerate of her. He suggested that it might be too soon for intercourse; he asked only for oral sex. She didn't know that fellatio was his principal sexual focus, that it always had been.

They spent the day of New Year's Eve visiting her family in Eugene. Randall told her he had arranged to rent a room from a divorced woman who lived with her young son, and Shelley went with him to Arden Bate's home on E Street in Springfield, just east of Eugene, where Randall gave Ms. Bates a check for his first month's rent.

Shelley hated to spend New Year's Eve without Randall, but he explained he had previous plans to meet friends in Portland

and go to a "forties costume party." She went to a party in Eugene, but she thought about nothing but Randall. He was too good to be true.

On New Year's Day, 1981, Shelley called Randall at his sister's home in Portland and told him that a friend of hers was coming up to Portland and that she could come along. He welcomed the suggestion and picked her up and took her out to TGI Friday. Providentially, Randall's sister was with their parents in Otter Rock, so the new lovers had another night together.

Shelley could hardly bear to get on a plane the next morning and fly back to New Mexico. But it was too soon for her to abandon college. Still, she knew they would be together again. She wished only that she hadn't forgotten the stuffed panda bear that Randall had bought her.

She wrote to Randall constantly, scribbling across the blank spaces of romantic cards. Her letters referred continually to how "exciting" Randall was. She vowed to enter a physical-fitness program so that she would be worthy of a man with so much athletic ability. She suggested plans that would let them meet again. She worried that most men might think she was coming on too strong, but Randall's letters to her were full of his affirmation of her plans. She had been dumped on by men before, and she was frightened. But not frightened enough to hold back on her confidences to him. She signed her letters "Your lover always," and each communiqué was more affectionate than the last.

Randall called her often, and he sent cards and letters too. He encouraged her commitment to him. She wrote that she was proud of him for searching for a job so diligently, and assured him that she would always be there for him if he ever became discouraged. No man could ask for more. A beautiful, intelligent, faithful woman loved Randall Woodfield.

"By the way, *I love you!*" she wrote. "I feel so lucky to have you in my life. I hope you are always there with me. . . . I have been looking for someone like you all my life—and now I've found you. Thanks for walking into my life, Randall."

The lovers were not separated long, although it seemed forever to Shelley. On January 30, 1981, Shelley flew into San Francisco to wait for Randall, who was driving down the coast to meet her. It was an idyllic three days. They spent the first night at the Hilton next to the airport, and then went to a cheaper motel in San Bruno to spend Saturday and Sunday night. They called it their "Love Boat" weekend. They went to Fisherman's

Wharf. Randall wanted to visit Alcatraz, and they toured the island prison for a couple of hours. They were typical tourists, two young people in love. Shelley was a little put off when they never engaged in normal intercourse, but she was so in love with Randall that she thought that would happen all in good time. Perhaps he had her on a pedestal, and felt that oral sex was all that they should do until they were married.

And they would be married. She was sure of that. On Saturday morning Randall bared his soul to her. He told her that he had been in prison and that he was on parole. He told her about his days with the Green Bay Packers and about his disappointment when it was over. Her shock about his criminal record dissipated rapidly; it was something from the past, and she knew that it would never happen again. And then he proposed to her. She said yes at once. They didn't set a date, but they discussed a late-summer wedding, or perhaps a Christmas wedding. They would definitely be married by Valentine's Day 1982. Randall called his friend Ralph in Los Angeles and asked him to be the best man. He called his parents in Otter Rock and told them he was engaged to be married.

After such a perfect weekend, Shelley hated to leave to fly back to New Mexico, but she had to wind things up at the university. All in all, the weekend had turned out better than she could ever have imagined. She'd known Randall for only a month, and now they were engaged. He took her to her plane and told her he would be driving back to Eugene up the I-5 freeway so that he could stop off at his sister Susan's home in Mt. Shasta and tell her the news about the wedding.

Shelley was home in Albuquerque by ten that Monday evening, February 2. Randall called her collect at midnight and told her he was only an hour and a half away from his sister's house. He would talk to her soon.

When Randall hadn't called her again by Wednesday, February 4, she tried to reach him in Eugene. He wasn't there. She was frightened and thought he might have been in an accident. She kept calling throughout the night, and she finally reached him on Thursday morning.

Randy said he'd had a pleasant visit with his sister, her physician husband, and their children, which was true; he had stopped to spend a short time in Mt. Shasta. As far as any trouble on the road, all that had happened, he said, was that he had gotten a ticket for speeding on the way home, and he thought he would buy a radar detector. Shelley didn't ask him why it had taken him two whole days to get home; she assumed he'd spent the time visiting his sister. He didn't actually say he had, but that seemed the likeliest explanation for his delay in calling her.

After the San Francisco weekend, Shelley's studies disintegrated; all she could think about was being with Randall. He called her every other day, or she called him. It wasn't enough. She couldn't bear the thought of Randall all alone in Eugene, discouraged about his lack of a job, and herself, just as lonesome, wasting time in New Mexico.

It helped a little when Randall sent her a dozen yellow roses on Valentine's Day. She put them in a vase where she could look at them when she wrote to him. "I feel like I've just begun on a very happy trail through life. Thanks!''

Shelley didn't know that Randy had remembered a dozen or more women for Valentine's Day, that each message was intimate, suggesting that a further relationship seemed almost a certainty. She had no idea how many women waited for a call from Randy.

Randy Woodfield was very thoughtful that Valentine's Day. He also sent an arrangement of red roses and white carnations to his parents, who were celebrating their thirty-fourth wedding anniversary. The flowers reached them in Reno, the first stop on an extended trip that would take them to Tokyo. His mother was especially touched by the gesture. They had been through much grief over Randy, and now it seemed that things were going to be all right after all. He was engaged to a fine young woman and talking enthusiastically about finishing his college degree at the University of Oregon. In the meantime, he had enrolled in a bartending school in Portland—which he would attend sporadically, even though he now lived in Eugene.

The Woodfields flew off to Tokyo with Randy's flowers carefully packed in damp paper, assured that all was well.

No one seemed to wonder that Randy could afford to send seventy-five dollars' worth of yellow roses to his fiancée and an expensive floral arrangement, plus champagne, to his parents even though he had no job and had had no employment for some time.

By the end of February, Shelley Janson missed her fiancé so much that she called him in tears. They agreed that they had to be together, and Shelley made plans to withdraw from school on February 24, pack her belongings, and drive to Eugene.

Shelley actually headed north on March 4, but when she got to Eugene, her world and everything she'd hoped for in the future had shattered into a million pieces.

10

Dave Kominek and Monty Holloway had received the information from Shasta County, California, that indicated that a suspect who sounded just like *their* suspect had struck in California along the I-5 freeway from January 28 to February 4, 1981. They also received copies of almost identical case reports from agencies ranging from Eugene, Oregon, to Seattle, Washington, and its suburbs. That meant that they probably were tracking a man whose geographical parameters included eight hundred miles of freeway, vast stretches of fast roads that allowed him to attack and be long gone by the time police were called. He had killed at least three times already. He had raped most of his victims.

And nobody knew who he was. But he had a nickname now: he was the "I-5 Killer."

Kominek was sure that the same man had used his silver gun on Shari Hull and Beth Wilmot in Salem after the attack on Merrisue and Megan Green in Corvallis. Perhaps his crimes against the Green children bothered him. Perhaps he was tired after "working" night after night all along the freeway. Four days had passed between the Corvallis incident and the carnage in the TransAmerica Building in Salem.

Corvallis police never located the missing phone receiver. They had found that someone had deliberately unscrewed the porch light on the Greens' front porch, and they tried to lift fingerprints from the bulb, but found only smudged glove prints.

There was no respite at all after Shari Hull and Beth Wilmot were shot; indeed, the next report in sequence had come in from Vancouver again. At seven-thirty on Monday, January 19 (as Beth lay under heavy guard in Salem Memorial Hospital), the man with the curly dark hair, the regulation false beard, and ski gloves robbed the Vancouver Skating Rink. The rink office was deserted except for the female cashier, seventeen, and three boys ten and eleven years old, one of whom had come to the rink that night to celebrate his birthday.

The man held out a silver gun, demanded the money in the cash register, and left after warning the cashier and the boys not to watch where he was going.

On January 26 he robbed the Dari Mart in Eugene at eight-fifteen in the evening. Again, he used Band-Aids over his nose. The twenty-three-year-old female clerk said he'd worn a brown corduroy or suede jacket with a hood and sheepskin lining. Again, no one saw a car.

Kominek turned to Holloway. "That's the pattern so far. It's quiet from here to Eugene after January 26. But it looks like that's because he was in California for the next several days. Almost two dozen cases that *have* to be the same man. There may be more that we don't even know about yet. What do we do now? Plant a stakeout in every fast-food spot between Canada and Mexico? *If* anybody had that much manpower, we might stumble onto him in a year or so. He's killed already; he's not liable to stop."

District Attorney Chris Van Dyke agreed that the time had come to coordinate the investigation in person with the California investigators. On February 6 Van Dyke, Kominek, and Holloway chartered a private plane and flew to Medford. There they met with detectives from the Shasta County Sheriff's Office, the Redding Police Department, the Yreka Police Department, and the Ashland, Medford, and Grants Pass police departments. Chris Van Dyke and the Marion County detectives presented the facts of the cases that they had come up with. And then the Shasta County investigators discussed their cases. They had conferred with the police north of them. There were *more* incidents to discuss.

The Shasta County investigators presented the information they had gathered that seemed surely to be the violent handiwork of the same suspect. The cluster of attacks in California and southern Oregon had occurred in a time frame that marked the man an insatiable sex prowler. Sergeant Rusty Brewer and investigator Ron Kingsley described attacks that were like carbon copies of those Kominek had received from Washington and northern Oregon. They went over the Eckard-Jarvis murders again for the benefit of the group.

Donna Eckard and Janell Jarvis had been alive six P.M. on February 3 (when Kristin talked with her mother on the phone), and their bodies still warm at nine P.M. (when Kristin discovered the murders).

"Now it looks like that wasn't the first hit on the third," Rusty Brewer said.

It seemed impossible, but the Shasta County sergeant said they had found another case on February 3 whose M.O. was almost identical. Earlier on the same night, a woman and a teenager working at the Burger Express restaurant in Redding had suffered an ordeal at the hands of an unknown suspect.

Marie Sloane, forty-six, owner of the Burger Express, was in the kitchen, and Lia Morris, eighteen, was at the front counter when a man with dark wavy hair walked in. He was over six feet tall and wore a wool cap, a windbreaker, faded jeans, and expensive jogging shoes. His hands were concealed by blue gloves with gray trim. Lia Morris looked up to take his order and saw that he was pointing a silver revolver at her. The man placed himself in a position where he could watch both women, and then he turned to Mrs. Sloane.

"Sit down, and you won't get hurt," he ordered.

Mrs. Sloane instructed Lia to get the money out of the cash register. The girl complied and handed it to the gunman.

He told Mrs. Sloane to lead him, with Lia in tow, to the bathroom. She obeyed, and the man told the shop owner to kneel down on top of the toilet. He taped her hands behind her back and then taped her ankles together. When she was helpless, he taped her mouth shut with a broad strip of tape. And then he turned to Lia and barked, "Take your clothes off."

While he was waiting for the teenager to remove her clothes, the gunman fondled Mrs. Sloane's breast, but went no further. He was waiting for Lia. Then he ordered Mrs. Sloane to get off the stool and face the door. When she said she couldn't move, he helped her to the floor and warned her to keep her face toward the door.

In the tight confines of the restroom, the intruder then turned to Lia Morris. The girl sobbed, terrified, but there was nothing her employer could do to help her. The gunman forced the girl to fellate him, but he did not ejaculate. He pushed her to the floor facedown and attempted anal sodomy. Still not satisfied, he demanded oral sex again. Finally he climaxed.

Finished with his victims for the moment, he fastened his clothes. They thought he was going to shoot them, but, providentially, Mrs. Sloane's husband stopped by the burger shop to check on her. She heard him outside the bathroom door, pushing against it, and then the man with the gun calmly saying, "It's busy."

Their captor opened the door and held the gun on her husband, forcing him into the bathroom. But he did not shoot them; they could hear his steps running away.

The women had come very close to death, but they were lucky. Lia Morris was taken to a hospital for treatment, and the Sloanes estimated their loss at two hundred and thirty dollars.

Within the next hour, someone shot and killed half of the Eckard family in Mountain Gate, less than ten miles away.

Yreka, California, is seventy miles north on the I-5, located on the other side of the Shasta National Forest, twenty miles south of the Oregon border. Almost exactly twenty-four hours after Donna Eckard and Janell Jarvis had been shot to death, Jessie Clovis, twenty-one, got into her Maverick after buying cigarettes at a liquor store in the north end of Yreka. She was about to start the car's engine when a man who looked to be in his mid-twenties suddenly opened the driver's-side door. She whirled, surprised, and saw a dark man who wore a green down jacket.

"Move over," he said. "I've got a gun."

She moved over and he said, "Don't look at my face."

She stared instead at the gun, and saw what seemed to be a small silver revolver with white grips. All she could think was: I can't believe this is happening.

She slid her eyes sideways, and she could see that the man wore blue jeans and running shoes. She let her eyes move up, and could see his sports gloves, a watch cap, and the wide swath of tape covering the bridge of his nose. He did not realize that she had seen him.

The man adjusted the seat to fit his long legs, started the engine, and backed the car out. He made a right turn on North Main Street and headed north toward Highway 263.

"May I have a cigarette?" she asked.

"No. And don't look at my face. Do you have any money?"

"A twenty-dollar bill."

"Is it in your purse? Get it for me."

She fished out the bill, and asked him if he wanted the change too, but he said she could keep that.

It wasn't money he was after anyway. He wanted to know the whole history of her sex life. Did she? How many men had she had? She said she didn't know. About how many? Jessie Clovis finally said, "Two," and began to cry.

"Stop crying. I'm not going to hurt you."

He ordered her to lie down across the seat so that her head was in his lap. She had to brace herself with her hand on the dashboard to keep from falling to the floor. He asked if she'd ever given oral sex before, and she said no. He forced her to unzip his pants, and she cried harder. Her tears seemed to anger him, and he demanded that she stop crying.

"Do what I say. You understand that, don't you?"

He asked if he could touch her breasts, continuing to use gutter language, but he hadn't really sought permission; he was already fondling her.

He seemed to want approval. He wanted her to tell him how much she was enjoying what he was doing. He squeezed her breasts until they hurt, and she obeyed and she said what he wanted her to say. She lied and told him that his hands pleased her.

"Do you let your boyfriend do this to you?"

"No."

"Why not?"

"Because it's wrong."

He was silent for a short time as the car hurtled down the highway, but the man had plans for Jessie. He ordered her to touch her own body intimately, and she pretended to do so. Now he ordered her to fellate him. She refused, and he grabbed her by the hair and bent her over his penis. She gagged, and that pleased him.

"I'm bigger than your boyfriend, aren't I?"

Jessie lied and said she guessed so.

Her abductor gave directions, demanding that she do this . . . and this . . . to him to stimulate him. She was sure she was going to die if she didn't do everything he asked. At length he ejaculated into her mouth and hair. She fought to keep from vomiting.

They were still racing down the highway, getting farther and farther away from populated areas. He promised her that there would be more; he insisted that she masturbate herself so she would be moist and ready for him. He was obviously having a good time, and he seemed almost casual about what he was doing to her. He kept her pinned flat to the front seat of her car so that no car passing by could see her.

She felt his thigh harden as he braked, and heard him say, "Oops . . . gotta turn around."

The car stopped and made a U-turn. She hoped and prayed

that they were heading back toward Yreka. It seemed to be only four or five minutes before she felt the car slow again and pull off to the side of the road and stop.

"Take your pants off, and your underwear, and your shoes," he ordered. "Now, get in the backseat. But keep your head down and don't look at my face."

The dark man told Jessie Clovis to bend over so he could enter her from the rear. She obeyed him, but he was annoyed because he hadn't achieved a second full erection.

Slowly he became erect, and now he toyed with her. "I could either come inside you or pull out and make you drink my come. It's up to you."

She could not bear to fellate him again. Resignedly she told him to ejaculate inside her. But he was playing a sadistic game; he'd only wanted to find out which act would upset her the most, and she'd given him his answer.

He demanded that she swallow his ejaculate. She started to cry again, and he barked at her to stop. Her sobs spoiled the game. It seemed necessary for him to be accepted as if he were truly her lover. She tried to pretend; she wanted to live.

"That was good, wasn't it?"

She nodded, wary of angering him.

"Now," he said, "lie back down."

She saw something in his hand, and knew that now he was surely going to shoot her with the silver gun. But he held only a roll of white tape. He showed her the tape, and she saw that it was half gone. He taped her wrists together so that she couldn't move, and then he took a rag and wiped the seat clean of any fingerprints he might have left.

"Don't go to the police," he warned. "If you do, I'll just say that you picked me up hitchhiking and you asked for it. They'll believe *me*. That would be an embarrassment for you."

Jessie lay weakly on the rear seat as the big man climbed back into the front and started the car, heading toward Yreka.

"Why did you do this to me?" she asked finally.

"Because all women are alike," he snorted. "They only give you pussy when they want it. My girlfriend was a waitress and fooled around behind my back. She attracted a lot of men, and that made me jealous. I'm a very jealous guy."

Jessie tried to keep him talking so he wouldn't stop the car and rape her again. "Why did she do that to you?"

"Because she was a bitch. She put out only when she wanted to. Like you—you should give it to your boyfriend all the time."

She moved slightly to relieve the pressure on her wrists and shoulders. He heard her.

"Don't move!"

"Are you going to kill me now?"

He laughed. "No. I'm not that kind of a guy. Do you think I'm that kind of guy?"

"No. No, of course not."

She asked what he was going to do with her, and he replied that he would drop her off in front of the store. She asked for her clothes so that she wouldn't be left naked on the streets of Yreka, but he refused, saying that she might try to get away.

And then she could see streetlights through the car windows, and felt the car stop. He was gallant now. He explained that he had stopped between some parked cars so that no one could see her.

"Okay?" he asked cheerfully. "Now, don't report this to the police."

"I won't," Jessie Clovis lied.

The dark man reached back and grabbed her breast and shook it lightly. And then he was gone.

Jessie raised up in the backseat and saw his broad shoulders disappearing toward Sambo's Restaurant by the I-5. She struggled to get the tape off her wrists.

It took her fifteen minutes before she was free. Trembling, she threw her clothes on and drove to her home. Then she called the Yreka Police Department.

She described her rapist. "Twenty-five to thirty. Six feet tall, 175 pounds. Brown hair. Short beard and mustache. Tape or Band-Aid over his nose. Blue watch cap, green jacket, blue jeans, white tennis shoes. Nickel-plated revolver, approximately four- to six-inch barrel."

The description was beginning to sound familiar.

Rusty Brewer told the other officers at the Medford meeting that the Shasta County investigators had found more cases, all of them along the I-5 freeway, and all within a week of the double murder in Mountain Gate.

On January 29 a twenty-year-old clerk working alone in Winchell's Donut Shop in Grants Pass, Oregon, had been accosted by a man who fit the familiar description. He had robbed the shop of seventy dollars and fondled both the clerk and a teenage customer.

Only an hour later, the man with the tape on his nose held up the Richards Market in Medford, Oregon, thirty-five miles south on the I-5. He used the same silver revolver.

The investigators at that first meeting had little doubt that they were all looking for the same man. The physical description, the M.O., and the connection to the I-5 freeway all matched. That was circumstantial evidence, very strong circumstantial evidence, but only probable.

The next day, lab reports gave the investigative team absolute physical evidence correlation. *The bullets found in the bodies of Donna Eckard and Janell Jarvis matched exactly the bullets removed from Shari Hull and Beth Wilmot. They had been fired from the same gun.*

And there was more; the surgical adhesive tape that had been used to bind the victims in Grants Pass, Medford, Redding, Yreka, and Shasta County not only matched in all classes and characteristics but also had come from the same roll! The torn edges could be approximated.

By coordinating their efforts, the investigators could have a virtual army of detectives working against time to catch this sexual sadist who apparently thought no one had connected his myriad crimes. Given the magnitude of the danger the suspect posed, was the "army" big enough?

On the trip back from Medford, Kominek made a wager with Holloway. "Where do you think he'll hit next? I'll put my money on Albany or Salem."

"I'll match you," Holloway responded, "but I say Corvallis or Eugene."

That very night, the I-5 Killer demonstrated that his trackers understood his pattern very well, but he neutralized the bet: he hit Corvallis *and* Albany.

On February 9 he appeared at a fabric store in Corvallis at eight P.M. He robbed the clerk of three hundred dollars, threatening her with a small silver gun. Then he forced the thirty-year-old clerk and her female customer into a back room, where he taped their hands, ankles, and mouths with surgical tape. When they were helpless, the now familiar sexual abuse took place. The clerk was fondled as she lay helpless. Then the robber masturbated himself against her face.

On that same night, the suspect bound and sodomized two young women at an Albany laundromat ten miles east of Corvallis.

Considering the circumstances, Holloway and Kominek were chagrined to find that they had been right on target in pinpointing their quarry's next hits.

*   *   *

In Salem, Dave Kominek fashioned a map that showed the broad blue ribbon of the I-5 freeway as it unfurled from northern California to Bellingham, Washington. He tacked it on the wall of his office and then placed Polaroids of all the composite pictures from the cases they knew about thus far next to it. They were so alike. In some, the suspect wore a hood, in some a watch cap. Rarely, his own curly dark hair showed. Sometimes he was clean-shaven, but most of the composites showed a beard, just as the majority of them featured patches of tape across the nose.

Dozens of pairs of dark eyes stared back at Kominek and Holloway, mocking eyes that seemed to say, "Catch me if you can, you dumb bastards."

Kominek stared back, and vowed softly, "You got it, baby."

11

After Shelley Janson left to return to school in New Mexico at New Year's, Randy had begun his new life in Eugene. He moved into the room he'd rented through an ad Arden Bates had placed in the Eugene *Register*. Arden was twenty-nine, divorced, and had a six-year-old son, Mickey. The rent on the neat rambler on E Street was three hundred and fifty dollars a month, and she was finding it hard to make the payments. She and Mickey didn't need the third bedroom.

Randy had left Medford after celebrating Christmas with Ralph, and gone to Eugene, where he'd rented a room at the New Oregon Motel. Then he'd gone through the ads looking for a place to live. He called Arden Bates, checked the place out, and decided it would do fine.

The next day, he'd met Shelley for the first time at O'Callahan's. On New Year's Eve he had gone back with Shelley and paid for the first month. It had been a busy two days for him, moving to Eugene, falling in love, and arranging his new living quarters. Somehow, informing his parole officer that he was moving had slipped his mind. Judy Pulliam assumed that Randy still lived in the Portland area.

Arden had made it plain right from the beginning that she wasn't advertising for a sex partner; she told Randy that if he had any ideas about that, that her house wasn't the place for him. He'd responded that sex wasn't what he was looking for either; he only wanted a room to live in.

It had proved to be a satisfactory arrangement. Arden Bates was a little overweight and a little old for Randy's tastes, and he made only desultory passes at her. She found him an easygoing "laid-back" kind of guy, and didn't expect any trouble from him. He told her that he was out of work and living on ninety dollars a week unemployment compensation, but that he had

112

money and she wouldn't have to worry that he could pay his share of the rent and the utilities.

"If anybody asks you what I do for a living," he kidded her, "just tell them I do bookkeeping for you."

She laughed. She didn't really care where his money came from as long as he met his obligations.

Six-year-old Mickey liked the new roomer, and Randy often played ball with the neighborhood youngsters, who were really impressed when he told them that he'd played with the Green Bay Packers. He showed them the Packers sticker on the back window of his gold Volkswagen Bug. On one occasion he took the neighbor kids to see the Harlem Globetrotters play basketball.

Actually, Randy seemed to be the perfect roomer; he wasn't around that much. Arden worked six days a week, and when she *was* home, Randy was usually gone. He took many overnight trips. He told her to tell anyone who inquired about him that he was out applying for jobs. She wondered when he found the time to look for work. He worked out often at a health club, and he signed up to play basketball with a team sponsored by a local optical firm. He told her he would be attending the University of Oregon when the spring term started.

Arden also marveled that Randy lived like a playboy, even though he had no visible means of support beyond his unemployment checks. He brought home prime steaks to cook, and several cases of beer at a time. He bought a forty-dollar plant for the living room. When his car was in the shop, he took taxis. He had the Volkswagen fitted out with five stereo speakers and a "fuzz-buster" to detect police radar traps. He talked a lot about his girlfriend, Shelley, in New Mexico and told Arden that he was going to send her a round-trip plane ticket to come and see him. He bought presents often for Shelley too, and mailed the mementos of his devotion to her.

Arden saw Randy snort cocaine, and she knew that that was a very expensive habit. In the evenings that he was in town, he patronized bars like De Frisco's, the Pour House, the Tavern on the Green, or O'Callahan's.

Arden noticed that Randy seemed addicted to the telephone; he made long-distance calls as easily as most people called across town. Her phone bills were huge, but Randy always paid his share, so it didn't concern her.

Her roomer seemed obsessed with communication in all forms. First, it was the phone, and then it was the mail; Randy hated to leave the house until he'd picked up his mail. And he did get a lot of mail, not only from Shelley but also from other women.

Sometimes Arden wondered just how committed Randy was to his New Mexico girlfriend. If he did love her as much as he claimed, he wasn't demonstrating much fidelity to her. His landlady saw that Randy was fascinated with teenage girls. What he did outside the house was his own business, but she was annoyed when she saw him coming on to her sixteen-year-old baby-sitter. Arden came home a few weeks after Randy had moved in and found him in bed with the teenage sitter. Arden expressed her disapproval, and wanted to take the girl home, but Randy had said, "No, she doesn't want to go home," and closed the door to his room.

The girl developed a tremendous crush on Arden's thirty-year-old roomer, and Arden found her with a naked Randy three or four times more when she was supposed to be baby-sitting.

Still, Arden talked with the girl and figured out that actual intercourse hadn't taken place. Then she tried to convince Randy to leave the girl alone, saying, "Why do you bother with her? She doesn't even give in to you."

He only shrugged.

On two occasions he brought women home. First, it was two young girl hitchhikers he'd picked up. One girl looked about sixteen, and the other said she'd just turned twenty. He'd taken the girls into his room for several hours, and then told Arden he was leaving to drop them off at Lane Community College in time for their evening class there.

There was another woman, a pretty dark-haired young woman in her early twenties. Arden was up when the pair walked in at eleven-thirty one night, and she tactfully left them alone and went to bed. When she woke up, it was after three and the television in the living room was sending out a steady drone. She looked for Randy but he was nowhere in the house. He was home the next day. She didn't ask him about the girl; it was really none of her business. Their agreement was that she would go her way and he would go his.

In spite of his constant womanizing, Arden found Randy's demeanor around women quite gallant; he treated them politely and deferred to their wishes. Still, she termed him a "Mr. Ego" when she watched him posing and preening in front of women like a high-school kid might to get attention.

Arden planned to move from the house on E Street on April 1, and until then her living arrangements were fine with her. She knew nothing about Randy's background, and she didn't care to know. He paid his share, and he wasn't underfoot much of the time. When he was home, he was invariably pleasant, and nice to Mickey and the other kids. It was working out well.

As for Randy's life during the first months of 1981, he *did* write and call Shelley often, and he *did* send her presents, along with declarations of his love. While Shelley dreamed of marrying him and bearing his children, while she started to play tennis and do aerobic exercises so that she would be worthy of him, and while she gazed at his pictures unable to study, Randy continued to prowl looking for other women.

He apparently could not stop; he was as addicted to the conquest of women as some men are to heroin. And no matter how many he seduced, it was never enough. He still felt empty.

If a day went by when he didn't have a date, or two or three, he was depressed. He was nice to girls, he bought them drinks, and he didn't bring up sex in a raunchy way. He could not understand why they rejected him when he wanted to get closer. He could not see that he skipped vital steps in the courting process. High-school girls might fall for his brand of "instant love," but girls with any experience at all saw how superficial he was. Superficial and a little weird.

He had to find more women. He looked in the bars, he looked on the freeway. He was living two lives now. He had been polite and considerate to women, and it had gotten him nowhere. He found far greater pleasure in taking what he wanted. After each incident in which he made helpless women do what he wanted, he felt better for a while.

But for such a little while.

On Friday, February 13, 1981, Randy found himself on the I-5 freeway south of Seattle headed back to Portland. He spotted a pretty girl driving in front of him, and pulled in close behind her. She was an eighteen-year-old student heading home to Salem. She noticed the man in the gold Volkswagen Bug with the Oregon plates pull alongside her several times. He smiled and pointed off the freeway, motioning with his hand as if he held a drink. She shook her head no. He was not that easily discouraged, and pulled off near the Thunderbird Motel in Kelso, apparently expecting her to follow. She grinned and sped up.

It wasn't long before she saw the gold Volkswagen in her rearview mirror again; he had raced to catch up with her. He pulled up into an adjacent lane and smiled broadly, pointing again to the side of the road. When she didn't respond by pulling off, he drifted back behind her. She wasn't alarmed; she was intrigued. The man was good-looking, and she was tempted to stop and talk with him.

They were close to Vancouver when she finally pulled into the Whimpy's Burger Stand lot and waited for the dark man to join her.

She found him very nice. He told her he was twenty-five and that he lived in Portland with his sister. He said he'd been a bartender but he'd had to quit because someone was selling illegal drugs in the restaurant where he worked. He mentioned Eugene and said he would be going to the university there. It was really an innocent encounter, she thought; they never even got out of their cars. But she did give him her phone number in Salem.

That was all Randy needed. Over the Valentine's Day weekend he called her several times. Her stepfather answered the phone and talked to Randy at two-thirty A.M. on Sunday, February 15, but refused to call his daughter to the phone. Whoever the guy was, he sounded very intoxicated.

Randy called again at eleven that Sunday morning and asked her to come to his suite in the Marriott Hotel in Portland. She said no.

It didn't matter; Randy was pursing a woman, and nothing would deter him. He looked up her phone number in a reverse directory and found out her address and last name. He began to send her cards. She thought his letters were rather strange. She never dated him.

But she remembered him.

So many women would remember Randy Woodfield, remember dates and places and things he'd said. In the end, it would be women who would help to trap him, women who could place him in areas where it was dangerous for him to have been remembered. He left his name with them almost compulsively. He told them too much about himself, never worrying that he might have left a trail for someone to follow.

12

Valentine's Day was an important holiday for Randy Woodfield; it was the ultimate romantic date. He tried to make sure that none of his women would forget him, sending out dozens of cards, and, of course, the yellow roses to Shelley. He planned to spend that weekend in Beaverton, Oregon, his old stomping grounds, and he wrote to several girls there, promising that he would take them out to dinner when he was in town. He planned to rent a room at the Marriott Hotel in Portland and throw a party on Saturday, February 14. He was running true to form; most of the girls who received Valentine cards were very young, some of them still in high school.

Randy had one platonic female friend in Beaverton, Dixie Palliter. Dixie had a steady boyfriend, but she liked Randy and was an avid listener when he discussed his escapades and his problems with women. She assured him that she would be able to spend some time with him while he was in Beaverton. He planned to call the girl from Salem he'd met on the freeway in Washington, and he also expected to see another of his old prison buddies.

Randy had so many tentative dates for that Valentine's Day weekend in Beaverton that he could not possibly have kept them all, but he wanted to be sure he had all bases covered.

The captain of detectives in the Beaverton Police Department was Dave Bishop, a tall, handsome man nearing forty. Bishop, gruff-voiced and punctilious about detail, had risen rapidly through the ranks in the Beaverton department. He was a superior detective and an indefatigable investigator. His brains and his dedication to duty made him a likely candidate for an administrative office. They also made him a likely candidate for ulcers—which he had. The cop's occupational hazard.

On that Valentine's Day in 1981, Dave Bishop was attending a religious retreat at St. Ignatius in Portland. He had looked forward to two days without urgent phone messages. Two days without dealing with the mechanics of death and violence.

But early Sunday morning, Bishop received a call from his office. "We have a dead body, with suspicious circumstances."

The body was that of Julie Ann Reitz. Julie Ann Reitz, who had been one of Randall Woodfield's admirers, if a long time back; Julie, who had once called him an "asshole" when she found him with another woman.

Julie, who still lived with her mother and a female roommate in a plush duplex on S.W. Cherryhill Drive in Beaverton, had celebrated her eighteenth birthday only two days before. She had had plans to attend several Valentine's Day parties on Saturday night, although she wasn't going with a date. Both her mother and her roommate were also away until the early hours of Sunday morning.

When her mother returned home, she found all the lights blazing, and then she saw, on the stairway of the town house, Julie's slender naked body. Thinking at first that the girl might have fainted, or even passed out after drinking more than she could handle, her mother rushed to help her up. But up close she could see that Julie's long light brown hair was stained mahogany with her own blood. She thought that Julie must have struck her head on the newel post and been knocked unconscious. But Julie did not respond to any stimuli, and her mother dialed frantically for help.

Ambulance attendants saw almost at once that Julie Reitz hadn't fallen; she had been shot—a near-contact wound to the head—and she was dead. The body was left on the stairway, and Beaverton police were called. Uniformed patrolmen verified that this, indeed, was a homicide, and cordoned off the crime scene to await detectives.

Captain Dave Bishop and Detective Neal Loper took charge of the case.

There were no signs of struggle. It looked as if Julie had been running down the stairs toward the front door when she was cut down by bullets. Likely her killer had been just behind her, and he—or she—had stopped the victim from flinging open the door to run for help.

Julie's mother and roommate said that the door to their home was always locked and that Julie would not have let a stranger in, particularly not late at night. That meant, surely, that her murderer was someone she had known and trusted. And if she'd known her attacker, he might well have felt killing her was the only way to keep his identity secret.

Like most teenagers, Julie had trusted a lot of people. Because she had been beautiful enough to be a model, Julie had had many male admirers. She dated frequently, mostly men near her own age.

Julie had graduated from high school just a month before her murder and she had been working as a clerk in a children's clothing store, Kids for Sure.

In an effort to retrace her activities on Valentine's evening, Loper and Bishop talked with her friends. She had been seen at several parties that Saturday night, and the last time anyone had seen her was around two in the morning. There had been no arguments, no incidents at all during the evening that might spark murder. The last time anyone saw her, Julie had indicated that she was on her way home.

In talking with Julie's friends, Dave Bishop learned that an older man, a man in his forties, had been attracted to her, and had insisted that she accept expensive presents from him. She had not been even vaguely interested in him. The detective captain wondered, however, if the man might have taken the rejection badly.

It was as good a place to start as any. On Sunday evening the man was located in an expensive Beaverton restaurant. He was haughty when asked to leave his steak dinner to speak with detectives, but Bishop informed him quietly that a murder investigation took precedence over his meal. He could talk there, or he could talk at headquarters. Meekly the man followed Bishop out of the restaurant.

He was able to present a solid alibi for his time on February 14.

A young man was located who had spent time with Julie at a Valentine's party.

"I was with her at ten, but that was the last time I saw her. I didn't take her home."

The youth passed a polygraph test. Three other teenage boys who had been with Julie at various times during the crucial evening were given polygraphs. All of them passed.

An autopsy on Julie's body produced a bullet from deep in her brain. It was a .38, the kind of bullet used in Smith and Wesson .38 Specials. Time of death was estimated as having occurred between three and four A.M. on February 15. Acid-phosphatase tests were positive for the presence of male ejaculate, and the man who had raped Julie had left behind the semen that marked his blood as Type B with no PGM enzyme factors. There was not enough fluid left to isolate positive or negative RH factors.

Sheets from Julie's bed were stained with the same type of semen. Both Julie's mother and her roommate were adamant when they said that Julie had not been sexually active in recent months. The semen stains on her sheets had to be fresh.

It was impossible to tell whether intercourse had taken place before or after the victim's death.

Dave Bishop is a "charter," a detective who believes that if only enough information is gathered and recorded, the truth will eventually surface.

"We had a huge office," he recalls, "and we soon had all the walls covered with butcher paper. Every name, every connection— no matter how slight—to the victim was jotted down. I want to see what I'm doing, study it, read it, *talk* to it. If you can see it written down, sooner or later the common denominator is going to jump out at you."

Within a week of the murder, Bishop's crew of detectives had questioned over a hundred people, taken reams of statements, and given three dozen polygraph tests—all of which cleared the subjects.

And all for naught—or so it seemed.

One bit of information listed on the chart came to the Beaverton detectives through a circuitous route. A woman who worked in the lunchroom of a school in Aloha, Oregon, had overheard a conversation among several teachers. One of the teachers' sons, a student at Beaverton High School, knew someone who had seen a Volkswagen Bug driving up and down the street in front of Julie Reitz's town house very late on Valentine's night. The car had finally pulled over to the curb and the headlights were flashed off and on.

Pretty thin stuff, but the words "Volkswagen Bug" were printed on one of Bishop's butcher-paper charts.

Neal Loper and Dave Bishop continued to question friends of Julie Reitz, and then friends of friends, always with the same question: "Will you list for me everyone you can think of that Julie knew? Will you try to remember where she went, and with whom? Even if it doesn't seem important, we want to know."

The butcher paper inched around the Beaverton office, and the blank spaces on the paper filled up. If a name appeared twice, it

While a student at Portland State University, Randy Woodfield was arrested for indecent exposure.

Woodfield sent this photo, probably taken in 1978-79, to numerous unsuspecting penpals.

Randy doesn't smile for the camera as he is arrested and booked into the Marion County Jail (Salem, Oregon) in 1981.

The lighted windows of the TransAmerica offices allowed Woodfield to spot Beth Wilmot and Shari Hull from the I-5 highway.

The killer entered easily through the open door.

The two young women's clothing and shoes were scattered through the employees' lunchroom. The paramedics' supplies lie beside them.

Police found Shari Hull's Bronco in the parking lot—engine running, victims' purses inside.

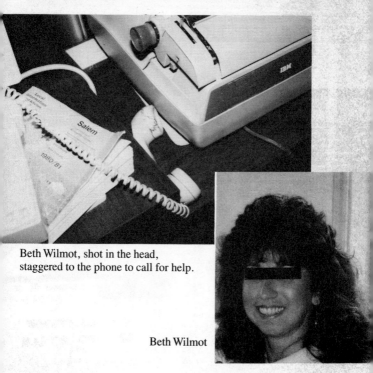

Beth Wilmot, shot in the head, staggered to the phone to call for help.

Beth Wilmot

The gold "Champagne Edition" Volkswagen in which Randy Woodfield cruised the I-5 highway, looking for victims.

Arden Bates's house in Springfield, Oregon, where Randy rented a room.

A detective searches the fireplace in Arden Bates's living room. Officers believe evidence was burned there.

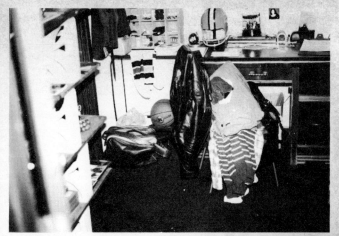

Randy's bedroom in the Bates house was full of sports gear and memorabilia.

In the pouch of Woodfield's racquetball bag, police found a .32 caliber bullet that linked him to four victims.

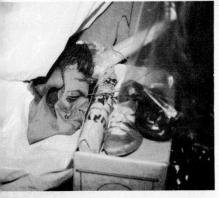

Police found a mask and other items at the bottom of Randy's closet.

The motel where Woodfield lived in early 1981. He brought his new girlfriend, Shelly Janson, there on the first night they met.

A quartet of tired detectives in Springfield in March, 1981, after a night of surveilling Randy. Dave Kominek is in striped shirt, far right.

Detective Dave Kominek

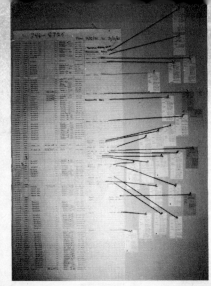

Randy Woodfield left a trail behind him with his long-distance phone calls. Police used this chart to link him to crime sites.

Beth Wilmot and several other victims chose Randy Woodfield (#5) out of this line-up. The others are police officers chosen to fit his description.

This map shows the I-5 Freeway Corridor from Redding, California, to Bellevue, Washington, with numbers indicating twenty-two attacks from rape to murder. Next to the map are the composite drawings made from victims' descriptions. Some show the killer with a fake beard and tape, others without.

was starred. Somewhere, Bishop believed, there was a connection, if they could only link the correct factors.

Forty-five miles southeast of Beaverton, in Salem, Dave Kominek decided that another joint meeting was needed.

In Oregon, the state attorney general's office is available to assist city and county jurisidictions with criminal investigation and prosecution. Kominek talked with Bob Hamilton, chief assistant attorney general in the criminal division. Hamilton had lost the election for Marion County district attorney in a close race with Chris Van Dyke, but there was no enmity between the two attorneys. Hamilton agreed that the I-5 Killer case was one to which the state office should offer whatever assistance it could.

Kominek organized a joint meeting to be held in Roseburg, Oregon, and Bob Hamilton served as chairman of that session. The attorney general's office would print and disseminate information on the I-5 Killer to all agencies who might be involved. The Oregon State Crime Lab would handle all the evidence turned up in that state's cases, and the Department of Justice Crime Lab in Redding would evaluate evidence from California crimes. All Washington evidence would go to the Western Washington Crime Lab in Seattle, whose director was famed criminalist George Ishii.

A massive force of detectives, forensic science experts, and prosecuting attorneys was about to concentrate all its efforts on one man. The need for haste had accelerated. The roster of crimes was growing.

In going over new cases sent to him, Dave Kominek could see that the I-5 Killer had apparently returned from California on February 4. Wherever the man's home base was, it had to be located midway up the Oregon coast. He seemed to work north, south, and west of that general location.

On February 12 the suspect had headed north again. It was a busy night for him, frightening proof that his crimes were accelerating.

He started in Vancouver at a quarter to six in the evening, when he robbed the Sassy Dress Shop on Main Street of fifty dollars and bound the elderly clerk with adhesive tape.

An hour and a half later, he was in Olympia, Washington, a hundred miles north on the I-5 freeway. He forced two teenagers into a freezer of a drive-in restaurant and subjected them to sexual abuse before cleaning out the cash register. He left his victims locked in the almost airless freezer.

By ten P.M. he was in Bellevue, Washington, confronting two employees at a Dairy Queen as they were counting the day's receipts. He grabbed the stack of bills, locked the male employee in the freezer, and turned to the young woman.

Five minutes after the bearded man with the Band-Aid on his nose left, his third set of victims in one night called the Bellevue Police Department. The case was assigned to Detective Gary Trent. The assailant was long gone; he had used his standard escape route, the I-5 freeway.

The composite pictures drawn in Vancouver and Olympia and Bellevue were almost identical. And they were, of course, almost identical with all the other composites.

The atmosphere at the Roseburg conference was tense; instead of the new information on the suspect they'd hoped for, the officers attending were hearing only about more cases—unsolved cases. Dave Kominek described the I-5 Killer's M.O.:

"The subject hits various businesses in the evening hours, normally between five P.M. and eleven P.M., with emphasis on the early-evening hours. He goes in when there is a lull in business. We believe he is armed with a thirty-two-caliber silver revolver. In most instances, he ties or tapes his victims—with hands crossed behind their backs and ankles crossed. He usually picks businesses with young women on duty, and often with two young women. He has them disrobe, but he only unzips his trousers. He forces victims to masturbate him or to perform oral sodomy. With older females he usually only fondles. He invariably takes his victims to the back of the building where they cannot be seen from the street. He sometimes removes the telephone receiver to prevent victims from calling for help."

Kominek wrote on a blackboard:

Tape on nose.
Green jacket or windbreaker-type jacket.
Hood or ski cap.
Fake beard.
Gloves—ski, sporting, driving.
No odors detected.
Soft-spoken, rarely uses profanity.
Macho—considers his penis is large, and brags about it.
When he leaves, orders victims to count to 100 or 500.
Vehicle thought to be left several blocks away.
White male—25 to 28.

5′ 11″ to 6′ 1″, medium build.
Dark hair, possibly curly.
Dark eyes—"sad eyes" or "tired eyes."
Good-looking. Possible acne scarring.
Weapons: .32-caliber 6-shot revolver, nickel- or chrome-plated.
Smith & Wesson model 60 stainless-steel .38 Special 5-shot
with a 3″ barrel, wood grips.
Vehicle: Volkswagen Bug???

There was a tentative psychological profile. The handouts
noting the profile were stamped "Confidential." No one but the
detectives should know that much about the suspect at that point.

"Subject is a male Caucasian, possibly recently divorced or
separated from girlfriend. Released within the last year from
some type of institution. Has a very macho image of himself. Is
the type to drive a four-wheel-drive or sports-type car. Uses false
beards as a possible macho symbol. The Band-Aid is simply to
hide behind. This man is probably the type who would be
considered a very nice person by the people next door. Primary
motivation is sexually related. Subject is a loner and possibly has
latent homosexual tendencies."

"Our man has herpes," Kominek continued. "Several of his
victims have contracted the disease after being sexually abused.
As far as we know, he has never attempted normal intercourse;
his fetish is oral or anal sodomy. I don't have to tell you how
frustrating this investigation is. We know what he looks like, we
know his patterns, and we even know where he hits—but he's
playing cat and mouse with us. When we're looking in Oregon,
he's in Washington or California. He may act like a monster, but
he looks like the guy next door. There are probably a lot of
people who know him well, who think he's a great guy—people
who are going to be struck dumb when we catch him. He's as
dangerous as any subject most of us will ever encounter, and
he's stepping up his attacks. He's killed at least three times, he's
attacked children, and he's attacked women. He's in some kind
of sexual frenzy. Let's go get him."

The detectives at that Roseburg meeting could not know just
how closely the profile correlated with the characteristics of the
man they sought. He could not know just how much they knew
about him.

He thought he was home free.

Each agency attending the joint meeting was given the responsibility of checking out and eliminating suspects in cases in their

jurisdictions. Information on every suspect who could not be eliminated would then be forwarded to Dave Kominek in Marion County. A photographic mug lineup with all the composites to date would be sent to all agencies concerned.

When the meeting was over, each investigator knew what all of the others knew. They knew so much . . . and yet so little. They didn't have a name. They didn't have a face.

Marion County District Attorney Chris Van Dyke called a news conference; he could not possibly warn all of the women in Oregon, but he hoped his words might alert some of them to the danger. Van Dyke's usual broad smile was absent as he talked to reporters and television cameras. He told the press that there had already been two dozen incidents of sexual attack on young women who lived and worked near the I-5 corridor.

"Unfortunately, the common thread that runs through a lot of these cases is a situation where *two* women are together in isolated laundromats, businesses, their homes, and places of employment."

Van Dyke said that authorities had real fears that the killer might strike again in Salem within the next few days. He stressed that he did not want to create a climate of fear but that he had no choice but to warn women.

Monty Holloway spoke up. "He's probably one of those individuals that, when he's caught, all of his neighbors will say: 'I can't believe it. He's such a nice guy.' "

"He could be *your* next-door neighbor," Kominek added.

Women *were* afraid. Teenagers working in fast-food outlets and convenience stores near the I-5 jumped at shadows. More calls came into police departments, but no one really knew who the killer was. None of the information helped.

The murder of Julie Reitz on February 15 did not seem to be connected to the epidemic of violence along the freeway. Julie had been killed in her own home, and almost certainly by someone she knew. The I-5 Killer, on the other hand, seemed to choose his victims in a totally random pattern. Furthermore, Beaverton was west of Portland, and not on the direct route along the I-5.

Dave Bishop and Neal Loper worked long hours on their case. Dave Kominek and Monty Holloway continued to work seven days a week on trapping the I-5 Killer. The Marion County detectives had never heard of Julie Reitz; the Beaverton detectives *had* heard of the I-5 Killer, but the M.O. wasn't right for their case.

The man with the Band-Aid disguise continued to attack women.

Three days after Julie Reitz died of a bullet in her brain, a customer walked into the 7-11 store on Coburg Road in Eugene at three-twenty-five in the morning. He waited patiently for the clerk, but no one appeared to wait on him. And then he heard a muffled thumping sound coming from the back room. A little uneasy, he walked back and found the female clerk lying on her stomach, her hands and feet bound tightly with surgical tape, and a swath of the stuff over her mouth. Quickly he freed her and called the Eugene police.

The I-5 Killer had struck again. This time, he had stopped at sexual molestation.

Detective Ron Griesel of the Eugene Police Department took over the investigation at three-thirty that morning. Griesel spent most of the night going over the 7-11. He gathered what slight physical evidence he could find. There were no usable fingerprints. There *was* adhesive tape in the storeroom, and more of it was found in the street outside the convenience store. There were a Band-Aid box and a Band-Aid, thrown away when the robber was through with them. Saline swabs were brushed across the victim's nipples on the faint chance that the suspect's blood type might be isolated in the saliva he'd left there.

Griesel found what might have been a real bonus: the television camera that constantly scans the aisles and counters of all 7-11 stores. Several frames from the videotape were snipped and then frozen. But when they were blown up, they proved to be disappointing; in some of the frames, the man was out of sight below the counter. In others he appeared only as a tall, slender figure in a dark jacket whose hood obscured his features. He was as elusive on videotape as he had always been.

There seemed to be no end to it. The map on Kominek's office wall had new flags marking new incidents, more drawings of the familiar bearded face. The man had been prowling for more than three months, and the weary detective wondered if they were any closer to catching him than they had been at the outset of the probe.

As if to thumb his nose at the police again, the suspect hit three days later; he didn't even bother changing cities. He had varied his pattern only a little; he was working later. Three in the morning at the 7-11. This time, a little after nine at the Taco

Time on River Road in Eugene. The two teenage girls on duty were back in the kitchen area, and the place was empty of customers. The girls were wary; they'd read about the I-5 Killer and they were nervous whenever the business lulls came.

They heard the front door open and looked up to see the tall dark man in the khaki jacket and watch cap walk directly into the food-preparation area. They couldn't see his hands; he had them jammed in his pockets.

Seventeen-year-old Connie Soldano didn't wait to see what he wanted. She bolted and ran toward out the back door.

"Stop!" the man shouted, and she half-turned and saw that he was pointing a little silver pistol at her. She kept on going, expecting to feel a bullet in her back.

And then she was free.

She ran into a neighboring Dairy Queen and grabbed the phone to call the Lane County Sheriff's Office. She felt guilty, leaving her friend alone, and she begged the operator to send help at once.

The big man had turned his attention to his lone captive.

"You! You squat down on the floor and don't move."

Terri Brady did as she was told, and the man ran out. Moments later the Taco Time was surrounded by police officers. Terri signaled to them that the robber was gone.

And he was—completely gone. No car. Nothing left of him but a wadded-up piece of surgical tape that he'd tossed away onto the parking lot in mid-flight.

There would be only one more. Time was running out for the I-5 Killer.

On February 25 he found a setup that appealed to him. He appeared in Corvallis at a small restaurant at eight minutes to six in the evening. The employees were two pretty teenage girls, one of them the daughter of a Corvallis police officer.

The man watched from his vantage point outside the restaurant, marking time until a customer picked up his order and left. Eighteen-year-old Jill Martin walked outside the restaurant and around to the back of the building where the restrooms were. As he had done before, the bearded man forced his way into the restroom.

Jill Martin resisted—until she saw him cock the hammer of his silver gun. When he had climaxed, he laughed as she spat his ejaculate on the floor, and then he bound her hands and feet with tape and left her alone in the dark room.

It took Jill fifteen minutes to free her feet. She could not get the tape off her hands, but she stumbled to the door of the restaurant and kicked at it until her friend heard her and let her in.

The semen found on the bathroom floor by Corvallis detectives was tested by the Oregon State Crime Lab. It was the ejaculate of a man with B-negative blood with no PGM-enzyme characteristics.

Kominek and Holloway read this last report, and Kominek slammed it on his desk.

"Enough! Dammit, that's enough! It's time our side got lucky."
And finally it did.

13

In Beaverton, Oregon, Captain Dave Bishop and Detective Neal Loper were as stymied with the progress of their murder case as Dave Kominek and Monty Holloway were with the stalemate in tracking the I-5 Killer. While both departments were peripherally aware of the other's investigations, all the detectives were working around the clock on their own cases. Anyone who has not been caught in the vortex of an intensive murder probe can never really understand what is involved. Detectives' lives are literally put on hold while they work day and night in a boiler-room situation where nothing else matters. They eat, sleep, and breathe the details of the homicides and their minds are a jumble of possibilities—most of which are reviewed, analyzed, and then discarded. If they make a mistake, even one, there is the dread possibility that someone else is going to die, and it will be their fault—or they will believe it is their fault.

Bishop's ulcer flared up, and he gulped antacids and ignored it. Both he and Loper saw their homes infrequently, and then only to catch a few hours of sleep. The memory of Julie Reitz's body on the stairway of her own home haunted them. The thought that someone had held a .38 to the back of her head was ugly. The pretty, slender girl could not have been much of a threat; she had clearly been shot either because someone hated her so much that he wanted to destroy her or, more chilling, because he wanted to silence her.

They kept coming back to the concept that Julie's killer had to have been someone she knew. They were sure they had already cleared the most likely suspects. That meant that it must have been a man who moved just outside the edges of her usual life, someone from her past that most of her friends had forgotten about—or even someone she had recently met.

Neal Loper questioned one of Julie's close friends again.

"Think. Could there be any man Julie knew so slightly that you may have forgotten him? Someone who didn't seem important?"

"No . . . Wait! There was a guy . . . Randy. He was a lot older than Julie."

"Tell me about him," Loper urged.

"He worked at the Faucet Tavern. His name was Randy Woodfield. That was last summer. Julie went out with him—maybe once or twice. He came on too strong, and she told me she didn't want to date him again—but then she said they were going to be friends."

"She hadn't mentioned him lately?"

The girl shook her head.

"What kind of car did he drive?"

"Let me think. Yeah . . . yeah, it was a Volkswagen Bug, I think. Kind of a gold color."

The information went up on the charts in Bishop's office: "Woodfield, Randy. 25–27? Faucet Tavern bartender. Volkswagen?"

And then the name came up again. One of Julie's girlfriends recalled that Randy Woodfield had asked to sleep over in Julie's town house. She explained that he'd taken Julie out and gotten her a little intoxicated.

"He crawled in bed with us and fooled around with Julie—but nothing really happened."

Randy Woodfield's name was jotted down again.

On February 27, when Woodfield's name was mentioned a third time, as someone who had been seen around Beaverton on the Valentine's Day weekend, he made the charts again. A three-time winner . . . or loser.

Coincidence? Perhaps. But detectives look at coincidence differently than a man on the street would. Coincidence can raise a warning flag. Bishop took a marking pencil and drew lines connecting the three notations.

"Let's see what else we can find out about this Randy Woodfield."

Neal Loper talked in depth with the young woman who had mentioned Randy as someone Julie had once dated. Yes, she was positive that Julie had known Randy. In fact, he'd tried to make it a point to keep in touch with Julie. "He's been to her house a couple of times."

"Would he know her phone number?" Loper asked.

"Oh, sure. I'm sure he would."

"Do you know where Randy Woodfield is now? Does he still work at the Faucet?"

"No. He got fired last fall. He was into a lot of things that weren't quite . . . legal. The last I heard, he was living in Eugene someplace and going to bartending school."

Loper called a girl who had mentioned that Woodfield was supposed to be in Beaverton on the weekend of February 14–15. Her opinion too was that Randy had been very interested in Julie Reitz.

"I met Randy last spring," the high-school senior said. "His parents live down at Otter Crest, and his sister lives in Portland. He went to bartending school in Portland, and then he moved down to Eugene to go to the University of Oregon."

"You hear from him lately?" Loper asked.

"He sent me a valentine from Eugene and said he'd be in town over Valentine's Day. He said he wanted to see me—but he didn't call."

Tactfully Loper asked if the informant had ever been intimate with Randy Woodfield.

"Yes. Once or twice. Maybe a few more times," she said without embarrassment.

"Was he strange, kinky at all?"

"No. Nothing like that. Just normal. He's a nice guy. He did tell me once that he'd been in trouble for burglary a long time ago."

The teenager discussed her impression that Randy had been interested in Julie Reitz, and she betrayed no jealousy about that. As far as she knew, he'd called Julie several times.

"He told me he was really serious about seeing her. He's kind of a persistent guy, but Julie told me she didn't want to see him again—that she didn't want a relationship with him."

"What kind of a vehicle does Randy have?" Loper asked.

"It's a gold Volkswagen Bug—fairly new, and it has a sun roof and it's kind of bashed in on the front."

Loper and Bishop found Randy Woodfield interesting. He had admitted some kind of criminal record to several friends, and he'd apparently betrayed an interest in pursuing their victim. Loper talked again with Julie's roommate.

"Randy?" the girl said. "Sure, he's been here, but Julie didn't like him."

"Would she have let him in if he came knocking on the door late at night?"

"Probably. She didn't hate him. She just wasn't interested in having a relationship with him. He was older, quite a bit older—and he was pushy. But I think she might have let him in.''

When Loper talked next to one of Randy Woodfield's former fellow employees at the Faucet, he learned of Randy's obsession with young girls and of his anger at women he'd dated when they rejected him. That didn't necessarily stamp him as a killer, but it piqued Loper's interest.

The next step was to find out just what Woodfield's criminal record entailed. On February 28 Judy Pulliam, Randy's parole officer, returned Loper's call.

She related Woodfield's record, and Loper listened with fascination. There had been more than burglary charges—a great deal more. Woodfield had been arrested and convicted of sexual crimes, not once but many times. The exposing had escalated to the incident in the park with the Portland policewoman, and he'd spent time in the penitentiary.

"There's more," Pulliam said. "That's why I'm so concerned, now that I hear about your case. Randy Woodfield was a suspect in at least three homicides in Portland. Darci Fix and Doug Altic last Thanksgiving Day, and Cherie Ayers a month before that. He was questioned, but he was never charged."

"You say you've had him in your caseload," Loper prompted.

"Yes, but he wasn't very amenable to supervision, and I've been concerned. He moved down to Eugene without permission. He waited a long time before notifying me of his address down there. It was only then that he requested permission to have his case transferred. I've just transferred his case down to Tony Meyer, an investigating parole officer in Eugene.''

All of this was absorbing for Bishop and Loper; once the name Randy Woodfield had been mentioned, a fountain of information followed. They obtained a mug shot and description of Woodfield and saw a very muscular, handsome man. Portland Detective Bob Dornay acknowledged that Woodfield had been a suspect in the Ayers case and that he had refused to take a polygraph. He had finally been eliminated as a suspect because of his blood type: B negative.

That blood type might have eliminated him in the Ayers case; it put him square in the ball park in the Reitz case.

Randy had told friends in Beaverton that he was going to rent a room at the Marriott Hotel and throw his own Valentine's party on February 14. That he had stayed at the Marriott was verified by hotel records. The Marriott was very close to the town house where Julie had been shot.

"Let's go talk to him," Bishop said. "If nothing else, we can eliminate him if he can come up with an alibi that works."

The Beaverton detectives called Tony Meyer, Randy Woodfield's new parole officer in the Eugene area. Meyer said that he had an appointment with Woodfield at eight on the morning of March 3 for a routine parole check-in. It was agreed that Bishop and Loper would be present at that meeting. Judy Pulliam would also attend.

Whatever might come out of that meeting, it was essential that Dave Bishop and Neal Loper confront Randy Woodfield. At the very least, the man was a convicted sexual deviate, an ex-con with a cavalier attitude about his commitment to parole; at the very most, he might be a murderer.

The I-5 Killer case was the furthest thing from their minds; they wanted only to solve the murder of Julie Reitz.

It was mere coincidence that, on March 3, 1981, the I-5 investigators had scheduled another joint meeting. That meeting was held in Eugene. Although they had no way of knowing it, all of the principals—except for the victims—gathered in Eugene, Oregon, that Tuesday morning. The Eugene Police Department opened their offices for the third joint meeting. It wasn't that there was much new information; it was just that the agencies involved in the search for the I-5 Killer felt that a brainstorming session might help. On the face of it, they seemed no closer to catching the phantom gunman than they had been four weeks earlier. In reality, if it had been a game of blindman's bluff, they were red-hot.

There had been several robberies by the man with the Band-Aid on his nose in the Eugene area, and surveillance stakeouts had been in operation since February 19. Oregon state troopers had worked twelve-hour shifts observing likely targets for the I-5 Killer. They'd staked out the Grocery Cart, Tom's Market, Dunkin' Donuts, the Dari-Mart, the A & W Drive-in. Hundreds of man-hours were involved, long, boring hours for the troopers sitting in sneaker cars staring through the windows of the brightly lit fast-food spots . . . waiting.

Only the night before, on March 2, Trooper Marlen Hein and Corporal A. Gale Lively thought they might have been onto something. They were positioned inside the Dari-Mart at eight P.M. when they saw a man who matched the description of the suspect walk into the store. He seemed very nervous, and he kept glancing toward the storeroom area, where the troopers were hidden. At length the man made a purchase and left. They could not stop him; he hadn't disobeyed the law in any way.

But they remembered him.

At the March 3 meeting, a technician from the Oregon State Crime Lab announced that there was no doubt they were looking for a man with type-B blood. Tests on all the semen that had been left never varied.

"We can eliminate any suspects who don't have this type blood," Kominek told the group. "Only nine to ten percent of the population have type B. That will cut down considerably on the paperwork. We're going to ask all of you to send your existing information to me at the Marion County Sheriff's Office. It will be programmed into a computer and checked against all suspects."

In addition, it was agreed that information released to the press would include nothing but location of incident, type of crime, and description of the suspect.

The media weren't going to like this. They were already badgering detectives for more information on the I-5 Killer, but it was essential to hold back those things known only to the killer and his victims. Should they ever get to the stage where someone confessed to the crimes, such privileged information could sort out the "crazies" from the real thing.

At the end of a long day, Kominek and Holloway drove back to Salem.

They might well have avoided the drive north. Within hours, they would be speeding back to Eugene.

14

Neal Loper and Dave Bishop arrived at the Lane County Corrections Office in Eugene, and met with Judy Pulliam and Tony Meyer at eight-thirty A.M. on March 3. They waited in vain for their first glimpse of the man who had once dated Julie Reitz. Randy Woodfield did not appear for his scheduled appointment.

Bishop and Loper contacted Detective Doug Ashbridge of the Springfield Police Department, told him of their interest in Woodfield, and Ashbridge drove by the residence on E Street. He reported back that Woodfield's gold Volkswagen was parked in the garage and the curtains of the house were drawn.

Since Randy wouldn't come to the parole officers, it was decided that they would go to him. This would be a way for Captain Bishop and Detective Loper to talk with him about the Julie Reitz case. The two parole officers, accompanied by Neal Loper and Doug Ashbridge, walked past the yard with its picket fence and knocked on the front door of the neat rambler.

No one answered.

"He's in there," Ashbridge speculated. "His car's still in the garage."

They pounded on the door and the front window. After a long time a sleepy-faced Randy Woodfield opened the door. He did not seem alarmed to see his parole officer or the strangers who accompanied him. He invited them in.

"Where were you, Randy?" Meyer asked. "I waited for you this morning."

"I thought my appointment was for this afternoon—or maybe it was for tomorrow."

Meyer let it go. He introduced Loper, and the Beaverton detective explained that he was investigating the murder of Julie Reitz and that their probe had to include all those who had known Julie.

Randy shook his head in confusion. He told Loper that he couldn't place the name, that he didn't know anyone named Julie Reitz and he couldn't see what he might have to do with her murder probe.

Loper responded casually, although he felt a thrill of excitement; he had witnesses who had assured him that Julie and Randy *were* acquainted. "Why don't you come down to the Springfield Police Department and we can talk about it? I have a picture of Julie back at the office. Maybe that will refresh your memory?"

"Give me a minute to get dressed, and I'll go with you," Randy said, still without any outward display of anxiety.

At the Springfield station, Neal Loper advised Randy of his rights under the Miranda and Escobedo decisions.

Randy said that he understood his rights and had no objection to talking with the detectives. It was just that he didn't know anyone named Julie Reitz.

Loper held out a picture of Julie, one of her graduation photos.

Randy studied a picture of Julie and said that, yes, now he recognized her. He'd gone out with her once. He said he'd met her when he worked at the Faucet, and he admitted frankly that he'd been fired from the tavern the previous October.

Randy said he'd been to Julie's town house only once, and that that had been several months back. "It was just a small party with her roommate," he recalled. "I don't remember her roommate's name. There was nothing heavy about me and Julie; we were just friends."

"Have you ever had sex with Julie Reitz?" Loper asked.

Randy shook his head. "Never."

"Did you see Julie Reitz over Valentine's Day weekend?"

Again he shook his head calmly. He hadn't seen her, and he hadn't called her. He hadn't seen Julie for months.

"Could you recall your activities over that weekend?"

Randy said he could. He had gone to stay at his sister's home in Portland, had gone out "partying" Saturday night—the fourteenth—and arrived back at his sister's home around four in the morning.

"You say you went partying? Could you be more specific?"

"I met a friend at the Marriott—him and his wife—and had a few drinks. Then I went to several other spots in the Portland area and had more drinks. I met a girl. Her name was Jeanie, but I can't recall her last name. She tripped around with me after that.

We went to Baxter's Corner, Frank Peters' Inn, and the Greenwood Inn. We stayed there until the bar closed."

"Where does this Jeanie live?"

Randy shook his head. "We just made small talk. I never asked her last name or anything about her. I don't know where she lives."

"You hadn't heard about Julie Reitz's murder?" Captain Bishop asked.

"No. I didn't know anything about it. Didn't hear it on the radio or the TV or from anyone."

Pressed for information that might help in the investigation of Julie's killing, Randy reiterated that he had known Julie only casually, that he hadn't even thought about her for months. There was no way he could be involved in her murder. The closest he'd been to her house on Valentine's Day was the Greenwood Inn.

"I didn't even know she was murdered until you guys told me about it."

"Do you own any weapons, Randy?"

"No, none."

Bishop and Loper asked Randy if he would be willing to give samples of his hair—both head and pubic—and blood for analysis so that he could be absolutely eliminated as a suspect in the Reitz case.

"Will you take a polygraph test?"

At first Randy agreed to cooperate, but then he equivocated. He thought perhaps he should call his attorney. The Beaverton detectives offered to make the call for him, but he decided he didn't need an attorney. They talked more about the evidence samples they needed, and the lie-detector test. At length Randy decided that he wouldn't cooperate.

"It's just against my principles to do that."

Bishop and Loper backed off. Parole officers Pulliam and Meyer talked to Randy next, suggesting that it might be better if he returned to Portland to live, where he would be fulfilling the stipulations of his early parole.

"I don't want to do that," he said. "But of course I will if I'm ordered to move back."

Randy was beginning to betray some nervousness. He decided he might cooperate with the detectives about the polygraph, but as soon as he said yes, he changed his mind again.

"I'd rather move back to Portland," he said vehemently. "I'd rather go back to the penitentiary before I'd do that."

An odd overreaction.

Neal Loper left the interview room for a short time, leaving Randy alone with Bishop. Casually Bishop suggested again that Randy could clear himself of any connection with Julie's murder if he would be willing to give hair and blood samples.

Randy was getting nervous, beginning to trip himself up. At one point he blurted to Dave Bishop, ''Just because I had sex with her . . . I wouldn't have killed her. . . .''

He had given away too much. He had denied sexual intimacy with the victim. Now he had admitted it.

Bishop let it pass. Given enough rope, Randy Woodfield might just twine it around his own neck.

Randy seemed relieved when the questions ended, and he consented readily to have the residence on E Street searched.

''Go ahead and search,'' he said. ''I'm curious to see what you could possibly hope to find. I have nothing to hide.''

Neal Loper, Doug Ashbridge, and Detective Tom Maloney of the Springfield Police Department conducted this first preliminary search. While Randy Woodfield watched, Neal Loper retained the following items and logged them into evidence:

Item 1: One set of bedsheets and a mattress pad from subject's bedroom. On mattress pad some dried blood. Sheets contain many head and pubic hairs.

Item 2: One set of sheets from hamper next to bed.

Item 3: One brown wallet containing identification and a receipt for the purchase of a gun. (.22-caliber handgun from G.I. Joe's Store in the Portland area.)

Item 4: One smoking device, (Bong) with residue.

Item 5: One box of athletic adhesive tape.

Item 6: A paper bag containing a .38-caliber or .357-caliber gun-cleaning kit.

Item 7: A cocaine snorter (from vehicle glove compartment).

Item 8: One box of firecrackers out of the glove compartment of vehicle.

Asked about the gun-cleaning kit, Randy seemed evasive; he thought it was probably something he'd used before he'd gone to prison in 1975 and that it happened to still be among his possessions. The item seized that appeared to bother him the most was the adhesive tape. He questioned the detectives closely about why they would have taken something as prosaic as adhesive tape as evidence. They replied casually that it was something that might prove valuable to them.

Indeed, when Loper had seen that tape, bells had rung in his head. He had come down searching for some clue to Julie Reitz's murder only. But he and Bishop, like every lawman in the state, had seen the composite pictures of the I-5 Killer, the man who invariably disguised himself with the use of tape or Band-Aids across his nose, the man who bound his victims with the same tape.

Was it possible that they had stumbled across a much bigger fish than they realized? Randy Woodfield's verbal consent to search his home had given them a great legal boost. Had they come in with a search warrant, they would have been able to seize only those items specifically listed in the warrant. But Randy's own assumption that he had nothing to fear from the cops had allowed them to seize anything they found. He seemed nervous about the tape, very nervous, but he dared not refuse to let them take it. There had been six rolls of tape in the box; one was missing. They could see that Randy was trying to pretend he wasn't antsy about the tape.

He failed in that area. The man was clearly covering up something.

What was it?

Randy Woodfield drove off in his fancy gold Beetle. Legally, he was free to go. He had lied initially about knowing Julie Reitz, but it was within the realm of possibility that a man who dated scores of women *might* forget the name of one. The adhesive tape might match the torn edges of bonds retrieved from victims, and it might not, but lab analysis would take time.

Clearly Bishop and Loper needed more information. They drove back to the little rambler in Springfield.

Randy Woodfield's car was neither in the garage nor parked on the street near the house on E Street an hour later when Dave Bishop, Neal Loper, and Doug Ashbridge set up a discreet stakeout so that they could observe the comings and goings of the occupants.

Three P.M. No sign of activity.

At three-thirty-four a small boy hopped off the school bus and headed for the front door. The detectives spoke with him, and he told them he was Mickey Bates, six years old. "My mom's at work," he said. "I stay with the neighbors till she gets home."

Mickey told the investigators that Randy had lived in a room in their house for about a month.

"Where does he go when he goes to work?" Bishop asked.

The boy shrugged. "He doesn't work. He plays ball with us."

"Have you ever seen any of Randy's guns?" Loper asked. "Does he have guns like the cops do on television?"

"No. Randy doesn't have any guns."

The boy skipped off, unfazed at the sight of three detectives watching his house.

At five-twenty-four Arden Bates drove up. The trio of detectives identified themselves and explained they wanted to talk with her about her roomer, Oddly, she did not seem surprised to find that police were checking on Randy. She had become a little suspicious of his activities herself, she said.

Arden explained that she'd met Randy by placing an ad in the paper seeking a roomer. She didn't know where his money came from; he had said that he received a small stipend from state unemployment, and she thought maybe his parents helped him out. "But he spends an awful lot of money," she blurted. "I don't know where it all comes from."

"What does he do with his time?" Bishop asked.

"I think he goes to college—or is planning on going to college."

"What about girlfriends? Women?"

"I've seen a few he brought to the house."

"They stay overnight?"

"I don't think so. I go to bed early because I work hard. But . . . no, I don't think so."

And then the vital question regarding the Julie Reitz case.

"Do you know where Randy was over Valentine's Day weekend?"

"I think it's quite possible he went to Portland."

Bishop had an inspiration, one that would prove to be the turning point not only in his case but also in so many others. He asked if Randy Woodfield ever charged long-distance phone calls to Arden's bill, and she said that he did—often. "He calls long distance all the time."

"Would it be possible for us to take a look at your last phone bill?"

"Sure. It's in the house."

Arden handed Bishop the phone bill with calls billed through the middle of February. He scanned it quickly, looking for calls to Beaverton. There were none. But one entry caught his eye. There was a third-party charge from Mt. Shasta, California, billing the call to Arden Bates's phone. The date was February 3. Something clicked in his head. "Shasta" and "February 3."

The I-5 Killer was supposed to have hit near Lake Shasta in the early part of February!

Bishop looked up suddenly and saw Arden Bates staring back at him. She was shivering involuntarily.

"It's him, isn't it?" she breathed. "Randy's the I-5 Killer, isn't he? I've been afraid of that, but I didn't want to say it out loud."

Bishop would neither confirm nor deny his own feelings. "Can we have this phone bill?"

"Sure, take it."

"We'd like to talk to you down at the police station, Mrs. Bates," Bishop said quietly. "I think it would be wise if you and Mickey moved out of here for a while. Can you find another place to stay for a few nights?"

She nodded, rubbing the goose pimples that dotted her arms.

"Good. The sooner you and Mickey can get out of here, the better."

Doug Ashbridge arranged for a continuous surveillance of the residence by Springfield police. It was not yet time to arrest Randy Woodfield; that would be premature. But the officers wanted to be sure where he was.

Arden Bates threw some clothing into an overnight bag and hurried her son out to her car. She turned back and looked at Dave Bishop and Neal Loper. "You know, he's a really nice guy. I liked him right away when he came to rent the room. If you met him, you wouldn't even think he could do anything violent. You don't think he ever would have hurt us, do you? You don't really think it's him, do you? This is just a maybe, isn't it?"

Loper smiled at her. "It's just a maybe. We only want to be absolutely sure you and Mickey are safe. When we check out the phone numbers, and when we talk with some of the other detectives on the case, we'll know more."

"But," she argued, "if he was a killer, I would have known it, wouldn't I?"

"I don't know," Loper said honestly. "That's what we're trying to find out."

15

Back at the Springfield Police Department, Loper and Bishop put through an immediate call to Redding, California. The phone call from Mt. Shasta might prove to be the one clue that scores of detectives in the Northwest had been seeking. When they reached Detective Ron Kingsley at the Shasta County Sheriff's Office, they asked him to check the reverse directory there to see where Randy Woodfield had been when he made a phone call and charged it to his landlady's Eugene number.

Loper told Kingsley the phone number. "Our man made that call from Mt. Shasta on February 3, shortly after nine P.M."

"That's the night of our double homicide in Mountain Gate!" Kingsley responded.

"That's why we thought this was so important," Loper agreed. "Call us back when you trace the number."

Kingsley called back within minutes. The call had been made from a phone booth in Jerry's Restaurant in Mt. Shasta. "It's just a fluke that you picked up on it," Kingsley explained. "The name 'Shasta.' Actually, Mt. Shasta is more than fifty miles north of our crime scene, up the I-5. The timing's right. Our victims were killed between six and nine P.M. Keep in touch."

"You bet. We'll pass information along the minute we get it."

Dave Bishop and Neal Loper had gone to Eugene to eliminate Randy Woodfield as a suspect in the murder of Julie Reitz. Instead of eliminating him, they'd found he looked good. Now, eight hours later, they found themselves deep in the middle of the biggest case going in Oregon, Washington, and California. Was it possible that Randy Woodfield *was* the I-5 Killer?

Dave Kominek and Monty Holloway had barely arrived back in Salem after the day-long meeting in Eugene when the call came from Dave Bishop and Neal Loper.

"Can you get back down here? We may have something for you. We have a suspect under surveillance who may look awfully good to you. The man looks like your composites, and we can place him in Shasta County on February 3."

Kominek and Holloway didn't stop to change clothes. They expected to be back in Salem later that night. They called Lieutenant Kilburn McCoy to tell him they were heading back to Eugene and that they'd keep him informed. Kominek left Salem with seventeen dollars in his wallet and no credit cards; he didn't expect to need much money during one evening in Eugene.

He didn't know he wouldn't see Salem again for almost a week.

When the Marion County detectives reached the Springfield Police Department, the probe went into high gear. They talked with Arden Bates and went over the dates when Randy Woodfield had been away from her home. Every out-of-town crime had occurred on those nights. According to Mrs. Bates, Randy was an inveterate traveler on the I-5 freeway.

Kominek looked at the mug shot of Randy Woodfield, and the skin prickled on the back of his neck. He saw that the eyes, the facial features, the coloring, the hair, the thick neck, and the broad shoulders were just like those of the composites he had begun to see even in his sleep.

Randy Brent Woodfield. An ex-con who'd been sent up for robbery, but the man's criminal history had revealed that there had been oral-sodomy charges which were dropped. That would explain why Kominek and Holloway hadn't found Woodfield's name in their massive search of parolee records; they'd been checking murderers and sex offenders. The sex charges on Woodfield hadn't been in the computer.

And there was more, so much more. According to medical records at the Oregon State Penitentiary, Woodfield had B-negative blood, just like the phantom man they'd been seeking; he drove a Volkswagen Bug, and, perhaps most telling, Neal Loper had seized a large roll of adhesive tape when he searched Woodfield's bedroom.

Dave Bishop held out the phone bill that Arden Bates had turned over to him. "He made a lot of calls."

Excited, Kominek ran his finger down the list of calls. On January 18, the night Shari Hull and Beth Wilmot had been shot, Randy Woodfield had called a Salem number at 9:01 P.M. from Independence, Oregon. He'd called a Newberg number an hour and a half later from Woodburn, north of Salem on the I-5. God, the man left a blueprint of his travels up and down the freeway! On January 28 he called to Medford, and there were collect calls from Medford, Grants Pass, Ashland, Yreka, and Redding between January 29 and February 4.

Kominek had memorized the roster of crimes and their dates, and the calls followed the lineup perfectly.

It was going to take thousands of man-hours to find out whom Randy had visited along the freeway and to verify his locations, but the hole in the dike was there.

The torrent of information had begun to flow.

The meeting in the Springfield police offices was fraught with subdued excitement and tension. Attending were detectives James Callahan, Jerry Smith, Doug Ashbridge, and Chief Brian Riley from the Springfield department; Pat Horton, district attorney of Lane County; Tony Meyer, Woodfield's Eugene parole officer; Detective Ron Griesel from the Eugene Police Department; Dennis O'Donnell from the Oregon State Police in Eugene; Chuck Vaughn and Jim Pex from the Oregon State Police Crime Lab; Captain Dave Bishop and Detective Neal Loper from the Beaverton Police Department; and Dave Kominek and Monty Holloway from the Marion County Sheriff's Office in Salem.

The lawmen stared at the blackboard in front of them and watched the damning circumstantial evidence against Randall Brent Woodfield mount, bits and pieces supplied by various detectives.

Arden Bates: Subject conducts his activities late at night. Subject leaves her residence on dates corresponding with the attacks by the I-5 Killer.

Subject drives a Volkswagen Bug.

Subject was in Mt. Shasta just after California murders in Mountain Gate.

Subject en route to Medford at time of Medford and Grants Pass robberies.

Subject's prior behavior pattern fits psychological profile established for the I-5 Killer.

Beaverton victim shot in the back of the head. Previous victims have been shot in back of head, temple, or right side of head.

Subject fits same physical description of I-5 Killer: 6′ 1½″, 170 pounds, athletic.

I-5 Killer wore gloves similar in all respects to racquetball gloves. Subject plays racquetball frequently.

Subject has B-negative blood, according to prison records.

*   *   *

It looked promising. Hell, Kominek thought, it looks perfect. The thing to do was to move immediately for a search warrant of the house on E Street and gather more physical evidence before Woodfield had time to destroy it. Dave Bishop agreed with Kominek, as did Ron Griesel of the Eugene Police Department. They could get a search warrant easily enough with Pat Horton, the Lane County district attorney, right in the meeting.

And then the specter of territorial rights raised its ugly head. Some of the authorities in the Eugene area were bristling; their feeling was that the detectives from Beaverton and Salem were treading on their turf. Bishop and Loper had informed the Springfield Police Department of their intent to question Woodfield, but they had not told Eugene and Lane County authorities before the fact. This suspect might well have committed offenses in other areas, but he was in Lane County now, and whatever would be done with him should be up to Lane County. D.A. Pat Horton was not amenable to direction from detectives from other jurisdictions. He wanted them to play a waiting game. Horton pointed out that Woodfield was home, asleep probably, in the house. He was under constant surveillance by officers watching in sneaker cars. If he left the house, he would be followed. There was no tearing hurry now.

Horton would not be talked out of his stance. There was a question as to whom the subject belonged to. He was a major catch. The jurisdiction that actually arrested him could count on headlines and kudos.

Now the jealousies flared up. A turf war. It had happened in Los Angeles when county and city wrangled over whom Charlie Manson belonged to, and it had happened in the Ted Bundy case when dozens of departments sought him.

Horton was adamant that they would do it his way. Lane County would call the shots.

The days that followed would be, perhaps, the most agonizing of the entire probe for Kominek and Holloway. Parole officer Tony Meyer said he would be willing to arrest Woodfield, as he had violated his parole by moving to Eugene without permission, but Horton vetoed that. The Marion County detectives thought they had their man, but they were being blocked from moving in and arresting him. Bishop and Loper figured that Woodfield was the man *they* sought. It was not a situation of give and take; it was a tug-of-war, and Randy Woodfield was the prize.

Springfield Police Chief Brian Riley, described by Kominek as ''probably the most professional police chief I've ever encountered," tried to calm the troubled waters. The meeting broke up at three A.M. on that first night. It was finally agreed that Woodfield would be left alone—but watched—and the detectives would meet again the next day.

Chuck Vaughn and Jim Pex would work all night to analyze the blood and semen stains and to try to match pubic hairs found on Randy Woodfield's sheets to hairs retrieved in the assault on the two young girls in Corvallis. Monty Holloway would fly out to Spokane, Washington, at five A.M. in a state-police plane through a driving snowstorm to contact Beth Wilmot so that she could look at a mug lay-down which included Randy Woodfield's picture. Dave Kominek would stand pat in Eugene; he could not risk driving back to Salem for fear the suspect would again slip through his grasp. D.A. Horton had promised that Kominek and Ron Griesel would be allowed to interview Woodfield the next day.

Kominek put in a call to Portland to Detective Sergeant Rod Englert of the Multnomah County Sheriff's Office. "Rod, get down here," he said fervently. "We're going to need you as a referee. Your county is one that *doesn't* want the I-5 Killer, so you can be an impartial mediator. I think we've got him. I'm sure of it, but we may be losing our momentum."

"I'm on my way," Englert promised, already shrugging on his clothes.

And then Dave Kominek realized, at four A.M., that he had no funds, not even enough to get a cheap motel room. Chief Brian Riley grinned and offered him the hospitality of the Springfield jail for the four hours until dawn. Not fancy, but warm and dry. Kominek accepted. A jail bunk was better than the backseat of his car.

Exhausted, Kominek fell fast asleep on the hard bunk. As a professional courtesy, the cell door was left wide open. The fact that a killer who had dismembered his wife was just down the corridor was the least of Kominek's concerns; the mutilation killer's cell was locked.

Kominek laughs when he remembers the comedy of errors that ensued. "I snore like a truck, and I woke up to see the female dispatcher from Springfield staring at me with a look of panic on her face. She hadn't seen me come in, she didn't know who I was, and she thought that I was a dangerous felon lying there snoring in an open cell, likely to wake up at any minute and run amok. Luckily somebody told her I was one of the good guys."

Kominek started his second day in Eugene with only three hours of sleep in thirty-six hours.

Marion County D.A. Chris Van Dyke drove down to Eugene from Salem to back Dave Kominek. The district attorney from Corvallis, Peter Sandrock, with his investigator, Randy Martinek, arrived from that city to attempt to issue a search warrant on Woodfield's home.

D.A. Horton was still insisting that there would be no action. Woodfield was to be observed, and that was all. Around-the-clock surveillance continued. Randy Woodfield was followed surreptitiously wherever he went. Tempers were unraveling on that second day. When Horton said that he thought he would send all outside detectives home and turn the investigation over to his men and the Oregon State Police, Kominek and Bishop neared their boiling point. What Horton was suggesting was akin to calling a hunting dog out of a fox hunt after he'd finally run his quarry to earth.

"It was our case," Kominek says quietly. "Monty and I had worked it for months, day and night. We had all the information, we were closing in, and we were told to go home and let somebody else take over."

The press had picked up the scent, and they hovered outside the Springfield police offices, which had become the focal point of a circus of black comedy.

The pressure to move was accentuated by the avid interest of the media. Since a news story had appeared in Salem on March 4 saying that Kominek and Holloway were on the way *north* into Washington State to check out leads there on the I-5 Killer, reporters had not given much weight to the activity in Eugene. But then a reporter who knew him spotted Kominek in Eugene. The Oregon press knew that Dave Kominek headed the I-5 task force. That had to mean that something big was coming down, that possibly police had homed in on the I-5 Killer. Reporters demanded quotes. If the I-5 Killer was in Eugene, they argued, the public had a right to know.

Indeed, the whole case was almost blown when a television news crew unknowingly parked next to Randy's gold Volkswagen in a theater parking lot while he was inside watching a film with one of his girlfriends. Watching police waited, hoping that their suspect wouldn't emerge from the theater, spot the TV crew, and be alerted that he was under surveillance. Officers rushed the reporter and cameraman away, giving rise to more questions from the crew.

If Randy *knew* that he was the focal point of such a massive investigation, he might destroy every scintilla of physical evidence.

All Randy really knew was that Beaverton police had connected him only tenuously to Julie Reitz. He thought he had carried off that interview rather well. He was a little nervous when he realized that Arden Bates and her son had left the house. He wondered why Arden was gone, but it wasn't a big worry. Arden knew nothing at all about him.

On March 4 the Eugene *Register Guard* carried a banner headline across the top of the front page: "POLICE HINT OF BREAK IN BANDIT CASE." The paper hit the street at twelve-thirty in the afternoon.

Forced to do something to stall the press, Chief Brian Riley held a news conference.

"The investigation has taken a significant turn today," he said carefully. "But it is not over by any stretch of the imagination. There is a lot of hard work left to be done. No charges have been filed."

That afternoon, the papers and a television anchorman announced to the public—and undoubtedly to the suspect—that police were questioning a man named "Randy."

Reporters tried to find out just who Arden Bates might be and where she might have gone. They found the house on E Street and camped out alongside the surveillance officers, waiting, like everyone else, to see what would happen next. What had begun as a methodical, careful investigation was rapidly turning into a Keystone Kops comedy. The Springfield neighborhood was crawling with reporters, each hoping to find out more about the man named Randy who lived there. Neighbors were being interviewed about what they might know of the occupants of the house at 3622 E Street. They commented cryptically that Arden Bates and her son, Mickey, had lived there. "But they're not there now; nobody knows what happened to them."

Neighbor boys told reporters about the nice guy who lived there, an ex-pro football player whom they all liked. It was hard for the press to contain itself.

Inside his house, Randy Woodfield stayed behind drawn curtains. He called Shelley in New Mexico and told her to come ahead on up to Eugene. He told her nothing about the trouble; he only told her that they would have to live in Portland because his parole officer was hounding him. Joyously she packed her car, rented a trailer, and began the long drive to Oregon. She had not the slightest idea that her best beloved was the focal point of the most massive police investigation in Oregon history.

At noon on the third day, Dave Bishop and Dave Kominek "pulled the plug" on District Attorney Pat Horton.

"It was our case," Kominek recalls. "We said the hell with it, and we moved. The press could sense it. Suddenly everybody was doing something. We told people who would do what and who was going to go where. We couldn't just sit there and watch Randy Woodfield."

The break with Horton was complete, but Kominek felt he had no other choice. Bishop backed him. Van Dyke backed him. Englert backed him.

At a quarter to two on the afternoon of March 5, Dave Kominek came face to face with Randy Woodfield for the first time. He and Ron Griesel of the Eugene Police Department knocked on the door of the house on E Street. Woodfield opened it and ushered the two detectives into the living room. He was calm, and he was polite. He nodded slightly when Kominek told him that his appearance and physical stature matched those of a man they sought.

And indeed Woodfield did resemble the composite in every detail. Kominek was astounded to see this man in person. He thought he could have picked him out of a crowd anytime. The man was muscular, obviously an athlete, and he could have posed for the composites retrieved from all the cases up and down the I-5. The Marion County detective waited for Randy Woodfield to speak.

Woodfield did not seem overtly hostile, but he betrayed anxiety when he demanded to know why the Beaverton detectives had taken his gun-cleaning kit and his athletic adhesive tape. "They took all the rolls I had. I can't understand it; one roll should have been enough."

Was it possible that Randy Woodfield was savvy enough about physical evidence to know that torn edges of tape can be matched absolutely to the roll from which segments have come? Kominek replied that he could not comment on Beaverton's motives.

"I'm probably going to be violated on my parole, and it's not my fault. She told me I had to go back to Portland, and I was going to leave this morning, and then they told me I could go later," Randy complained. "The police are following me around. I think it's the Beaverton guys. The neighbor kid came over and said the police were watching me and they think I'm the I-5 Bandit.''

"Did the Beaverton officers look through your house here?" Kominek asked.

"Yes, they did.''

"Would you have any objection to our taking a look?''

"No. I'll show you around.''

Randy gave Griesel and Kominek a guided tour. He showed them his Green Bay Packers souvenirs, and he bragged about his gold Volkswagen, explaining that it was a limited-edition Super Beetle. "A friend did that damage to the front end. I may sue him, because he wasn't covered by insurance.''

"What made you decide to move down to Eugene?" Griesel asked.

"I was trying to find work so I could go on to college at the same time. I've applied for jobs at O'Callahan's, De Frisco's, the Atrium, and the Tavern on the Green. I'm going to get my degree in P.E., and I hope to manage an athletic club—like one that has racquetball, for instance.''

The conversation moved along easily now. The detectives could see that Randy was in his element when he talked about sports, and they threw out questions. He brought up the Packers and said he probably should have stayed with basketball instead of football. The three men discussed topics that all men talk about, and Kominek had a little trouble now believing that Randy Woodfield could be the man he had sought for so long. Woodfield certainly *looked* just like the man they were looking for, but the guy was calm, pleasant, companionable. Could they have zeroed in on the wrong man after all? It would be a long time before Kominek could be sure; he would have to wait until, in this conversation, or the next, or the next, Woodfield either vindicated himself or wove himself a trap.

Kominek asked Randy about his prior arrest record, and Randy admitted the exposing incidents and the armed robbery that had sent him to prison. And then Randy soberly explained that all of his sexual problems were in the past. "I'll never do that kind of stuff again. I don't have a problem anymore.''

Kominek glanced casually around the room. His heart sank when he saw the fresh ashes in the fireplace and the can of lighter fluid on the hearth. "Looks like you had a fire,'' he remarked.

"No. The landlady's kid plays in the fireplace a lot. He

probably left that stuff there. The wood in the garage is so green, we have to use lighter fluid to get it going.''

Kominek let it pass. Whatever had gone up in flames, it was too late now—too late unless the lab guys might be able to retrieve something from analysis of the ashes. Probably the fake beard, the hats, the hooded jackets were gone forever. *Damn*.

''Your landlady's not here?''

Randy shrugged. ''I don't know where she is. I haven't seen her in two days. I'm probably going to get evicted. Do you know where she is?''

''I think the Beaverton police have talked to her. They probably know where she is.''

''Are you going to violate my parole?''

''I don't know,'' Kominek said truthfully. ''I hear they found a bong or some dope or something when they searched your room.''

Randy said nothing. Most men would be sweating buckets by now, but Woodfield continued to be soft-spoken and amiable. When he talked about sports, he took on a kind of glow. He was a likable man. Kominek could see why others—men and women— might be drawn to him. He had somehow expected a rougher, cruder man.

Randy's friendly acquiescence disappeared, however, when Kominek pressed a little harder.

''Randall, would you give us a hair sample—so we could eliminate you as a suspect in the the I-5 case?''

''No, I wouldn't do that.''

''Would you submit to a polygraph?''

''No.''

''Could you account for your whereabouts on certain dates?''

''Only if I could find notes on the dates you might be interested in.'' Woodfield stood up. ''I think I've answered enough of your questions. I can't see what this has to do with me.''

Dave Kominek advised Randy Woodfield of his rights under Miranda. ''Do you have any questions?''

''No, I understand.'' Randy signed the Miranda card, but only with his first name. Oddly, considering how much he hated the diminutive of his name, he signed it ''Randy.''

Kominek asked if Randy had contacted anyone in Salem recently, and he replied that he had a grandmother and an aunt and uncle there, and that he tried to keep in touch with them.

''Have you ever been to Corvallis, Randy?'' Griesel asked.

''Never. I don't know anyone in that area.''

"Have you ever been to Seattle?"

"No."

"Tacoma?"

"My best friend lives there. He's an assistant professor at Pacific Lutheran University, and the long-distance track coach."

"How long since you've visited him?"

"I can't recall. He came to Portland to visit me."

"How about Albany? Ever stopped for coffee or anything there?"

"No. Don't know anyone there."

"When was the last time you went to Portland?"

"Last weekend. My parents just got back from a tour of Taiwan."

Asked about his female friends, Randy told them about Shelley and about a young woman who worked as a baby-sitter in Eugene. The conversation about girlfriends eased the tension in the room a little. And then Kominek asked a question that made Woodfield tighten up again.

"When was the last time you were in Redding?"

"Redding? California? I can't really remember. It's been quite a while."

"We understand you made a trip to California. You didn't stop in Redding?"

"I told you I don't remember."

He was lying. Every line in his body said *lie*. He froze up almost imperceptibly when the towns where major assaults had occurred were mentioned.

Kominek saw Woodfield's unease and deftly switched topics. "You have any other kinds of tape around here?"

"Strong tape—like they use for packages. Strapping tape."

"What kind of hat do you usually wear?"

"I don't wear hats. They smash my Afro down."

"Is that natural curl or a permanent?"

"It's naturally curly." He was lying again. Why? "I'm going to get it cut today because my girlfriend is coming up."

"Have you ever had sex with a girl in this house?" Griesel asked suddenly.

"No. I never had sex with my landlady."

"When *was* the last time you had sex?"

Randy stared back at Kominek. "That's none of your business. I think I've answered enough questions."

"We're taking you into custody on parole violation," Griesel said, slipping handcuffs on Randy's incongruously slender forearms.

"I expected that. I'm not going anywhere," Woodfield said calmly. "I might as well go with you."

When they headed for the Springfield police station, Dave Kominek's elation at having the prime suspect under arrest was considerably dampened by the memory of the ashes he'd seen in the fireplace on E Street. There had been a lot of ashes; Randy Woodfield could have burned items that might have been pure gold as evidence. Sure, Horton's surveillance tactics had kept Woodfield under constant observation—he hadn't bolted and run—but all the officers in the world watching him could not have stopped him from destroying evidence.

Too late now.

16

On this, the third day of the intensive investigation in Eugene, Randy Woodfield was placed in an interview room in the Springfield Police Department. The room had a one-way-mirror viewing area, and conversation could be monitored by someone outside the room. Beaverton detectives Dave Bishop and Neal Loper, and Detective Sergeant Randy Martinek of the Benton County Sheriff's Office in Corvallis listened as Kominek and Ron Griesel talked with the tall, curly-haired suspect. Would he say something, betray guilt in some slip of the tongue? He seemed relaxed; if he was not actually enjoying the session with Kominek and Griesel, he was certainly not showing outward tension.

Again Randy Woodfield was advised of his rights under Miranda and asked if he wished to consult an attorney. He did not want an attorney but he asked to call a young woman who could contact his friends. "I want Jennifer to get hold of Shelley. Shelley's on her way up here from New Mexico with a U-Haul trailer."

"What's Jennifer's number? We'll call her and you can talk to her."

Randy shook his head. "She's hard to get hold of. She's a college student."

"You're sure? We'll call anyone you like."

"I can call her later. Ask me what you want to know."

Kominek began. "Randy, we're basically trying to pinpoint where you were on certain dates and times."

"I could give you any information you need to prove I'm innocent if I have to."

"If you're innocent, we could check out those dates and locations to verify your innocence, and that could establish alibis for you. It would help us too; we need this information now to move ahead with our investigation. If we can eliminate you as a suspect, we can keep on going looking for the man we're after," Kominek said.

"I know my parole is going to be violated," Randy said. "I know I'm going back to the joint."

"Whose fault is that?" Griesel asked.

Woodfield winced. "My own. It really doesn't bother me, but it looks like my world is going to be inside for quite a while."

"If you were sure you were going back, why did you wait for us at the house today?" Kominek asked.

"It wouldn't do any good to run, so I just waited for some officer to come and get me."

Randy's reaction was rather flat; he was portraying himself as the poor beleaguered ex-con whose only crime had been moving without notifying his parole officer. He was sorry for himself, but said he assumed that's the way things went for ex-cons.

"Have you been working at all down here, Randy?" Griesel asked.

"Not yet, but I've been looking for a job. And I've been playing basketball."

"What kind of shoes do you wear for basketball?"

Many of the victims had mentioned that their attacker had worn sports shoes, but Kominek made it sound as if it were a throwaway question.

"I like Nike high-tops. My ankles are weak. I had to have special shoes smuggled into the pen. I got in trouble—but they smuggle dope and other junk in, so high-topped basketball shoes aren't really a major crime. Basketball weakened my ankles, and I hurt my knees playing football. Outside of that, I keep in pretty good shape."

"You ever have a vasectomy?" This question seemingly out of left field from Griesel.

"No." Woodfield's muscles tensed. "You going to take my blood today?"

"We might. Do you have any objection to that?"

"I don't want to let you take blood today."

"You ever have gonorrhea, any kind of V.D.?"

"I really screwed up when I got out of the pen—got in a hurry and caught herpes." Woodfield smiled conspiratorially—males talking together about male interests.

Kominek felt a rush. Beth Wilmot had developed herpes nine days after she was attacked. He kept his face bland.

The detectives offered to get some food for Randy, but he said he didn't like jail food.

"We can send out for something."

"No, I don't want to put anyone out."

"You say you play basketball?" Griesel asked. "For what team?"

"Columbia Optical."

"Could you tell us what nights you've played? Have you missed any games?"

"I missed some, but I couldn't tell you specific dates."

"What kind of jobs have you been looking for?"

"Tending bar. I just finished a bartending course in Portland, where I learned to make any kind of drink you might ask for. I hope to tend bar nights so I can go to school."

"You learn how to make a Freddie Fudwarmer?" Griesel asked with a grin. Both of the detectives were holding back, asking ten inane questions for every query on the vital issues. It was agonizingly slow, this process of interrogation, but they could not rush into the heart of what they needed.

"I think that's your basic Harvey Wallbanger with a sillier name."

"You consider yourself a religious man, Randy?" Kominek asked. "Were you involved in religion while you were in the joint?"

"Yeah, I was into religion a lot then." The suspect stared at his hands. "But somewhere along the line, I guess I just told God to take a backseat."

The room swelled with silence. And Randy volunteered his feelings about the power of women over prisoners in the penitentiary. "They had women guards watching me when I had to take a piss. They had these nurses in group therapy wanting us to share our sexual fantasies. They wouldn't share theirs with us, so why should I tell them mine?"

"Do you feel uncomfortable around women?" Kominek asked.

"No—not at all. I like women."

Kominek switched gears again. "Do you think your basketball buddies would remember which games you were at, and which you missed?"

Randy shrugged. "They might; they might not."

"What position do you play?"

"Center. I'm their high scorer; everybody passes me the ball. I know what I'm capable of doing. It's a matter of being in control at all times, especially in sports. If you don't have control, things go to shit.''

"You feel 'up' when you're competing? Does it make you more aware of things around you?"

"Oh, sure. The roar of the crowd and all that. I thought I might be slower in my rookie games at Green Bay, but with forty thousand people watching, it actually speeded me up. I like that. I like to be active, working or playing sports. Sitting around these past couple of months in Eugene has been hard on me. I'm really looking forward to getting back to college. I like studying— except for economics.''

"Randy, we have a problem that you may be able to help us out with," Kominek said. "We have the records from Arden's phone. You called from certain cities in California and other places in southern Oregon where some of our crimes occurred, and you charged those calls to Arden's phone. We've got toll calls listed that you made in Independence and Woodburn, Oregon, on the night that Shari Hull and Beth Wilmot were shot near Keizer, outside of Salem. You seem to have been in several areas on the same days our crimes occurred.''

"I called Shelley in New Mexico and charged it to my home phone.''

"Were you in Salem on the Sunday night of January 18?''

"I might have been. I stop there often, and I call often and charge it to my home phone.''

"Try to remember. The records say you made calls to Salem at one P.M., two-forty-two P.M., and five P.M. on January 18. You made a call from a booth in Independence—just south of Salem—at nine P.M., and from Woodburn—north of Salem—at ten-thirty P.M. Do you know where Keizer is?''

Woodfield nodded.

"Did you drive from Independence through Salem toward Portland on the I-5 that Sunday night?''

The suspect nodded again.

"Then you would have had to pass through Keizer. You would have been a few hundred feet from where our victims were shot in Keizer between nine and ten-thirty P.M. Our crime occurred in that time frame.''

Randy said nothing.

"Do you ever do anything that changes your appearance?" Griesel asked. "Change your hairstyle, wear a hat, anything like that?''

"No. My hair's naturally curly. I don't do anything to it.''

"You always look just the way we see you now?"

"Yeah . . . except for when I grew a beard in the joint. They didn't like it."

"Could you tell us a little about your habits? How late you stay out, what you drink—how much?"

Randy was more relaxed now. The conversation no longer dealt with the Salem murder. "I don't get drunk. When I drink, I drink beer. It makes me easygoing, maybe a little louder than I normally am. I'm usually home right after the bars close."

"Ever get in a fight? When was your last fight?"

"I don't get into many fights. I don't like getting hit on the nose. That smarts."

Randy grinned. He felt that he'd slid through the dangerous area of the interrogation. Again, they were only three men rapping.

"What attracts you in a female?" Griesel asked. "Myself, I go for the upper structure."

"Breasts aren't a big deal for me," Randy answered. "I like a woman with an athletic build. Women with nice asses are usually athletic. I like a woman who dresses conservatively—I don't like revealing clothing. That's not classy."

"You must meet a lot of attractive women tending bar."

"Right. Most places I've worked, everybody parties after hours."

Suddenly the conversation was no longer casual.

"Why do you think the Beaverton police are so adamant about your being a good suspect in their case?" Kominek asked.

"They were talking about Julie Reitz, and I knew her. She played up to me."

"How old was Julie?"

"Eighteen or nineteen, but she had I.D. that said she was twenty-one. I was surprised at how mature she acted for her age. But I didn't know her that well; I knew her girlfriend better."

"You ever date Julie?"

"I won't tell you that. . . . Well, it's not important anyway. I went to her house once after hours."

"You told us before that three women you knew had been murdered. Who were those women?"

"Yeah. Well, there was Julie. Then my best friend's ex-fiancée—Darci Fix. I knew her because my friend introduced us and we went out to dinner. But my friend broke off that relationship before she was shot. And then there was Cherie Ayers. I went to school with Cherie at Newport High School. She was killed in the Terwilliger Boulevard area in Portland. She was a good Christian girl; she helped us set up our class reunion.''

"How was it that you knew her in Portland? That was a long time after graduation."

"I just ran into her by accident. I think Cherie was going to school there."

"That's a lot of people to know—and have them all killed in the space of a year."

"Yeah."

"Captain Bishop and Detective Loper saw a gun-cleaning kit in your room. What did you use that for?"

"I never had a gun. I used some of the swabs from the kit with alcohol to clean my face."

It was a ridiculous explanation, but they let it go. "When you are in Portland," Griesel asked, "where do you stay?"

"With my friends or my sister."

"Do you think you might be able to remember where you were on these dates we're concerned about?"

"If I had to, I could prove it in court that I wasn't in those places."

Randy Woodfield was not emerging as a suspect who, faced with hard questions, would spill his guts. He was polite, soft-voiced, and cooperative—but only to a point. When the queries probed too closely, he threw up walls.

"It might be necessary to go to court," Kominek said. "On the night of one of the incidents in Corvallis, your landlady told us you didn't come home all night."

"I find that hard to believe. I've never been away all night—except when I was away on a trip."

"We'd be happy if you could give us alibis . . . but it seems evident that you can't do that. We think that you are the I-5 Bandit."

"I'm not pleading guilty to that one, and I'm not the I-5 Killer. I am not going to defend myself because I don't have to."

But then Randy began to explain where he had been in late January and early February.

"I travel a lot. I went to San Francisco on January 29. I drove down there to meet Shelley, my girlfriend. I stayed in Ashland at a friend's house on the way down. I spent the weekend with my girlfriend, and then I drove back up to Oregon."

"What would be the exact dates?"

A thin beading of sweat marked Woodfield's forehead.

"I can't be absolutely sure. I think I left for San Francisco on January 28. I must have been there around the thirty-first or the first of February. I got back to Eugene about the third or fourth. I stayed at my sister's in Mt. Shasta for one night on the way home, and I stayed one night with a friend in Medford on the way back. Look, I can't be expected to remember exact dates or times or locations. The past is history. I would like to help you more, but I can't do that at this time."

The interview had not gone as well as Randy had intended.

"Do you think you need an attorney now?" Kominek asked.

"No, I don't," Randy answered, but he gave the two detectives a name and phone number for his attorney.

"I'm going to call him for you," Kominek said. "We'd like to help you if we could—you're not giving us anything to go on."

Woodfield stood up. "How are you going to help me? You could put me away forever."

The interview was over.

A few miles outside of Eugene, Shelley Janson realized that she would shortly be seeing her lover. Her happy-ever-after love story was about to begin. She was as happy as she had ever been in her life. It had been a long, hard trip, pulling the U-Haul, but it had been worth it. She would be with Randall, and within the year they would be married.

But when she stopped at a pay phone to call him and tell him that she had arrived, the phone rang endlessly. There was no one home. She tried again later, and then again. She couldn't imagine where Randy might be. Finally she gave up and drove to her father's house.

She waited there for Randy to call.

17

Monty Holloway and pilot, Oregon state trooper Graning, had flown out of Eugene in a state plane at five-thirty A.M. on March 4. They contacted Beth Wilmot at ten after ten that morning in the Spokane airport. Ron Griesel had constructed a throw-down of Polaroid photos, including a picture of Randy Woodfield taken the day before, and Holloway held his breath as he watched Beth stare at the five photos. Randy was number three.

There was a long silence. Beth placed her index finger on Randy Woodfield's picture, but she said nothing for minutes. And then she handed the lay-down back to Holloway.

"I'm not sure," she said. "I think . . . Unless I'm sure, I won't pick any of them. I will have to say it's none of them."

Holloway felt crushing disappointment, but he could not urge Beth to reconsider. The game wasn't over yet. Beth had seen a man with a hood over his hair, and she had seen that man while she was in the grip of profound terror. The photo of Randy showed a man with a full head of dark hair, half-smiling at the camera. The voice, the mannerisms, the size of the man didn't show in the Polaroid.

"Beth," he asked, "will you come down to Eugene? We'll be having a lineup where all the victims can actually look at the man we have in person. We'd like you to be there."

"Which one is it? Is he one of those men I just looked at?"

"I can't tell you that. We want you to see him with an open mind. Will you come?"

"Of course."

It was too dangerous to fly Beth to Eugene in the small plane. As it was, Holloway and Graning were forced to set down when the plane's wings iced up while crossing the treacherous Cascade mountain range. Arrangements were made for Beth to travel to Eugene by bus.

*   *   *

Back in Eugene, detectives from eleven police agencies were working frantically to tie up all the tangled leads. Randy Woodfield was in custody, but on a basically fragile charge: parole violation. They had no gun, despite the media's hints that they had found one. They had very little physical evidence; they were sure that most of what they needed had gone up in flames in Arden Bates's fireplace. They had a prisoner who was, at the very least, reluctant to give them any information on his travels. They were hampered by the fact that they were working in the glare of press attention. One slip and the error would be emblazoned in headlines.

They had a tiger by the tail.

The little house on E Street was cordoned off by the police with rope, along with the lot next door to it. A huge sign was nailed to the picket fence: "NO TRESPASSING: INVESTIGATION SCENE—BY AUTHORITY OF THE SPRINGFIELD POLICE DEPARTMENT."

The only thing missing was hawkers selling balloons and hot dogs.

The detectives worked to make their case so strong that nothing could crumble it. First, there would be a search warrant of the premises where Randy Woodfield had lived. Next, every victim who could be located would be transported to Eugene to view a lineup. People who had been part of Randy's life during the previous months and years had to be contacted.

Not surprisingly, most of them were women.

Dave Kominek had finally received funds from home; he would no longer have to sleep in the Springfield jail, but it would be a long time before he returned to Salem.

The search warrant came first. On March 5, at six-fifty P.M., Benton County District Court Judge David Smedena signed the warrant:

YOU ARE THEREFORE COMMANDED to make immediate search of: the single-family wood-frame brown-colored home located at 3622 South E Street, Springfield, and the area immediately surrounding that dwelling in Lane County, Oregon,

TO SEARCH FOR: a false beard, white adhesive tape, silver pistol, blue jeans with a button above the zippered fly, a dark stocking cap, a blue or green waist-length jacket, a red-and-white-checked paper sack bearing the logo of "Fabric Patch," brown army-type boots, a brown waist-length jacket with hood, blue gloves, tennis or jogging shoes, a Smith and

Wesson .38-caliber revolver (or other small revolver), as well as head, facial, body, axillary, and pubic hairs, transferred clothing fibers, and semen stains on any underclothing and/or trousers as well as any ashes and unburned parts of material found therein.

In addition to the items listed, the detectives had the right, legally, to seize any articles not listed which were in clear view and seemed to bear a connection to crimes included in the I-5 pattern.

For the next four days, three dozen detectives and criminalists from state crime labs moved through the three-bedroom home. Each detective's entrance and exit was carefully monitored with date and time on a log kept by officers stationed at the doors. There was no sense of time for the investigators. The home's lights burned twenty-four hours a day. If anything of evidentiary value remained in Woodfield's residence, they would find it.

Eventually, sixty-four separate items were removed from Arden Bates's house—most of them useless for evidentiary purposes.

Criminalists in the lab would determine which evidence was important. For now, the search team had found interesting circumstantial evidence: many pairs of blue jeans, a hooded sweatshirt, a blue-maroon-and-white knit shirt, several pairs of sports shoes, a jogging outfit. All of it fit with the clothing worn by the man who had attacked so many women. But many, many men wore clothing like that. Some of the items bore dark stains. Would it prove to be blood? Was there some minuscule bit of evidence in that prodigious haul that would link Randy Woodfield with any of his victims?

There was.

One pubic hair seized under the search warrant from Woodfield's body was microscopically indistinguishable in class and characteristics from the single pubic hair found in the TransAmerica Building on the night of January 18 when the two were compared under a scanning electron microscope.

One lone .32-caliber bullet was found in the pouch of a racquetball bag in Randy Woodfield's bedroom. The Remington-Peters .32 Colt long bullet was a rare bullet, a very rare bullet. It was the same type of bullet used in the shootings of Beth Wilmot, Shari Hull, Janell Jarvis, and Donna Eckard. Only the one bullet, tucked away in a pouch of Randy's sports bag. Why had he saved it? Had he perhaps forgotten it, or was there some compulsive reason to save this one dread souvenir?

The rest of the evidence proved to mean nothing. The stains on Randy's clothing were not blood. There had been traces of blood and semen on Randy's mattress—but criminalists found there was not enough to test for origin.

Arden Bates told detectives that she had never used her fireplace, that the ashes found there had come from a fire after she and Mickey had moved out. But the fire had consumed whatever was burned there almost totally. All criminalists in the state-police lab could isolate were nails, melted glass fragments, bottle caps, aluminum foil, and metal lids. The supposition was that Randy Woodfield had been doing more than toasting marshmallows while surveillance teams had waited outside. There was no way now to know just what had been burned in that fireplace.

But the case was building, brick by brick. Senior Oregon state trooper Richard L. Davis had been sent off to check phone numbers Randy had called in Medford and to follow up on cards Randy had received from women there. Marion County Detective Jay Boutwell would interview the individuals whose phone numbers Randy had called in Salem on the afternoon of January 18 and on February 15. Neal Loper contacted Pacific Northwest Bell security and received the names and addresses of the subscribers for each number called.

Randy Woodfield's long-distance phone calls, made from pay phones and billed to Arden Bates's phone, when correlated with his constant contacts with the women he expected to be waiting by the phone for him, proved that he had been in the vicinities of the crimes he was suspected of.

"Once we had homed in on him, the case against Randy Woodfield became like a runaway landslide," Kominek recalls. "It took so long for that first rock to let go and tumble down the hill, but then everywhere we turned we found more things that tied Woodfield to our victims. Little pebbles of information grew into boulders. And everything pointed to Randy."

Lieutenant Kilburn McCoy and Detective Jay Boutwell interviewed two young women Randy had called continually on Sunday, January 18, Penny Hale and Lou Lester, and established that Randy had indeed been headed for Salem that day. The detectives heard about the "weirdo" who had followed the Salem girls home from TGI Friday in Portland on January 10.

"We tried to lose him on the road, but he stayed right behind us," Penny explained. "I gave him a cup of coffee, sent him on to Eugene—but after that, he kept calling me. I didn't want to see him again, and I avoided his calls."

Randy had apparently expected that Penny would welcome him with open arms. When she wasn't home to receive his calls on Sunday, he asked another girl to accompany him to Portland, but she too refused him.

With the information that two women had rejected his advances on the afternoon of January 18, one could surmise that a man of Randy's insecurities might have been quite angry as he drove along the I-5 through Keizer, Oregon.

Beth and Shari had been shot sometime between nine-thirty and nine-fifty-four P.M. on that Sunday.

At ten-thirty-one P.M., records indicated that Randy made still another phone call, from a phone booth in Woodburn, thirteen miles north of Keizer on the I-5. This call was to Moira Bandon, the woman he had lived with for a few months after he'd gotten out of the penitentiary in July 1979, the woman who'd forgiven him for giving her herpes.

Moira told Monty Holloway that Randy had asked if he could bunk on her couch that night because he had to take a bartender's exam in Portland the next day. Moira told Randy that she didn't have a spare bed *or* a couch, but that if he wanted to come up and sleep on her bean-bag chair, he could.

"He said he was in Woodburn when he called, and he got to my place between eleven and eleven-thirty."

"What was he wearing?" Holloway asked.

"Jeans, a blue or green pullover shirt, and a brown leather jacket. He wore Nikes—blue, I think, with either a dark blue or yellow stripe on them. He slept over, and he left about noon the next day. I saw his gold Volkswagen."

On Monday night, January 19, Randy had tried once more to call Penny Hale, this time from a booth in Tigard, Oregon, just south of Portland. Again Penny had declined to speak with him. She told Jay Boutwell that she had received one of his clever cards later that week, chiding her for playing so hard to get, but offering her another chance to "get close" to him.

Calls to Salem on February 15 had been made to a home where an eighteen-year-old girl lived. At first Jay Boutwell was extremely interested in this girl; her home was only three blocks from the TransAmerica Title offices.

The proximity of her home to the scene of the shootings on January 18 proved to be only a coincidence. The girl hadn't even met Randy Woodfield until February 13. She told Jay Boutwell about meeting the man named Randall on the I-5 freeway somewhere north of Tacoma on that afternoon. He'd been driving a gold Volkswagen with a Green Bay Packers decal on the window. She had never dated him, but she'd given him her phone number after he'd finally persuaded her to pull over north of Vancouver. She verified that Randall had planned to be in the Portland area over Valentine's Day and that he'd rented a room at the Marriott Hotel. "He called my house really drunk at about two-thirty or three in the morning on the fifteenth, and my stepfather talked to him. Then he called the next day. He never said anything sexy to me, but when he wanted me to come to his suite in the hotel, I thought he had something like that on his mind. He was very polite, and he was very macho. I never saw him in person except for that one time on the freeway."

So there was no connection to the Marion County case, but this girl's statements added to the supposition that Randy *had* been in Beaverton on the Valentine's Day weekend, and Boutwell sent the statement on to Dave Bishop and Neal Loper to add to the growing file they had on the Julie Reitz murder Valentine's night.

Phone records showed that another vital sequence of calls began on January 29 as Randy headed south toward San Francisco. Detectives had to prove that it *was* Randy who had made the calls trailing up and down the coast between the twenty-ninth and February 4. Senior Oregon state trooper Richard Davis located the women Randy had called.

Randy had, of course, kept the phone numbers of the women he had met at the Sandpiper in Medford during the Christmas season just past. He called Lynette Lacey on the way south, and told her that he was leaving for northern California, and suggested he stop by her house and sleep over on the way down. She declined. The next time she heard from him was on February 4. It was eleven P.M.

"He said that it was so foggy out, and that he was tired and he'd missed the off ramp and had gone to Gold Hill. He just wanted to come over and have a drink. I wouldn't let him, and he promised he would only sleep on the couch and not bother me. He just wanted to get some shut-eye. I still wouldn't let him come over. He said he'd been driving a long time, coming back from his sister's house. I can't remember where he said his sister lived. He said a couple of things that were a little bit screwy, you know, that just didn't make sense. He said 'Okay' when I wouldn't let him sleep here. He talked for about fifteen minutes and hung up. Then I got a letter from him a couple days after that saying he was sorry for bothering me, and that he wanted me to come up to Eugene.''

Next, Davis talked with Denise LeNoir, the young Ashland divorcée whom Randy had met on December 26, the same night he met Lynette Lacey. Randy had struck out with Lynette on January 29, but Denise had been more amenable, at least initially.

''It was a couple of weeks after I met him on the day after Christmas. I got a phone call one afternoon when I was home sick from work—that would have been around January 20— and he mentioned he was planning a trip and asked if he could stop by. I said sure, but just let me know. He said it would be within the next week or so, and sure enough, it was. I got a call at home late on the night of the twenty-eighth, and he was at the exit—the Ashland exit from the I-5—and he wanted to know if he could come over for coffee and wanted directions.''

Randy had told Denise that he was going to San Francisco to meet his friend Ralph. He also intended to visit his sister in Mt. Shasta, and he seemed concerned about snow on the mountain passes. Randy called his sister, in fact, from Denise's phone to find out about weather conditions, charging the call to Arden Bates's phone.

Denise told Davis that she'd begun to wonder a little about Randy's past. He told her he'd been in Portland to go to bartending school, but she knew such a school didn't involve much time.

''He left a big blank spot, you know, in his past. Like he wouldn't mention what he had done before that. He was very hesitant to talk about what he had done before that.''

Evincing great concern over the snowy pass conditions, Randy asked Denise if he could sleep on her couch. She felt sorry for him and told him he could. Then he suggested that they sleep together.

''He made the comment that there would not necessarily have to be any sex. He said, 'Don't you want a nice warm cuddly body once in a while?' I told him I did sometimes, but not with him. I told him if he wanted to sleep on the couch, he could, but that was all.''

When Denise told him she didn't want to sleep with him, he insinuated that she was either frigid or afraid—that something must be wrong with her. He told her about several young girls who were anxious to ''party'' with him, and said that all the girls in his neighborhood thought he was ''really neat.''

And then Randy had acted as though his proposition was only

a joke, but he still hinted that if he couldn't get to sleep, he would come upstairs and "bother" Denise.

He did not approach her during the night, and he laughed at her the next morning, saying, "Well, I didn't bother you, did I?"

"He was very calm about it," she told Davis. "He made insinuating remarks, but it was always a joke. He gave handfuls of candy to my kids; he had foil-wrapped chocolate candies in his pockets."

When Denise walked Randy to his car, she saw a teddy bear in the back of the gold Volkswagen and he told her it was a present for a friend. And then Randy had asked about a motel on the I-5: the Knight's Inn in Ashland. Davis was interested in this; this was the motel that was robbed five days later by a man with a silver gun and tape on his nose.

"He sent me a postcard later," Denise recalled. "It said something to the effect that he'd tried to get close to me, and I wouldn't allow it, and I didn't want romance, or something like that, and I knew where he was if I changed my mind."

Back in Eugene, Dave Kominek and Ron Griesel interviewed Randy Woodfield again the day after the search warrant was executed. They found their suspect more closed up than ever. He did not want to talk with them about anything—not even his prowess as an athlete.

18

Shelley Janson had pulled into Eugene on March 6, 1981, her U-Haul trailer full of her belongings, ready to move in with Randall. But now she could not find her fiancé. The phone in the house he shared with Arden Bates rang endlessly, and she could not imagine where either Arden or Randy had got to.

Finally, through friends, she learned that he had been arrested. Determined to find out how such an improbable thing could have happened, she called the Springfield Police Department and was put through to Beaverton Detective Neal Loper.

Shelley Janson met with Loper and Monty Holloway and consented to a taped interview about her relationship with Randall Woodfield. The detectives saw before them an exceptionally beautiful girl, slender, with long dark hair. They looked at each other and shook their heads slightly. Most men would have considered themselves lucky to be engaged to a woman like this. Their investigation suggested that she had not been enough for Randy.

Shelley came across as totally naive. Loper and Holloway were sorry that they had to explain the charges against her lover. Shelley agreed to have the interview taped; she had never been in any kind of trouble with the law, and she was open with the detectives.

The romance that she had found so perfect that it might have come right out of a novel was reduced now to two sides of a tape cassette that would become part of a police file.

Shelley told the truth. She believed that the truth would help Randall. She told the two detectives about the weekend she'd spent with her fiancé in San Francisco on January 31–February 1, only five weeks earlier. She had left him to fly back to New Mexico, and Randall had left to drive back to Eugene. Yes, she'd been terribly worried because she hadn't been able to reach him until Thursday morning, February 5. She'd been terrified that he'd had an accident.

But when she'd finally reached him, he was fine. He'd told her about a speeding ticket, about having to buy a new battery and tires. She thought he'd spent the extra time at his sister's house in Mt. Shasta. He had seemed a little tired on the phone, but he'd been explicit about his need for her, telling her how much he missed her.

"He told me that the trip back had been very expensive for him."

Shelley turned over a packet of Randall's letters to her; she was sure they would show what kind of man Randall was. He'd spent the time since she met him—two months—trying to find a job, trying to get back into college. He couldn't be guilty of what people were hinting. She simply refused to believe it.

Jack Woodfield came to the Springfield jail to see his son. The shock of the ordeal showed on the older man's face; it had seemed to the elder Woodfields that Randall had finally pulled his life together, and now his father was facing a situation that might break any parent's heart. Jack and Randy met in the presence of Dave Kominek. Randy slipped again when he explained his latest trouble with the law to his father. He said that he had been out with "a girl" the night she was killed in Beaverton and that the Beaverton police had questioned him about her death. He told his father that the girl had been to a Valentine's party that night, and he'd seen her after that.

Randy had never before admitted being with Julie Reitz on Valentine's night. None of the detectives had ever told Randy that Julie had, indeed, been to a Valentine's party that night.

He talked earnestly to his father of his innocence, apparently oblivious of the fact that he'd just contradicted statements he'd previously given to Dave Bishop and Neal Loper. At first he'd denied even knowing Julie Reitz. Then he'd admitted dating her at one time, and then he'd admitted having sex with her. Now he had told his father in Kominek's hearing that he'd been with Julie only hours before her murder.

Randy Woodfield continued to maintain his innocence to detectives when they questioned him, but he was getting progressively more tense—this despite his ace in the hole, which was his delusion that the women in his life would do anything for him, even lie if necessary.

One of Randy's Eugene girlfriends had gone to a detective and told him that Randy had confided to her that the police were following him because they thought he had killed a girl in Portland on Valentine's Day weekend. "He asked if he could count on me for an alibi. I told him that I wouldn't lie for him, and I asked him why, if he was innocent, he didn't just cooperate and tell the truth. He said he couldn't really do that because of the way he'd been spending his time. He dropped the conversation when I made it clear I wouldn't lie for him."

Randy had good reason to be nervous. With every day that passed, he seemed to be in a little more trouble. The lay-downs of mug shots that Kominek had sent to every agency involved had drawn several "hits." On March 7 the victims in Bothell, Washington, who had encountered the I-5 bandit on December 21, 1980, identified Randy Woodfield from the lay-down. Chief Rudy Plancich of Bothell obtained an arrest warrant listing Randall Brent Woodfield as the alleged perpetrator of those crimes.

Physical evidence was piling up, witnesses were verifying what lawmen suspected about Randy's travels along the freeway, and now the time was ripe for the lineup. Would any of the victims recognize Randy Woodfield as their assailant? The I-5 Killer's disguise had been very effective in altering his appearance—the beard, the tape over his nose, and the watch caps or hoods over his hair. But many of the victims had commented on the distinctive qualities in his voice, the soft, well-modulated tones that seemed to war with the ugly things he had said and done to them.

Monty Holloway and Dave Bishop worked to set up the lineup. The "cons" in the lineup would all be police officers, and for a very good reason. If it ever became necessary to regroup that lineup, the participants would be easy to find. If they chose other prisoners to stand beside Randy Woodfield, they would undoubtedly scatter to the four winds as soon as they were released from jail.

The officers chosen were from the Springfield Police Department, the Lane County Sheriff's Office, and Multnomah County in Portland. Woodfield, as well as all the other men in the lineup, would wear a short-sleeved pale gray Springfield jail shirt and dark gray trousers. Each man would be barefoot. Each had dark curly or wavy hair and wore a mustache. They all had wide shoulders and athletic builds. They were all between twenty-five and thirty-two. Kominek made the decision not to have the men wear fake beards and Band-Aid disguises; witnesses usually remembered voices, eyes, general bearing, and those disguises might only confuse them.

The investigators did not want to skip any vital legal steps. They contacted Woodfield's attorney and asked him to come to Eugene to okay the men selected for the lineup and to attend the lineup itself.

"They left out the number three," Kominek recalls, "because Woodfield had been number three in the lay-down shown to Beth, and that might have weighted it. They left out one because we didn't want someone to say 'Is this the *one*?' They tried to think of everything they could to make that lineup totally without prejudice."

The lineup was set for Sunday afternoon, March 8, in the Springfield Police Department. It had taken three days after Woodfield's arrest to round up more than two dozen of the victims assaulted by the I-5 Killer.

Before the lineup, the victims were led into a large room, where Ron Griesel made sure that they did not converse with each other. Each victim had a memory of what he or she had seen; the investigators wanted no transfer of information. The victims tried not to stare at each other and tried not to surmise what the others might be doing there. The tension in the room was almost palpable. Confronting a man who might be the one who had filled every one of them with abject terror—even seeing him through a glass wall—would be frightening.

And then the word came that the lineup was ready.

Shasta County Detective Sergeant Gene Farley and Captain Dave Bishop stood at the doors of the viewing room.

The lineup moved across the stage in the six-by-six-foot room at five-forty-eight that afternoon. Randy Woodfield was number five. Monty Holloway asked the six men to face front, turn left, turn right, turn so that their backs showed to those viewing them from behind one-way glass. He asked each man to repeat certain phrases: "Do what I say and you won't get hurt." "Where is the back room?" "Count to one hundred before you move." "Don't call the police." "Lay down on the floor. Look at the floor." "Put the money in the bag." "Does this feel good?" "Aren't I big?"

On the other side of the one-way glass, Dave Kominek stood just behind Beth. He could not see her face. She didn't move. She said nothing at all. It was impossible for him to sense what might be going through her mind. She was so still that he wondered if maybe this whole phase of the probe would be all for naught.

Dave Bishop and Chris Van Dyke were in a position from

which they could see Beth's face when the six men walked out onto the stage. Both Van Dyke and Bishop saw the color drain from Beth's face. Her normal olive skin had turned as pale as chalk, yet her expression was only one of intense concentration as her eyes scanned each man in the lineup. Van Dyke and Bishop looked at each other. Could this be it? They would have to wait until they saw whether Beth circled a number on her card.

When the lineup was completed, victims were taken one at a time into an interview room, where detectives Neal Loper and Ron Womack from the Beaverton Police Department, and Rick Burnett of Shasta County questioned them. All the interviews were taped, and each victim was asked to mark a card with the six numbers on it, and then to sign it.

Womack began the questioning with the victims from the Burger Express in Redding: the owner, her husband, and the teenage employee who had been sodomized and raped in the restroom. The owner picked number five (Randy Woodfield) because of his voice, his eyebrows, his facial structure. Her husband picked number five, but was not as sure. The rape victim could not make a choice; she had been so terrorized by the gun that she had obeyed her rapist's orders not to look at his face.

Jessie Clovis was next to mark her card. The rapist who had jumped into her car on the main street of Yreka had ordered her repeatedly not to look at him, but she'd recognized number five from his voice, his eyes, and his build. She had looked hard at him as he walked away after leaving her naked in Yreka.

"The voice stood out the most," she said quietly. "It just clicked in my head."

Now, the three young women from Corvallis—two from the restaurant, and one from the fabric store. Each of them circled number five. Again and again Rick Burnett, Neal Loper, and Ron Womack heard the same phrases: "His eyes." "I just got a feeling in my stomach when I saw him." "I remember that voice."

One of the youngest victims proved to be a most perceptive witness. Merrisue Green and her sister, Megan, the little girls who had been attacked in their own home in Corvallis, had viewed the lineup. Eight-year-old Megan told the detectives that she could not recognize the man who had attacked her, but ten-year-old Merrisue could. She drew a careful circle around number five.

"Merrisue," Ron Womack asked, "why did you circle number five?"

"Because when, uh . . . okay . . . at my house when he came in, he sounded exactly like him and he looked like him too. 'Cause his hair wasn't the same, but his face looked the same, 'cause I know that he could get his hair cut and his hair changed and stuff."

"Was he the man?"

"He sounds a whole bunch like him."

"What about the rest of them, the other five?"

"They didn't sound much like him. Not at all."

"So you could, by looking at them and listening to them, you could eliminate those guys?"

"Uh-huh." She nodded. " 'Cause some sounded kinda high-pitched and some sounded low-pitched and they weren't it. He was just kind of a medium."

"Besides just his voice, do you feel that he looked a lot like the man that was in your house?"

"Well . . . his hair didn't look the same. It looks the same color, but it didn't look . . . umm . . . well, it looked changed. His hair wasn't that way and he had a mustache before. He had sideburns, but he doesn't now. He sounded like the same. His facial bones and stuff looked the same to what I can remember."

"You're picking number five?"

"Yes. *Yes.* That's him."

Merrisue Green was a very intelligent, very observant child. Her attacker had apparently discounted her ability to perceive what was going on around her. But she had seen him and she had seen him without his false beard, without the tape across his nose. She had even memorized the length of his sideburns.

Next came the employees of the Dairy Queen who had traveled down from Bellevue, Washington, with Detective Gary Trent from that city's police force. The male employee picked the wrong man, but the girl who had been subjected to oral sodomy after the male employee was locked in the freezer recognized Randy Woodfield. Like most of the victims, she found that his eyes were unforgettable. And his voice. "That same tone value, not too many ups and downs. Not a real monotone . . . but not much inflection. It was the feeling I had when he talked."

The victim who had been sodomized in an Albany laundromat had reacted profoundly when she saw Randy Woodfield. She too circled number five. "It sure made my heart race when I saw him. I remember his eyes . . . and his nose. His voice."

Not all of the victims solidified the case against Woodfield. The girl who had been shot in the restaurant in Sutherlin, Oregon, wasn't sure which man in the lineup, if any, might have been the gunman. She finally picked number two—tentatively.

The desk clerk from the Knight's Inn Motel in Ashland, Oregon, didn't hesitate at all: "It's number five."

And so it went. The majority of the victims picked number five, some adamantly, some tentatively.

And now it was Beth Wilmot's turn.

"When it was Beth's turn," Kominek recalls, "we walked out of the viewing area into the interview rooms. I handed Beth the little card and asked her to circle the number that matched the man who had shot her—if he was there—and then sign it. She circled it and gave it to me. I looked down, and there it was: *number five.*"

Van Dyke stood by waiting. This was the most important victim as far as the probe went. This was the living victim whom the killer had left for dead, the one person who had seen him full face just before the act of murder. Would she remember enough?

"Tell us why it is you picked number five, Beth," Kominek said quietly.

"Okay." Beth had begun to tremble, and Kominek could see she was trying hard not to cry. "The reason is that he's tall and the way he was built. I checked his whole body out. His face. Just the way his face was. And I could picture him in a hood, and just everything about him. I chose him. That's why I chose him. His eyes. Everything."

"That's the man?"

"That's him!"

For the detectives, for D.A. Chris Van Dyke, it was akin to winning the Grand Prix. *They knew they had the I-5 Killer.* Beth's absolute identification had convinced them.

They discussed arresting him immediately for murder on probable cause, but they didn't want to risk the slightest chance of a reversal on a legal technicality. Van Dyke left at once to drive to Salem, taking Beth Wilmot with him. She didn't even want to be in the same town with Randy Woodfield.

Van Dyke went directly to his office to do the paperwork, working through most of the night. He obtained a district-court warrant early Monday morning, charging Randall Brent Woodfield with murder, attempted murder, and two counts of sodomy in the attacks against Shari Hull and Beth Wilmot. Van Dyke called Kominek in Eugene.

"We've got it, Dave. The warrant will be ready at ten-thirty A.M. You can arrest him then."

At ten-forty-four A.M., Captain Dave Bishop, Corporal Monty Holloway, and Detective Dave Kominek went to Randy Woodfield's cell and charged him with the four counts, placing him under arrest for charges far more serious than parole violation.

Woodfield looked at the three detectives. "I knew it. I knew last night that you guys were charging me."

It was almost impossible to judge Woodfield's emotions; he wasn't angry, and he didn't seem particularly anxious. He seemed to have known it all along. And then Randy shut up; he had nothing more to say.

Dave Bishop and Dave Kominek drove Randy Woodfield back toward Salem, where he would be placed in the Marion County Jail. They thought if they left right away they could have Randy safely in jail before the press got word of his arrest on murder charges. They didn't spot any reporters or photographers during the hour-and-a-half drive, but as they headed to the jail entrance with their barefoot prisoner in his white coveralls, the dark morning lit up. Photographers popped up everywhere, lined up three deep to get their first glimpse of the man who was rumored to be the I-5 Killer.

"Do you want your leather coat so you can hide your face?" Bishop asked his prisoner.

Randy shook his head. "It's too late. They've all seen me now anyway. Let's keep going."

While they were booking Randy into the Marion County Jail, he turned to the two detectives. "My only regret is that I didn't have a chance to shave or put on clean clothes before I had to face the news cameras."

But Randy was a crowd pleaser right to the end. He'd held his head high and grinned directly into the cameras.

The pictures turned out great, and they were flashed up and down the West Coast via news-service wires in time to make the early editions. The Portland, Seattle, and San Francisco six-o'clock news broadcasts all showed Randy Woodfield ambling into the Marion County Sheriff's Office. Randy was smiling broadly. He might well have been a sports star coming home after a triumphant game. Only he wasn't. He was quite probably the most prolific sexual criminal in Oregon criminal history. He would garner far more headlines over the next months and years in this role than he ever had as a star athlete.

Chris Van Dyke held a press conference, facing the packed room cautiously. He explained that additional charges might be forthcoming, although none were planned at the moment.

"Do you think there's a link between the Salem crimes and the I-5 Killer?" a reporter called out.

Van Dyke was not about to risk a premature tipping of his legal hand. "It really remains to be seen at trial whether or not there is a link between those—the various crimes. There are a number of similarities."

"Can residents along the freeway relax now?"

"Let's say that anyone concerned about Shari Hull's murder and the shooting of Beth Wilmot can rest more easily. Events last night convinced me to go to the grand jury. I can't elaborate. I simply made the decision we had a strong enough case to press charges here."

A month earlier, Monty Holloway had told the press that the I-5 Killer "was probably one of those individuals who, when he's caught, all of his neighbors will say, 'I can't believe it. He's such a nice guy.' "

And Holloway had been right on target. Reporters scattered to gather shocked quotes from people who had known Randy Woodfield. And all of them said essentially, "I can't believe it. He was such a nice guy."

In Eugene, Shelley Janson read the headline stories and stared at the pictures of Randy smiling at the camera as the two grim-faced detectives held his handcuffed arms. The text that followed was so devastating, she could not assimilate it. Randall had been charged with murder. The police thought that her Randall, her gentle, sensitive lover, was the I-5 Killer. She didn't believe it. It had to be some kind of grotesque mistake.

19

Even though Randy was locked in the Marion County Jail in Salem, the probe went on. There were so many crimes, so many victims, and so many ragged ends to be knit up into the fabric of the case.

Shasta County Detective Gene Farley contacted Randy's sister in Mt. Shasta to see if Randy had, indeed, stopped to visit her family on his trip to northern California. Susan, three years older than Randy, said that he had been there—twice. On the way down, he'd stopped on January 30 for lunch. He'd been wearing the blue plaid shirt she'd given him for Christmas, and blue jeans. He'd called to get Shelley's flight number, and then continued south. He'd come back before eleven P.M. on Tuesday, February 3. They'd sat up talking about his relationship with Shelley, although he had told his sister that he and Shelley were not engaged yet. (Shelley, of course, had flown back to New Mexico thrilled because she thought she *was* engaged.) Randy also talked about jobs he might get in Eugene, particularly a job working at a golf course. His sister said she'd been a little concerned about Randy's unemployed state but that he'd seemed confident that there was no problem. He hadn't seemed nervous, and he hadn't seemed tired.

"What time did Randy leave your home after his second visit?" Farley asked.

"Before noon the next day—February 4. He stopped by my husband's office to say good-bye to him."

Farley talked next to Randy's physician brother-in-law. Yes, Randy had left that afternoon to head back to Eugene after stopping at his office to discuss his relationship with Shelley.

Even though Farley had difficulty understanding how Woodfield—if he was the guilty man—could have been so calm in his visits to his sister's home, the times and locations all matched.

There had been the rape and robbery at the Burger Express in Redding early on the evening of February 3. Ten miles north, and an hour later, the double homicides of Janell Jarvis and Donna Eckard occurred. The Shasta County detective crew estimated that the killer had cleared Mountain Gate before nine P.M.

And Randy Woodfield had shown up to visit his sister in Mt. Shasta, sixty miles north of Mountain Gate on the I-5, before eleven! If, as Farley suspected, Randy had committed the ugly murders in Mountain Gate, they had not affected him any more than a rest stop along the freeway.

And then the next day. Randy had left Mt. Shasta in the afternoon after a cozy family visit, and headed north again. That evening, Jessie Clovis had been subjected to hours of sexual abuse in Yreka, thirty-five miles up the freeway.

Randy's relatives thought he'd worn a leather jacket when he visited them. The living victims in Redding and Yreka had described a green windbreaker. And a green windbreaker had been found during the search of the Bates home in Springfield.

Randy's sister and brother-in-law were stunned to learn on March 5 that Randy had been arrested for parole violation when a friend called from Eugene. They were shocked almost speechless when the second set of charges was filed on March 9.

Randy had seemed the same as always when he'd written to them in the first week of March. He'd talked of setting up a chess-by-mail game with a mutual friend, and about his new love. He'd sent a note to thank them for putting him up on February 3. He'd called the next day to say Shelley was driving up, asking if she could stay with his sister and brother-in-law. They had welcomed Shelley, and they'd been pleased to see that Randy had finally found a really nice woman to settle down with.

And now, like almost everyone else who was close to Randy Woodfield, they could barely believe he had been charged with murder.

There was one young woman who was not as thunderstruck by Randy's arrest as his other friends were. That was Dixie Palliter, twenty-two. Even before the lineup had taken place, Neal Loper had headed back to Milwaukie, Oregon, to speak with Dixie Palliter, the young woman everyone said was Randy's one platonic girlfriend. There were rumors that Dixie had accompanied Randy on at least one of his trips up into Washington State, that she had talked about helping Randy buy a gun. The G.I. Joe receipt Loper had found in Randy's wallet indicated just such a purchase. The .32 was missing, the .38 was missing, and so was the little silver gun described by so many of the victims.

Dixie had told Loper she had agreed to purchase a gun for Randy. "But I changed my mind, and I never picked it up."

Loper wanted to talk in depth with Dixie again; he was not convinced she was telling him the whole story. On March 10, armed with a grand-jury subpoena for the records pertaining to the purchase of .32-caliber ammunition from a G.I. Joe's store in Milwaukie, Oregon, by Dixie Palliter on December 19, 1980, Loper found that that purchase had indeed taken place. Dixie continued to deny that she had bought the ammunition. Other records verified that Dixie had also purchased a .22-caliber weapon on October 10 but that she'd returned the gun and gotten her money back on December 10.

On March 10 at six-thirty in the evening, Neal Loper of Beaverton and Jay Boutwell of Marion County contacted Dixie at her home.

Dixie Palliter, who worked as a Portland bus driver, told the detectives that she had met Randy Woodfield when he was a bartender at the Faucet Tavern a year before and that they'd become good friends. "That's about it. We just continued being really good friends."

Dixie was the first woman the investigative team had encountered who had had only a platonic relationship with Woodfield. Randy had been living with Lucy Grant in Lake Oswego and Dixie was going steady with a man when they met. "We got to be such close friends 'cause he was splitting up with Lucy at the time, and I talked with him about my problems with my boyfriend."

"So you had something in common?" Loper asked.

"Yeah. At first it was kind of like dates, except, you know, nothing ever came of it."

"Dixie," Neal Loper said firmly, "I don't think you've been telling us the truth. I think you know more about Randy Woodfield's activities than you're admitting. We've gathered a lot more information since the last time we talked."

Dixie Palliter became visibly nervous; the interview was not going well for her.

Well, there were some things she hadn't told them. Dixie was not very adept at remembering dates; she thought a robbery involving Randy had taken place around Christmas 1980. She admitted that Randy had mentioned robbing a Baskin-Robbins ice-cream parlor in Washington. "He said he went into a Baskin-Robbins and made a girl get on the ground and . . . I can't remember his words. I just know that he said he made her get on the ground and told her to put the money in the bag, and then he told her just to remain on the floor until he was gone."

Dixie thought that the robbery had occurred somewhere off the freeway near Seattle.

"Did he mention anything about disguises or anything?" Boutwell asked.

"Uh . . . he mentioned about a beard."

"Anything else?"

"Uh, hmmm . . . A Band-Aid over his nose."

"Did he say why he did that?"

"Well, I guess, 'cause that's so you can't be identified because the nose is supposed to give you away."

Asked if she had ever seen the beard, Dixie said no. Loper suggested that she was not a very good liar. Dixie's relatives had surmised to the detectives that Dixie might have been along on some of the robberies in Washington. But Dixie continued to insist she had not been with him. She *had* heard him talk about a silver gun, however. "He wanted to take it down to his dad's—that's why he needed the bullets—practice shooting. Another reason was that these guys that smashed up his car were giving him a bad time, and they weren't going to pay for it, so he said he wanted to flash the gun on them if they were going to try to beat him up or something. He said that he would just show them the gun, but he wasn't going to have bullets in it."

"He tell you about the 7-11 too?" Loper asked.

"Well, they showed it on TV, with that guy that was holding up one of the stores, and it showed him [on film from the hidden camera]. I think he had a cap on—that kind of looked like him; I don't know."

Dixie allowed that she was the "type of person you can confide in," but she balked at discussing any of the dozens of other crimes alleged to have been committed by Randy Woodfield.

Loper and Boutwell were convinced Dixie knew more than she was telling. She finally admitted that Randy had gone with her to buy a little silver gun and that Randy had chosen it. But she had returned that gun in December. She thought that perhaps he had used that gun when he'd gone to Washington. Later she admitted that Randy had another gun that she thought he'd obtained "through a private party." But she said she'd never seen it.

"Where did he get the gun?" Loper probed. "What private party? Tell me what happened."

"I don't know who it was. I swear to God I don't."

"Was it a dirty gun? Stolen? Clean? What?"

"Uh, oh . . . I think it was just . . . Maybe a friend; I don't know. See, I wasn't too interested. I didn't really want to hear all this stuff. I wasn't wanting to hear about all, you know, a gun and stuff, and I'm scared to death of guns myself. You guys act like I'm just . . . I am telling the truth. Get that lie detector in here so I can—"

All in good time, Loper promised her.

Dixie explained that she knew the second gun had been silver too, only because Randy had told her that it was. She kept repeating that she thought the gun had come from a "private party," but would say no more. The bullets she'd bought for him were for that gun.

Loper sensed that Dixie was holding back information, and he suspected that she might have actually "ridden shotgun" with Randy on some of his forays. But he doubted that she had been an active participant. Her value to the investigation was the information she had given them—and, hopefully, would continue to give them.

Like most of Randy's women friends, Dixie had been the recipient of gifts. He had bought her a phone, a sweater, given her eighty dollars for Christmas, and he often filled up the gas tank in her car. "He gave me those things just because I was a good friend."

"Where did he get all his money?" Loper asked.

"Well, I thought most of it was from unemployment. He was getting quite a bit from unemployment, and then when he was working at the Faucet and—"

"He tell you about ripping off the Faucet?" Loper cut in.

"Yeah."

"What'd he tell you?"

"He told me that . . . umm . . . that he had done it."

But no matter how much Loper and Boutwell pressed for details, Dixie evaded their questions.

"Let's talk about Valentine's Day weekend," Loper said.

Now they were getting into the Julie Reitz murder case, and the details of Randy Woodfield's movements on that day were vital to the probe. Dixie seemed to relax a little when the questioning concerning the guns stopped. She was willing to talk about that weekend.

"He called me up and came over and we went shopping and out to lunch about eleven in the morning on Valentine's Day. Down in Milwaukie, to the Blade Men's Clothing Store, and we picked out a sweater and a pair of pants for that night 'cause he was holding a party at the Marriott for whoever wanted to come."

Randy had changed into his new clothes at her house and left about six P.M. to go to the Marriott Hotel, but when Dixie had called his room at seven, he wasn't there. He did call her later and asked her when she'd be coming down. But Dixie said she had felt ill and that she never went. Randy kept calling her until about midnight. She didn't hear from him again until nine the next morning.

"He said he was going in the Jacuzzi and that he had to check out by three. Then he was going home."

Dixie and her boyfriend had joined Randy that afternoon for racquetball, and she'd found him just as he always was. He had mentioned to her, however, that he didn't need his gun any longer and that he'd thrown it in a river.

"Has he contacted you recently and asked you to provide him with an alibi?" Loper asked suddenly.

Dixie was silent for a few moments. "Well, he called me the day before they [the police] came to his house. He said he needed my help because they were suspecting him in that Beaverton girl's murder, and I told him, 'No, I can't help you about that.'

"I was really shocked, and I go, 'What? They're suspecting you of a *murder*?' and he said it was no big deal, that he just needed my help. Just as soon as I got off the phone, I told my sister that if he did call, to say I was away with one of my girlfriends somewhere."

"Did he ever tell you that he knew Julie Reitz?"

"No."

"Did you know Julie Reitz?"

"No."

Dixie said she had known about Darci Fix's murder, and about Cherie Ayers' murder too—through information from Randy—but only that they had been killed, nothing more.

Jay Boutwell asked Dixie about Randy's sexual preferences, and she appeared embarrassed. Finally she said that Randy seemed to be fixated on fellatio rather than straight intercourse.

"You've indicated that Randy did like girls," Boutwell said. "Did he ever tell you how many girlfriends he had?"

"He just dated. He had a lot of girlfriends he dated. Different ones."

"If you were to draw an opinion of Randall, how would say his opinion toward women is?" Boutwell probed.

"Well, I'd say he likes women a lot. He's crazy about them. He's just always talking nice about them whenever he's gone out with a girl; he's always said nice things about her."

"Okay. You feel that he feels he's been wronged by women?"

"He could have, yeah. He might have felt rejected a few times by some."

"Okay," Boutwell continued. "So you think that Randall liked girls, but you had a feeling that he thought he'd been wronged by girls . . . he'd felt rejection?"

"Maybe by a couple. Well, he used to tell me that he couldn't understand why girls stood him up. And I used to tell him I couldn't see why either, 'cause he was a good-looking guy. And he goes, 'You even stand me up.' But he said that didn't matter because we were just friends . . . and we kind of laughed about it."

"Did he describe to you what he meant by the words 'stand up'? Did he explain that to you?"

"No. He just said they'd stood him up. He just said he didn't know why. He said he was nice to them. He didn't know why they stood him up."

"He indicate how many times this happened to him?"

"Quite a few. He says girls always stand him up."

"Did you feel he had any hatred toward them?"

"No. He didn't ever seem like he hated them. Every time we ever went out together, he was always asking a lot of girls to dance, and he always seemed happy around them. Always had a lot to talk to them about, was always nice to them."

Neal Loper excused himself from the interview and went to a phone to call D.A. Chris Van Dyke.

"She's not telling us everything. She's holding back."

"Arrest her for hindering prosecution," Van Dyke decided. "I'll file a material-witness complaint against her."

A shocked Dixie Palliter was advised of her rights under Miranda. When she was placed under arrest, she suddenly remembered that she had, indeed, seen Randy Woodfield with a silver .32-caliber gun in his possession.

"But I only saw it once. He had it in the car, right after I brought him the bullets, and he was trying to put the bullets in the gun."

Later, however, Dixie admitted to the detectives that she had seen the gun again. She had seen Randy cleaning the gun sometime before Christmas 1980.

"You still say you never went to Seattle with Randy?"

She shook her head. "He asked me to go with him to see Tim so that he could comfort Tim because Darci got murdered. That was the week before Christmas. He also said that he was going to rob some stores because he needed some Christmas money. He told me about the Baskin-Robbins deal when he got back. He said he wore a Band-Aid over his nose, a stocking cap, and a beard. He said he always went to where girls were working because they were easier. He said he switched jackets sometimes."

Dixie Palliter was proving to be an essential witness. She was still holding back a little. Chris Van Dyke made the decision that Dixie would have to be granted immunity from prosecution for whatever part she might or might not have played in Randy's crimes. Dixie insisted to Van Dyke that that wouldn't be necessary; she was now telling the whole truth.

Dixie told Jay Boutwell and Neal Loper that she had begun to wonder if her good friend Randy might not be the I-5 Killer after she watched television news. She thought it was odd that all the places where the I-5 Killer had struck were places where Randy had been.

"I even mentioned my worries to him once, but he told me not to jump to conclusions. He wouldn't talk about it. He'd told me before that I shouldn't tell anyone about the gun. He told me that I should be quiet about anything he told me."

Dixie Palliter was given a polygraph test, which she agreed to willingly. She said that she wanted to clear her name.

Lieutenant Teuscher of the Oregon State Police administered the test at three P.M. on March 11.

Teuscher found that Dixie was deceptive in her negative responses to the following questions:

"Did Randy Woodfield tell you about killing anyone?"

"Were you with Randy Woodfield when he committed robberies or murders?"

"Did Randy Woodfield tell you where he threw the gun? Or were you with him?"

"Do you know the exact location where the gun was thrown or gotten rid of?"

"Do you know where Randy Woodfield purchased the silver gun?"

"Have you ever been in the state of Washington with Randy Woodfield?"

"How many times have you purchased gun ammunition for Randy Woodfield?" (When Dixie answered "Once," the polygraph's leads registered deception.)

"Did Randy Woodfield ever give you any money which was the proceeds of a robbery or theft?"

"Were you ever with Randy Woodfield when he committed any murders?"

Dixie still was holding back. And she always would. But she had, of necessity, been promised that nothing in the polygraph-test results could be used against her in a court of law.

The silver .32 would never be found. A hundred years from now, it will probably still lie in the muck at the bottom of some river in Washington, Oregon, or California. Still, having the gun itself would not be essential for conviction. The bullets taken from the heads of Beth Wilmot, Shari Hull; Janell Jarvis, and Donna Eckard, and the bullet retrieved after the nonfatal shooting of the girl in Sutherlin, Oregon, had all been fired from the same gun. The lands and grooves left by that gun's barrel were identical on the fatal bullets under a scanning electron microscope. Moreover, the lone .32 bullet found in Randy Woodfield's sports bag had been tested through neutron-activation analysis at Oregon State University and its essential elements were identical to the other bullets, suggesting that it had almost certainly come from the same lot as all the other .32 slugs retrieved. All Remington Peters long.

This brand of .32 ammunition is rarely sold. Even the biggest outlets for aumunition traditionally sell only one or two boxes of Remington Peters .32 bullets a year.

The bullet that had killed Julie Reitz had been a .38, probably fired from a Model 60 Smith and Wesson revolver. Shasta County Detective Craig Wooden contacted firefighter Steve Eckard again to ask what kind of bullets he had used in the weapon which had been stolen the night his family was killed.

Eckard said that he had loaded his own bullets. Wooden obtained some examples of those bullets and hand-carried them to Neal Loper in Beaverton. They were full lead slugs, and one of them was of particular interest. It was jacketed with three-quarters of an inch of copper and had a blunt-nosed lead end.

It was identical to the bullets taken from Julie Reitz's body.

It was only after Randy Woodfield had been arrested that the missing .38 Smith and Wesson stolen from Steve Eckard's home surfaced. And it was found as a missing gun might have been found in a detective novel. A boy playing near the banks of the McKenzie River, which divides Springfield from Eugene, glanced into the clear water and saw the shiny barrel of a revolver. He fished it out and turned it in to the Eugene Police Department.

The gun had a stainless-steel barrel, so it had not rusted; the serial number was easy to read. A Eugene detective, not actively involved in the Woodfield investigation, placed a routine call to California. "We've got a gun here that was probably stolen in a burglary in your state."

He read off the serial number. Within minutes the word came back. "That gun wasn't taken in a routine burglary—it came from a double homicide scene in Mountain Gate!"

Steve Eckard's gun had been thrown in a river only blocks from the house on E Street where Randy Woodfield had rented a room. Because the barrel was in no way corroded, the gun was still operable. The lands and grooves matched. The bullets from Julie Reitz's brain had been fired from that gun.

And yet, as damning as it might seem, the gun could only be used as circumstantial evidence. No one had actually seen the person who had thrown that gun into the McKenzie River.

The case against Randy Woodfield continued to grow . . . and grow . . . and grow. The phantom killer who had moved up and down the Pacific Coast, convinced that no one would ever identify him, had left all manner of clues.

Detective Ron Womack of the Beaverton Police Department had been given the assignment of talking with Nancy, Randy's sister who lived in Portland and with whom he had lived off and on when he was between jobs.

Nancy recalled that Randy had arrived at her home on Friday night, February 13. He had gone out that evening, and returned, she thought, very late. The next morning, he'd complained that he had a hangover. He had left that afternoon to have lunch, he said, with someone named Dixie. His sister had not seem him at all on Saturday night.

Asked if there were any guns in her residence, she produced a .22-caliber handgun which she'd found, still in its holster, where it had always been.

Womack had received a phone call from yet another of Randy Woodfield's roster of female acquaintances. This girl, Dru Casey, who had met Randy a year and a half before, reported that something odd had occurred at her home in Beaverton during the early hours of the morning of Valentine's Day, 1981.

"I was in bed at about a quarter to three in the morning. My boyfriend had just called me from eastern Oregon and asked me to drive over and go skiing. I told him I couldn't, and I went back to bed after I'd set my alarm for seven. Suddenly I saw someone walk by my bedroom window. I got out my can of Mace and went to the window. I saw a tall dark man outside, just a quick glance. I didn't recognize him as Randy Woodfield at the time. The man tried my front door, and I dialed the police department and ran out the back door. Officer Jim Johnson came out and he checked the house, but he didn't find anyone inside. But someone had ripped my phone out of the wall—*inside* the house—and the screen was off my bedroom window. We never did find out who the prowler was.

"Later, I found out that Randy Woodfield had been in Beaverton that weekend—and I wondered . . ."

20

The official indictment of Randall Brent Woodfield on murder and attempted-murder charges came down from the Marion County grand jury on March 16, 1981. Randy would continue to be held without bail. The court appointed a defense attorney for Randy, and he was given the cream of the crop: Charlie Burt. Burt, a former president of the Oregon state bar and the successful defense attorney in some of Oregon's most publicized cases, began at once to prepare a defense. Oregon justice moves swiftly; Randy Woodfield would stand trial within ninety days.

Randy pleaded innocent to all of the charges.

A public hungry for details about the handsome ex-football hero would have slim pickings. A Portland television station showed footage of a shiny silver gun, but it wasn't the gun actually used in Shari Hull's murder. Both Chris Van Dyke and Charlie Burt were angry that the broadcast had implied that the actual gun had been found.

Burt told the press that his primary duty was to see that Randy Woodfield got a fair trial, but he said he could find no cogent reasons for seeking a change of venue from Marion County. There had been so much publicity that there was probably nowhere in Oregon where potential jurors had not heard of his client.

"Where do you change it to—maybe Mars?" Burt asked.

Dixie Palliter remained in jail under $290,000 bond. Dixie's friends talked to the press and explained that she wasn't the "kind of girl who would go out and try to get in trouble, but she's rather naive."

Dixie's mother stressed that her daughter hadn't been that close to Randy. "He's been to the house a few times, but I think they're being a little harsh on her myself. She's never been in trouble. You can't help it if someone you meet commits a murder.''

If knowing a murder suspect was a felony, then there were several hundred young women in Oregon who could be in jail right along with Dixie. Pretty girls all over the state were staring at Randy's face on the news and shaking their heads. He looked familiar to a lot of them—some who'd turned aside his advances, some who'd dated him and found him a little weird, and a few who had actually fallen for him.

On March 19 the hindering prosecution charges against Dixie Palliter were dropped, and Dixie was held only as a material witness.

On March 24 Randy pleaded innocent to two counts of sodomy, two counts of attempted kidnapping, and one count of being an ex-convict in possession of a firearm in Linn County, these additional charges the result of his alleged crimes in Albany, Oregon.

He had also been charged with one count of robbery in the Baskin-Robbins holdup in Bothell, Washington.

Next came charges of sexual assault at the Dairy Queen in Bellevue, Washington, on February 12.

On April 1 Randy pleaded innocent to seven felony charges in Benton County, Oregon (Corvallis). There were two counts of sodomy and one count of burglary stemming from the attack on Merrisue and Megan Green in their home, robbery and sexual-abuse charges from the fabric store in Corvallis, and sodomy and kidnapping charges from the February 25 incident at the fast-food restaurant in the same city.

If murder charges were to be filed in Beaverton in the murder of Julie Reitz, and in Shasta County, California, in the double homicides of Janell Jarvis and Donna Eckard, the authorities in those jurisdictions were keeping mum about it. Murder trials tend to come about in order of time sequence. The Salem murder had occurred in January, 1981, and the California murders had been committed on February 3, with the Beaverton murder on February 14.

Marion County would have the first chance to confront Randy Woodfield with its case. However, it looked as though Randy Woodfield would spend the coming months in court *someplace,* no matter what the verdict was in the murder trial that lay ahead in Salem.

The Shari Hull–Beth Wilmot trial date would be set on May 5 in Marion County Circuit Court. Before those proceedings, Randy was brought down to Judge Wallace P. Carson's court in the green coveralls issued to all prisoners in the jail.

When he entered the second-floor anteroom, he saw that there were spectators in the courtroom and he asked to be returned to the jail. The request was granted, and he appeared a few minutes later wearing gray slacks, a sports shirt, and a white V-neck sweater.

Randy Woodfield would continue to be concerned about his appearance when the media were present.

The public had to make do with newspaper articles about Randy's apparel and about Charlie Burt's demands that certain evidence be declared "fruit of the poison tree"—that is, illegally seized—and that victim identification of his client in the lineup be excluded from the trial.

It was all part of the tactics that any good defense lawyer employs. No one could ever say that Randy Woodfield did not have adequate legal representation; Charlie Burt was one of the best.

And no one except the lawmen and the Marion County district attorney himself really knew what Chris Van Dyke's game plan would be until the actual trial began.

If Randy Woodfield's life was in limbo, so was Beth Wilmot's. It was arranged that Beth would work in the courthouse cafeteria; she would be the prime prosecution witness, and she had to remain in Salem. She also needed a way to make a living. And so, while the man alleged to have shot her stayed secluded in jail on the fourth floor of the Marion County Courthouse, Beth worked in the basement lunchroom, just down the hall from the detectives' offices where Dave Kominek worked. She was still frightened, and Kominek talked with her often, promising that everything would be all right.

The pretrial hearing began on May 28. Charlie Burt alleged that Randy had been illegally arrested and that the March 8 lineup had been improper. He insisted that the parole-violation charge had been a "sheer hoax," and he castigated Randy's earlier attorneys for advising the defendant to appear in the lineup.

"I would suggest that six months for contempt is better than life for murder."

Dave Kominek testified that Woodfield's identification by victims of the I-5 Killer was only one of *five* elements of direct evidence linking him to the shootings at the TransAmerica Building. He cited the pubic-hair match, the telephone records, the identification of Randy Woodfield by Marion County Deputy Bernie Papenfus as the man he'd seen near the shooting scene, and the bullet found in Randy's Springfield residence as the other four elements.

Kominek argued that the search of the Bates home had been legal and that Randy had been fully advised of his rights to remain silent under Miranda.

Only one victim witness was called to testify at this pretrial hearing: Beth Wilmot.

Beth described the events of January 18, and then Chris Van Dyke asked her: "Is that man in the courtroom?"

Beth rose from the witness chair and walked stiffly toward the table where Randy Woodfield sat. She stood directly in front of him, her hands clenched into fists.

Screaming, she cried, "I hate you! I hate you! I hate you!"

And then Beth walked back to the witness chair, sobbing.

Judge Clarke C. Brown asked the press to use discretion in reporting the scene they had just observed, but Beth's outburst was reported faithfully in evening editions and on the television news. There was too much drama for newsmen to resist.

The actual trial promised even more headline stories.

The trial loomed ahead, and both Beth and Randy had reason to dread it. He would be facing a life term, and Beth would have to repeat once again the terrible details of the attack she and Shari Hull had endured.

21

Randy Woodfield's trial on charges of murder, attempted murder, and sodomy began in earnest on June 9, 1981, in Marion County Circuit Court Judge Clarke C. Brown's courtroom in Salem. The corridors outside the windowless courtroom were clogged with would-be spectators, reporters, artists (because cameras are not allowed in Oregon courts), and law-enforcement personnel. No one—*no one*—would be allowed to enter the courtroom until his briefcase or purse was searched by Marion County deputies. Body "pat-downs" were accomplished by male and female deputies. Three armed deputies stood by inside the courtroom itself. Feelings about the brutal shootings in the TransAmerica Building were running too high to risk a replay of what had happened in Dallas when Lee Harvey Oswald was shot and killed by Jack Ruby.

Outside the Marion County Courthouse, magnolia trees, rhododendrons, and azaleas were in full bloom, but they were buffeted by torrential rains, the frigid wind belying the fact that it was June. Inside the wood-paneled room, the air was close and cloying. There was no sense of season at all. There was no coolness. But no one moved, and all the spectators seemed willing to endure the discomfort so that they might hear the details of this case that had not yet been revealed to the public. The courtroom was designed to hold only sixty spectators. Each of the four benches in the gallery was packed. The first two rows were reserved for the press, reporters, and artists who sat barely three feet away from the man everyone had come to see: Randall Brent Woodfield. Each time a reporter had to leave the courtroom to call in a story on deadline, he asked others to take notes for him. So much was happening so fast that none of the press dared risk missing something. The artists, considerably hampered by the cramped space, sketched continually nonetheless.

Images of the man everyone wanted to see took form again and again on their huge sketchpads.

But this Randy didn't look the way anyone expected.

Randy Woodfield had been touted in the media as a massively muscled professional athlete. The man in person seemed strangely diminished, not a superman after all. He scarcely resembled the cocky, grinning prisoner who had been photographed as he was led into jail in March. Three months behind bars can change a man.

Randy wore a gray-and-tan plaid shirt and gray slacks; the slacks were too big for him now, and his tightly cinched belt gathered up loose folds of cloth. His two-tone saddle shoes looked collegiate, but then, Randy seemed always to have clung to the glories of his college days. The schoolboy effect was marred by the manacles on his ankles.

Occasionally Randy's dark eyes glanced toward the gallery. His hair was still permed into tight curls, and his jaw showed the blue-black of a beard that must be shaved at least twice a day. His skin was muddy, pimpled, marked with old acne scars and the gray of jail pallor; he had not seen the sun for a long time. He sat slouched in his chair, shoulders bent, and he no longer looked either powerful or dangerous. He looked, if anything, humbled—a predatory creature brought down and caged in mid-rampage.

Those in the gallery seemed a little disappointed. They had expected someone different. They had expected to find the legendary "I-5 Killer" to be larger than life, and he was not. The defendant didn't look husky enough to play high-school football, much less for the Green Bay Packers. Indeed, he didn't look dangerous at all now.

Was he a killer? That was another question altogether.

The underlying tension and tragedy in a murder trial are always subtly hidden by proper courtroom procedure. The prosecution and the defense always begin with cordiality and politeness. As does the judge. The fireworks come later—if at all.

Charlie Burt and Chris Van Dyke could not have been more opposite in personality and appearance—Charlie, the old pro, a defense attorney who seldom lost, going into yet another murder trial in his long career, and Van Dyke, tall, exuberant, a Young Turk facing the first murder trial of his career.

Burt dressed in conservative three-piece suits, while Van Dyke occasionally would wear a sports jacket and slacks.

The young D.A. grinned often, and, as always, reminded the

gallery of his father with the physical similarity and the way he moved. But this was not a half-hour television comedy; this trial was deadly serious, and no one realized it more than Chris Van Dyke. The last seven months of his life had been totally taken up with this case. Like the detectives, he had had no real personal life, he had missed sleep, and he had agonized over the problems—first in catching the suspect and then in prosecuting him. No matter how many murder cases he might prosecute in the future, Van Dyke would never, never forget this, his first.

Judge Brown also had tremendous burdens on his mind; his wife was in the hospital, facing the possibility of quadruple-bypass heart surgery. But he kept those worries to himself.

The proceedings began in a most civilized manner. Judge Brown smiled at the defendant. "Good morning, Mr. Woodfield."

" 'Morning."

Randy Woodfield's voice was a surprise too; he sounded like a boy. The soft voice his alleged victims had described did not match the macho jock image.

" 'Morning, gentlemen," Judge Brown said to the opposing attorneys.

And now the jury selection began. There were fifty-five potential jurors in the first jury pool. The selection would move ahead tediously. Three of the would-be jurors were excused because they said they had already reached a conclusion as to the defendant's guilt or innocence. Several of them knew witnesses or relatives of the victims. And then there were the usual excuses: upcoming military duty, vacations, and one man who told Brown that he would be of "dubious durability" as a juror because he was "nursing a kidney stone."

Of major concern to both sides were the potential jurors' attitudes toward hypnotism, the credibility of physical evidence, and the reliability of witness identification.

A repeated question from Chris Van Dyke dealt with the ability of an individual to recreate in his mind something he has once experienced. The D.A. wanted jurors with eidetic imagery—who could literally "see" a memory on the "TV screen" of their minds.

Van Dyke questioned a former mayor of Salem, also a well-known sports referee: "Have you ever had anything happen to you that was so frightening or so wonderful that you can close your eyes and picture it again in your mind?"

The answer was, "No, I can't say that I can."

It was a fascinating question. Those in the gallery who did

"see" with their minds (almost all the reporters could) were surprised at the number of prospective jurors who could not. And it was essential to the prosecution that jurors could understand how Beth Wilmot had remembered the man who had shot her.

Chris Van Dyke asked one juror: "Would you remember a person who confronted you with a gun three and a half feet away in a well-lighted room and later killed your best friend?"

"Yes . . . I think I would."

Charlie Burt was going at it from the opposite direction.

"Do you think a person can think he recognizes someone and still be mistaken? There's going to be evidence that what she believes is not true."

Again and again, Burt asked various would-be jurors if they had ever approached someone they thought they knew, only to find out they were mistaken.

And so the jury pool moved through the witness chair, people of all ages from all walks of life—a pipe fitter, a meat cutter for Safeway, a retired gentleman. And finally a jury was selected. They were all Caucasian, four men, eight women, with one male and one female alternate.

The final list included: an Oregon Department of Justice payroll clerk, a teller at a Salem bank, a mathematician and freelance writer, two housewives, an employee of Crown Zellerbach, a data processor for the state of Oregon, an employee of the Oregon Department of Revenue, a sheet-metal worker, a mechanical draftsman, an insurance-company clerk, and a secretary for the Oregon State Department of Revenue. They ranged in age from twenty-seven to fifty-six.

The alternates were a forty-two-year-old female Greyhound bus driver and a seventy-year-old man retired from the hotel-casino business in Nevada.

A true cross-section of the Oregon population, they would decide Randy Woodfield's future.

The trial began on Thursday, June 11, 1981. Chris Van Dyke rose to make the opening statement for the prosecution.

"Despite his best efforts to disguise himself, a trail of evidence was left by Randall Woodfield. He left a 'road map' of evidence. The first thing he left behind was a living victim—who confronted that man eyeball to eyeball."

Van Dyke listed the evidence, circumstantial and absolute physical evidence, that the state would present to the jury:

The victim identification of the defendant in the lineup.

The bullets. Bullets removed from Beth Wilmot and Shari Hull were .32-caliber Remington Peters. A rare bullet—a .32-caliber Remington Peters .32 Colt long bullet—had been found in Randy Woodfield's gym bag. That bullet, when tested at the Oregon State University Neutron Activation Center, had proved to come from the same batch of lead as the bullets taken from the victims' heads.

The pubic hair found on the rug of the TransAmerica Building. That hair had been found "microscopically indistinguishable" from the pubic hair of Randy Woodfield.

Blood tests done on the swab of semen found in Beth Wilmot's mouth. The tests had shown that her assailant was either an A or a B secretor. Woodfield was a B secretor.

Herpes. Within two weeks after the shooting incident, Beth Wilmot had been diagnosed as having herpes. Randy Woodfield had herpes.

Telephone records. Telephone records from the home where Randy lived placed him at the scene of the TransAmerica shooting. Van Dyke gave the jury a precise timetable. Woodfield called a Salem number from a phone booth in Independence at 9:01 P.M. on January 18. The suspect entered the crime-scene building between 9:35 and 9:45 P.M. At 10:04 P.M. the defendant had been seen by Bernie Papenfus a mile from the double shooting. At 10:30 P.M. two phone calls were made from a booth in Woodburn, north of the shooting scene. "The driving times from all these sites correspond with the crime time," Van Dyke told the jury.

"The state has forty witnesses," Van Dyke said. "A trail of evidence was left which will point conclusively to Mr. Woodfield."

Defense Attorney Burt rose to give *his* opening statement.

Burt said that Beth Wilmot had "simply picked the wrong person." He disputed the use of the hypnosis session performed by Dave Kominek, suggesting that Beth had been confused by the session and that had caused her to select the wrong man.

Burt also told the jury that the scientific evidence had not been tested properly. He maintained that the bullets did *not* match, nor did the pubic hair, nor did the seminal fluid. "He couldn't possibly leave an A enzyme. He doesn't produce it."

And Charlie Burt had another ace up his sleeve.

There had been a particularly sensational shooting spree in Keizer, Oregon, on May 7, 1981, and Burt hoped to cast suspicion on that gunman, suggesting that that man, Lawrence Moore, might also be responsible for the attack on Beth and Shari.

On the Thursday night of the seventh, Moore, twenty, had

burst into the Oregon Museum Tavern and opened fire. Within seconds, four people were dead and nineteen wounded. Moore had pleaded innocent by reason of mental defect and was awaiting trial.

Van Dyke termed Burt's allusion to the Oregon Museum Tavern shooting case as a "red herring," saying that there was no evidence at all that might link Moore to the TransAmerica shootings.

When the trial was a week old, Judge Brown made his final decision on allowing the jury to view Moore. The decision was that they would not. "Mr. Moore will not be called as a witness in this case," Judge Brown said, "because I feel it is immaterial and irrelevant from the testimony I have received."

22

A trial is, in essence, the recreation of the crime the defendant is accused of, and of the investigation that followed. Beth Wilmot would have to live through it again, just as all the detectives who had sought the man who shot her would relive their months-long probe.

What it came down to was which witnesses the jury would believe. Charlie Burt had suggested that Beth's testimony would be a bid for sympathy, testimony from a young woman whose description of her attacker had changed from one version to the next. And, in a sense, that was true. Her description of the gunman *had* changed slightly in the five statements she'd been asked to give to various authorities. This variance would be one of the defense's strongest points. She had said during some stages after the attack that the man had dark brown hair, and during others, that he had had brown hair or light brown hair. But the *first* description, the description given to Liz Cameron, the Salem police dispatcher, the one that was freshest in her mind immediately after she was shot, was: "White male, about twenty-seven, five feet, nine inches to six feet tall, dark brown hair. Band-Aid on nose, jeans, leather jacket."

Chris Van Dyke pointed out to the jury that that inventory of characteristics closely matched the defendant.

Deputy Bernie Papenfus, who was not laboring under the disadvantage of a bullet in his head, had seen the running man just after the call for help came in. And Papenfus identified Randy Woodfield as the man he'd seen. Charlie Burt countered with the argument that no man could run that far that fast. But could an athlete in perfect condition have run 1.2 miles in six minutes?

Papenfus disagreed with Burt's time estimate. It was his understanding, he said, that Beth had waited at least five minutes in the TransAmerica Building before she called for help. "And I think track people can come close to that [time]."

Detective Jay Boutwell, who had ridden to the hospital with Beth, said that, by that time, she had trouble focusing her attention. He had suggested that Beth describe the gunman by comparing him with the people around her, and she'd had only himself and the two paramedics to compare her assailant with.

A nurse at the hospital testified, "She said it [the man's hair] was darker than Stuart's but lighter than Joyce's." (The paramedics.)

Dr. Robert Buza, the neurosurgeon who had taken the bullet from Beth's head, testified that the pain medication she was receiving when she described her attacker as having light brown hair "is known to cause temporary amnesia."

For spectators, the legal jousting was absorbing. Burt was good, very, very good. He was folksy and low-keyed and he explained to the jury that the defense had to play "catch up" after the prosecution had a head start. He would produce his own experts who were just as authoritative as the prosecution's experts were.

For the defense, Dr. Kay Carlisle, an expert on hair identification who worked at the Primate Center in Portland, would assert that the pubic hair could not be absolutely traced to Randy Woodfield—or to any human source positively. And that is true; hair and blood have not yet been isolated scientifically so that they can be conclusively traced to one source and one source alone. Forensic-science experts predict that, one day, both hair and blood *will* be traced to one individual, but that time is not yet here.

However, Steve Van Ootegham, a hair-and-fiber specialist from the Oregon State Police Crime Lab, would testify that the pubic hair found at the shooting scene and a pubic hair taken from Randy Woodfield's body were microscopically indistinguishable. "There would be only one chance in eight hundred that pubic hairs that look the same under a microscope could come from different bodies."

Dr. Stanley Abrams of Portland and Dr. Maurice MacDowell of Salem, hypnosis experts who had checked the tape made by Dave Kominek during Beth's hypnosis session, would testify for the defense that Kominek had "inadvertently destroyed her memory ability when he had told her that she would be able to see the gunman's face."

Dave Kominek took the stand to validate his expertise at

hypnosis. He explained that he had had eighty-eight hours of professional training in hypnosis and had used the art in about twenty police investigations. Burt objected on the grounds that Kominek was not qualified to testify as an expert; he was overruled by Judge Brown.

"Did you make any posthypnotic suggestions to Beth Wilmot?" Burt asked, suggesting that the hypnosis had caused Beth to identify Woodfield in the lineup on March 8.

"No, sir."

"Isn't it true that sometimes suggestions under hypnosis are purely accidental?"

"Yes, sir. But no names were mentioned during hypnosis, because we had no suspect at that time."

Dr. George Bischel, a Salem psychiatrist, testified that there was nothing improper about Kominek's hypnotic technique. Bischel, who has conducted at least a thousand hypnotic sessions, said that he had reviewed the tapes and transcripts of the Marion County detective's session with Beth and found that Kominek's approach was generally accepted as valid.

While this preliminary testimony went on for a week, all the policemen, experts, and forensic scientists laying out the structure of the case day by day, Beth Wilmot waited downstairs in the courthouse cafeteria. She was nervous, but she was anxious to testify. She had confronted Randy Woodfield three times now—once during the crime, once during the lineup in Springfield, and once during the pretrial hearings. Her fear of him had been defused, if only slightly. She would be in the same courtroom with him, but his legs would be manacled; he could no longer harm her.

Still, how many of us would choose to relive a nightmare, to confront the one thing that terrifies us the most?

All week, the spectators told each other that Beth Wilmot would be testifying at any moment; there was disappointment when she did not appear. The gallery was not nearly as interested in the forensic details as they were in actually seeing the young woman who had survived the shootings in January.

Many of them had *already* seen Beth without realizing it, not knowing that the pretty dark-haired girl sipping Cokes in the cafeteria was the prize witness they all waited for. This author talked with Beth in the court house cafeteria. Her hands trembled slightly, but her smile was open.

"I want to get it over with. I'm afraid, but, in a way, I'm

anxious to tell the jury what happened. I can't even be in the courtroom until after I testify, and it's so hard waiting. . . ."

On Thursday, June 18, the rumors were true; Beth Wilmot would be taking the witness stand.

Chris Van Dyke would make the questioning as easy on Beth as he could; Beth had met with him many times, and she liked and trusted him.

When Beth walked into the courtroom, there were slight gasps. She looked far younger than twenty-one. They saw a tall, very thin girl whose huge dark eyes seemed to dominate her oval face. She looked a little frightened, but the expression in her eyes was one of pure hatred. She stared down at Randy Woodfield, who seemed, at last, ill-at-ease as he slouched at the defense table.

If it were possible, the courtroom was jammed with more people than there had been before. There were nine reporters and four artists, their fingers flying over notebooks and sketchpads.

Van Dyke, whose every movement spoke of subdued energy, unfolded his long legs from the prosecutor's chair and walked toward Beth.

The district attorney began with the easy questions, asking her about her age, her occupation, and her close friendship with Shari Hull. Randy's eyes darted constantly from Beth to Van Dyke as he followed this testimony closely.

Beth trembled almost imperceptibly, but her voice grew in strength. She told about the janitor's job that she and Shari had shared. "We got to the TransAmerica Title Company office on River Road about nine-ten or nine-fifteen that Sunday night. We were done with our work in about twenty minutes. Shari started the truck. We were ready to go, but we noticed a window was dirty. I went to get the spray bottle. . . . When I came around the corner, he was standing there with Shari."

Beth described the man who stood there holding a gun. He'd worn jeans, tennis shoes, and a dark jacket with a hood covering his head. "He had a Band-Aid across the bridge of his nose."

"Is he in the courtroom?" Van Dyke asked.

"He is. . . . Right there," Beth answered. She pointed to Randy Woodfield.

"Are you sure?"

"No doubt. That's the one."

Randy's expression didn't change at all. But then, it seldom did; he spent most of his time scribbling notes on the yellow legal pad in front of him.

"How far away from you was the man when you first saw him?"

"About three feet."

"Were the lights on?"

"Yes. It was very bright. The gun barrel was aimed right at me when the man ordered us to get in the back room. He ordered us to take our clothes off and lie on the floor there."

Asked to explain what happened next, Beth bowed her head and started to cry. It had been difficult enough for her to give a full statement to Dave Kominek; now she would have to tell a packed courtroom the intimate details of the attack she and Shari had endured. But it had to be done. Beth told the jury that she and Shari had been forced to perform oral sex on the intruder and that he had commanded her to fondle Shari. He had also attempted intercourse with her.

Van Dyke led Beth gently through a recreation of the scene in which her best friend died.

"Shari was crying, begging him not to hurt her."

"Where were you at this point?"

"I had my face against the counter, and then I heard a shot. He shot her in the head. He shot me. He shot her again. He shot me, and she moaned and he shot her again."

Tears had welled up again in Beth's eyes, and she fought to retain her composure.

"I pretended I was dead. I was afraid that he would shoot me a third time. He shot Shari the third time because she moaned. I couldn't hear anything except for the ringing in my ears. I waited about five minutes before I got up, and then I went into the bathroom and looked in the mirror, and the whole right side of my face was swollen."

Beth explained that she had been rescued by the sheriff's officers and the paramedics and that she had spent the next several days in the hospital.

"Did you have any aftereffects of the attack beyond your head wounds?" Van Dyke asked.

Beth looked down. "Yes. About ten days later, I learned from a doctor that I had contracted herpes and that that is a disease usually transmitted by sexual contact."

Charlie Burt's job in cross-examination was difficult. A kind man, but a keen-minded attorney, he now had to play the "bad guy" in questioning a trembling, crying girl.

He asked her a little about herpes. It was clear that Burt hoped to suggest that Beth might have had herpes for some time—that she had suffered, not a first episode, but a *recurrence* of the disease after the attack.

She was adamant that she had never had it before the night of January 18. She described what she now faced for the rest of her life.

"It can go away, but you never get rid of it," Beth explained. "It's in your blood system. I can get something at the drugstore, but there is no cure."

"Did you have sexual intercourse in the month preceding the incident?" Burt asked.

"No."

"Have you ever had intercourse?"

Van Dyke objected, and Judge Brown sustained the objection. The sexual history of rape victims is often an issue in trials; women who have already endured a major psychic shock are put in a position of having to defend *their* morals. But Judge Brown was not going to allow this to happen to Beth Wilmot.

Burt's main thrust was not Beth's sexual history, however. He wanted to shake her on her memory of the man who had shot her. He questioned her repeatedly on the color of her assailant's hair.

"You said that your assailant had a hood over his head. Your best recollection is that you don't know what color his hair is, do you?"

"No . . . but his eyebrows were dark. I don't think he'd have blond hair."

"How many photographs of men did you look after the shooting?" Burt asked.

"About a hundred, but I didn't recognize any of them."

"When did you first see a picture of the defendant?"

"In March when Detective Holloway came to Spokane and showed me pictures of five men."

"Did you identify Mr. Woodfield at that time?"

"I made a tentative identification of one of the men, but I wasn't sure. I told him I didn't want to pick anyone out I wasn't sure of."

Van Dyke asked Beth what had caused her to pick Randy Woodfield from the lineup.

"His whole body—his forehead, his nose, his shoulders—just everything about him."

After two hours on the witness stand, Beth was excused. She had balked at giving her address at the time of the shooting, because she still visited there. and she was afraid. Local papers agreed not to print that address, and they kept the promise.

On the ninth day of the trial, Dixie Palliter—Randy's old friend from Beaverton—testified. Considerably chastened now, and no longer so anxious to protect Randy, Dixie told the jury that Randy had had a gun and that he'd told her he'd thrown it in a river after the shootings on River Road.

Evidence was introduced that he had acquired a box of the rarely sold .32-caliber long Colt bullets about a month before Shari and Beth were shot. "I bought a box of bullets for him on December 19 from the G.I. Joe store in Milwaukie. He checked to see if they would fit a silver gun he had with him. I saw him cleaning the same gun about the first week of January."

"Did Randy ever talk to you about disguises?" Van Dyke asked.

"He said something about a Band-Aid over his nose."

Van Dyke called gun-shop employees to demonstrate to the jury just how rare the .32 long Colt bullets were.

The manager of G.I. Joe's said that of the 3,039 boxes of ammunition sold in her store in 1980, only _four_ boxes were Remington Peters .32 long Colts.

The manager of a sporting-goods store in Salem said that his store had sold seven hundred and fifty boxes of pistol ammunition over a nine-month period.

"How many of those were .32 long Colts?" Van Dyke asked.

"Two. We have six boxes of that type of bullet on our shelves, and some of them have been there for twenty years."

It was to be a full day. Penny Hale, eighteen, who'd met Randy at TGI Friday in Beaverton on January 10, a week before the Salem shootings, described the hooded dark leather jacket he'd worn that night—very similar to the coat Beth had described.

Penny told the jury that Randy had followed her home, stayed until four A.M., and that she had avoided all his calls since. The calls that had trapped Randy by placing him in the vicinity of the TransAmerica shootings had been made to Penny's apartment.

"There were four or five calls on January 18," Penny testified. "The last call came at nine."

"Are you sure that call didn't come in around eight?" Burt asked.

"No, it was at nine," she answered firmly.

Dave Kominek took the witness stand again. He explained that the vital telephone calls had come from phone booths—at Independence at one minute after nine P.M., and then from Woodburn at ten-thirty-one P.M.

"Did you drive between those booths to estimate the time required?" Van Dyke asked Kominek.

"Yes, sir. I drove several routes from Independence to Salem, and from Salem to Woodburn."

"And what did you find, as regards to time?"

"Trips from Independence to Salem took between twenty-one and twenty-eight minutes."

The shootings, of course, had taken place just outside Salem between nine-thirty-five and nine-fifty P.M. Randy's driving time was, at the most, forty-five minutes from one phone booth to the other; that left almost an hour unaccounted for—more than enough time for him to have shot Shari and Beth. . . .

Captain Dave Bishop, who, along with Neal Loper, was the first of the hundreds of officers in the long probe to home in on Randy Woodfield, testified on this tenth day of trial: "I could see Beth Wilmot's face when she viewed the lineup. It appeared that she had seen a ghost. She was extremely frightened."

Bishop also told the jury that he had heard Randy admit that he had herpes.

The ends of the case had been so tangled, but now, in the courtroom, they were coming together in a pattern that made ultimate sense.

Almost every day of the trial now, there were enough histrionics to titillate the gallery.

Arden Bates, apparently consumed with guilt that she had helped the police trap her former housemate, testified that Randy was "one of the nicest people you'd ever want to meet" and described the weeks that he had lived in her home in Springfield. No longer did she see him as a womanizing macho man; she might have been describing the perfect boy next door. As she left the courtroom, she suddenly threw her arms around Randy and started to cry. She had to be pulled away from him by a courtroom deputy.

For Randy Woodfield, the trial must seem like a black-humor *This Is Your Life,* with D.A. Chris Van Dyke as the M.C. Many of Randy's old girlfriends testified, and now he watched as a former convict-buddy took the stand. When Van Dyke asked Tony Niri, twenty-nine, how long he had known Randy, Niri answered that he had known him "socially" since September 1975.

"Socially" in this case meant that they'd done time together in the Oregon State Penitentiary.

Niri said that he had seen Randy on occasion wearing a

hooded jacket, gloves . . . and a Band-Aid across his nose. He also said that he'd seen Randy carrying a dull chrome pistol around in late 1980, a "small revolver."

Charlie Burt, of course, took advantage of the fact that Niri was an ex-con, and ex-cons are notoriously suspect witnesses. When he asked the witness a question about guns, Niri said he really didn't know much about guns.

"You'd have to know something about guns to be an armed robber, wouldn't you?" Burt asked sarcastically.

"Not really," was Niri's mild reply.

The defense began its case on June 23. Charlie Burt worked hard to convince the jury that Randy Woodfield sat in the defendant's chair solely because he had been mistakenly identified. He went over the discrepancies in hair color again. He told the jury that Beth Wilmot's description, overheard by paramedics, fit Lawrence Moore, the suspect in the Oregon Museum Tavern slayings, far more closely than it did Randy Woodfield.

Indeed, the paramedics had actually *seen* a person on Church Street N.E., after they'd left the emergency room, who resembled the man Beth Wilmot had described. The man had looked more like a picture of Lawrence Moore, according to the medics.

The usual "war of the psychologists" took place. Dr. Maurice McDowell told the jury that he didn't believe anything "pertinent" had resulted from Kominek's hypnosis of Beth.

And then Burt called Kay Carlisle, the scientist from the Oregon Regional Primate Research Center in Portland.

"I don't believe hair should ever be used to identify a person," Carlisle said. "The only exception would be a case involving congenital abnormalities where rare types of hair were produced."

Carlisle said she had examined the same hairs that Ootegham had and that she couldn't even say for sure that they were pubic hairs, much less identify the person they'd come from.

It was really a matter of *which* experts the jury would believe.

Shelley Janson was standing behind her fiancé. She still did not believe that Randy had anything to do with the shootings on January 18, 1981, or, indeed, with any of the other crimes he had been accused of. Although it must have been exquisitely embarrassing for her, Shelley took the stand and told the jury that she had known Randy since December 30, 1980, and was prepared to answer questions about their most intimate relations.

In answer to Burt's questions, Shelley said that she had been intimate with Randy several times.

"And did you contract herpes?"

"No, sir. I did not."

"Have you ever seen Randall with a hat on?"

"He never wore either a hat or a hood. It would look funny on his hair."

This statement seemed to be straining at gnats. If Randy Woodfield had used hats and hoods as a disguise, he probably had done so to *change* his normal appearance, and "looking funny" would not have mattered.

In reality, Shelley had seen her lover such a pitifully few times—a few days at the end of December and a weekend in San Francisco. After that, she had only seen him behind bars. It would seem impossible for Shelley to know what his usual habits were, or what he usually wore on his head.

For Shelley, who had seen her dreams of the future vanish like smoke, the only small comfort was that she had not contracted her fiancé's herpes.

The trial had been going on for more than two weeks now, and tempers were eroding. At times, Chris Van Dyke and Charlie Burt appeared to be about to leap at each other's throats, arguing, and, according to Judge Brown, playing up to the press.

"Both of you are attempting to try this case in the newspapers," Brown snapped. "I'm telling you, we're going to quit talking to the press!"

The jury didn't hear that exchange, nor had the jury seen any media coverage of the case. But the public was lapping it up.

Randy Woodfield had scrupulously avoided looking back at the gallery during the entire trial. But on June 25 he had to face them head-on. Randy was going to testify.

It was risky. Most defense attorneys urge their clients not to take the stand; it gives the prosecution too many opportunities to ask embarrassing questions on cross-examination. But Randy wanted to testify in his own behalf. He wanted to explain just where he was on the night of January 18, 1981.

Randy seemed almost nonchalant as he took the stand, as if he had no part in these proceedings. He did not, however, look at the jury while he testified, a definite error for the defense in body language.

Burt quickly asked Randy about his previous convictions for robbery and indecent exposure. If Burt brought out his client's criminal record first, it would take the option away from Van Dyke, and it would show that the defense was not trying to hide anything from the jury.

Randy told the jury that he had been driving between Springfield and Portland on the night that Beth and Shari were attacked. That trip would have taken about two and a half hours, if one went by way of Independence. And, of course, that would have accounted for Randy's time during the vital period between nine-thirty and ten P.M.

Randy said he'd stopped at a bar in Independence and had several beers that night. However, on cross-examination, Randy told Chris Van Dyke that he couldn't remember where the bar was, or what its interior looked like. "It was just one of your average bars."

Randy admitted that he had stopped in North Salem on the way from Independence to Woodburn. He had bought beer at a convenience store, made a phone call, and looked at some new cars in a car lot.

No, he didn't own a coat with a hood. No, he had never worn Band-Aids on his nose.

Yes, he had bought a silver-plated pistol from an acquaintance in the fall of 1980, and he admitted that a friend had bought him a box of shells, but he'd told his friend later that he'd thrown the gun away.

"I wasn't supposed to have it," he said, adding that he was already having problems with his parole officer because he changed addresses so often. "I didn't want to go back to prison."

Randy testified that he had at one time feared that he had herpes and that he'd told a friend about it. "But none of my girlfriends ever complained that they had caught it."

He was on the stand only thirty minutes, and he had said nothing that might truly help his cause. His alibi, even viewed generously, was weak.

Reporters speculated in print about Randy's demeanor during this long trial, a trial that could put him in prison for life. He appeared to them as if he were only an observer, not the defendant. He was handsome, he dressed nicely, and he had pretty, well-dressed girlfriends. He didn't look the way killers are supposed to look.

But then, few killers do.

The trial was winding down. Dr. Stanley Abrams from Portland arrived, directly from a week-long meeting of the Northwest Polygraphers' Association, to repudiate the validity of eyewitness identification.

"Eyewitness testimony is very poor—particularly in an emotional situation," Abrams said.

In answer to Burt's questions, Abrams said it was possible that

Beth had identified Randy in the police lineup because he was the only man in the lineup whose picture she had seen earlier.

On cross-examination, Van Dyke asked Abrams to examine the lay-down of photos that Monty Holloway had shown to Beth at the Spokane airport.

"The most significant thing, I think, is the hairstyle," Abrams said. "Only one other person in this group has an Afro that resembles Woodfield's."

"Would you point out the photograph of the defendant?" Van Dyke asked.

Abrams picked the wrong man!

"You mean another person looked more like Woodfield in the throw-down than Woodfield in the lineup?"

Asked to try once more to pick the defendant, Dr. Abrams again picked a wrong man!

Abrams smiled, embarrassed. The gallery broke into titters, and Chris Van Dyke, turning away so that the jury could not see him, broke into a wide grin.

The defense's own witness had scored a big one for the prosecution.

Late on Thursday, June 25, Chris Van Dyke presented two rebuttal witnesses. A Portland woman who had been training Randy in the art of bartending said that she had often seen him wearing a waist-length leather jacket with a hood.

A Salem physician testified that herpes is transmitted through sexual contact but that a herpes carrier does not always infect his partner. If the disease is in remission, the carrier is not infectious.

It was all over but the final arguments, and they would come on Friday morning. Judge Brown turned to the jurors. "Bring your toothbrushes and pajamas tomorrow."

The jury would be sequestered during deliberation. If they did not reach a verdict by Friday evening, they would spend the weekend, perhaps the next week, away from their homes.

Chris Van Dyke spoke first. He suggested that Woodfield's manner on the witness stand had hardly been that of an innocent man. "It was the demeanor of an arrogant, cold, unemotional individual."

And then Van Dyke went through the damning testimony and physical evidence that had come out during the protracted trial:

Positive ballistics and hair comparisons; eyewitness identification by a victim who had been left for dead; friends who had seen Randy with a Band-Aid for disguise; friends who had seen Randy wearing the hooded leather jacket.

According to Van Dyke, everything presented had led directly back to Randall Brent Woodfield as the man who had shot Beth Wilmot and Shari Hull.

Burt contended that Beth Wilmot's descriptions of her attacker had varied a good deal and that the description had grown more detailed as time went on. "She's simply been adding to it because people have been pestering her."

Charlie Burt proposed that Randy's activities on the night in question were such that he could not have been in Keizer at the time the attacks took place. He had been traveling, Burt said, during the time he was supposed to have been in the TransAmerica Building.

"Hair is a valuable tool," Burt said scathingly, "but only if you want to nail someone."

Chris Van Dyke had one more chance to speak to the jury. "Randy Woodfield says he can't remember any details of the tavern. If *I'd* been accused of murder, I'd make darn sure I'd remember where I was!"

There was one aspect of the case that no one has ever been able to explain, and Van Dyke admitted that he couldn't either.

"I can't tell you why someone who seemed to have everything going for him would commit murder. . . ."

And then it was over—all over except for the deliberations of the jury.

It took them only three and a half hours, and only one vote. The decision was unanimous on that first vote: guilty. Guilty of murder. Guilty of attempted murder. Guilty of two counts of sodomy.

Beth Wilmot and Shari Hull's mother were in the gallery when those verdicts were read. They both broke into tears.

But later, as she reached the second-floor elevator, Beth Wilmot was, at last, smiling.

"This is the happiest day of my life," she said.

An equally happy Chris Van Dyke gave credit for the strong prosecution case to "high-quality policework and a very courageous victim." He estimated that the case had occupied his life full-time for two months and that it had cost an already financially pressed county a quarter of a million dollars.

But for Randy Woodfield it was only round one. Many, many trials lay ahead of him. Charlie Burt told reporters that Randy seemed to have accepted the verdict, that he understood that was the way the judicial system worked, and that he did not seem bitter.

Indeed, in a letter written to a friend a few days later, Randy sounded anything but bitter. Once again he was counting on God and religion to see him through, although Shelley was visiting him and writing him often.

He wrote that he was awaiting another psychiatric evaluation for his PSI (pre-sentence investigation) report. He then expected to gear up for the next trial, to be held in Albany.

He vowed he would seek psychiatric help from the state mental hospital because he was now convinced (once again) that his penchant for robberies and sexual assaults was something he had no control over. He compared the period just past to a dream from which he was slowly emerging.

Whatever the courts and the psychiatrists at the state hospital should decide, Randy wrote that he had focused on his future. He would work hard, wherever he was, to seek the Lord and become a minister.

Randy had told Dave Kominek in Springfield that he had "told God to take a backseat." Now, as always, when Randy was backed to the wall, he talked fervently about religion and seeking psychiatric help.

He asked his friend to read Romans 8:28: "And we know that all things work together for good to them that love God, to them who are called according to *his* purpose."

Those who had sought Randy's conviction and imprisonment felt the same way.

23

During the summer of 1981, the months that followed his conviction on all charges in the first trial in what promised to be an almost endless series of trials, Randy Woodfield existed in a kind of limbo. He had not been sentenced, nor would he be until the fall. Whatever the sentences would be, he surely faced years and years in prison. Randy continued to read his Bible, and to send scores of letters out to friends. He was once again the pious, subdued Randy. All of the rampaging sexual attacks had apparently become, in his own mind, only "a dream."

He, the *real* Randy, was coming back to reality, a reality that he seemed to have fashioned for himself. If his crimes had taken place while he was in a dream or a fugue state, then no one could blame *him*.

And surely he would not have to take any responsibilities for his attacks on women; those attacks had been committed by the "dream" Randy.

Oddly, Woodfield seemed to bear Dave Kominek no particular grudge, no more than a player on a losing football team might resent his counterpart on the winning squad. Kominek's side had won this one. The detective and the convicted killer talked in Randy's cell sporadically during the weeks after the Hull-Wilmot trial. On one such visit that took place just before sentencing, Kominek suggested to Randy that he might venture some hypotheses about the Darci Fix-Doug Altic murders. Randy made no objections, and sat back to listen to the detective's theories.

"This is strictly between us, Randy," Kominek began. "But this is the way I think it happened. I think you were very, very angry with Darci for dumping your friend, Tim Rossi. I think you were even so angry that you thought she should die. You were disgusted with the kind of woman who would walk off and leave her boyfriend hurting. It happened to you, and you didn't like the fact that Darci had done it to Tim. I think you went to her house last Thanksgiving Day . . .''

Randy didn't move; he held his muscles taut, waiting.

". . . You had a gun with you. I think the gun was the .357, the one with the interchangeable barrels that belonged to Tony Niri, your friend from the joint. You saw Darci and Doug having a great time, not caring about what they'd done to Tim. And you put the gun to the backs of their heads and you blew them away. Then you found Darci's gun—the little silver gun her father had given her and you took that. I think you used that little silver gun a lot. When it got too hot to keep, you threw it in a river. Isn't that right?''

Randy's dark eyes bore steadily into Kominek's. He was silent for seconds, minutes—and then he nodded slowly.

It was a moot victory for Kominek. A small personal satisfaction that one part of the puzzle had been clarified. "But we couldn't use it," he recalls. "Those other guns were gone—probably forever. Still, when I laid out the Fix-Altic murder case to Randy, he never contradicted me. I'm still convinced he killed them.''

Kominek also suspected that Woodfield had killed many, many more women than he had ever been accused of. There had been four murders of pretty young women in Huntington Beach, California, homicides that occurred during a period when Randy visited there.

There were the unsolved murders of Marsha Weatter, nineteen, and Kathy Allen, eighteen, in Washington State. The girls' homes were in Fairbanks, Alaska, but they'd been traveling in the Continental Forty-eight when they vanished. The pair was last seen hitchhiking two miles west of Spokane at the junction of Interstate 90 and U.S. Highway 2 on March 28, 1980. They were seasoned hikers who considered themselves capable and strong; they carried full backpacks as they held their thumbs out.

A college student recalled having given Marsha and Kathy a ride from Missoula, Montana, to Spokane, and they indicated that their plan was to hitch to Seattle, 270 miles west. From there, they planned to catch a flight home to Fairbanks on March 31.

But they never made the plane, and they never came home again.

Months later, long after the volcanic eruption of Mt. St. Helens on May 18, 1980, the bodies of Marsha Weatter and Kathy Allen were discovered close to the I-90 freeway, buried beneath the fine gray ash that blanketed Eastern Washington when Mt. St. Helens blew. Like the victims of ancient Pompeii, the girls had lain buried, not by any human hand, but by nature. They had each been shot in the head.

Late March, 1980, was just before the time Randy Woodfield started working at the Faucet Tavern. He was between jobs, he had no steady girlfriend at the time, and he was a constant traveler on his days off.

Even so, it was a fairly remote possibility to conclude that Randy in his gold Volkswagen had veered off his favorite North-South I-5 corridor to troll for female victims two hundred miles away from Beaverton. The Weatter-Allen murders have never been solved, and they remain a question mark in Dave Kominek's mind.

Another darker question mark is the murder of twenty-one-year old Sylvia Durante, a beautiful young cocktail waitress at the Red Robin restaurant, a popular "yuppie" super-hamburger/watering hole in Seattle. The Red Robin was located just off I-5 in the University of Washington district, hard by the Lake Washington Ship Canal Bridge. It was crowded every night and packed to the rafters on weekends.

Sylvia's body was found in the bedroom of her apartment in December 1979. Investigating Seattle Homicide Detective Gary Fowler noted marks on her ankles and wrists that suggested she had been bound before she was strangled.

There were flowers from a secret admirer nearby, and there was no apparent forced entry. The victim had undoubtedly trusted the wrong man, invited—or allowed—him to visit her at her home.

Sylvia Durante was a lovely brunette, a vibrant girl—filled with joy for life, and, like Shelley Janson, she had been actively seeking the one right man for her. Sylvia preferred dark-haired, muscular men. Randy Woodfield fit her qualifications precisely. But did Sylvia Durante ever meet Randy? No one will ever know.

There is no physical evidence linking Randy to Sylvia Durante's murder. However, traffic citation records indicate that Randy Woodfield was in Seattle during the week before Sylvia's death. He had even played Good Samaritan to a young nurse whose car ran out of gas shortly after she left work on the night shift at the University Hospital.

The nurse had been wary of the big dark-haired man at first, but he'd been so boyishly charming that she'd finally relented and locked her car, allowing him to drive her home. He'd been such a gentleman and had rescued her from a long hike in the wee hours; she even gave him a kiss good night.

The University Hospital is located a scant half-mile from the Red Robin. And the Red Robin is to the University District what

O'Callahan's and De Frisco's were to Eugene, *the* yuppie pick-up spot. Randy would have gravitated to it like a beacon in the night.

A close perusal of the voluminous files on the Durante case, however, elicits no mention of a "Randy." There *is* a letter that Sylvia wrote to a cousin, a letter in which she writes enthusiastically about meeting an interesting man from Portland—a man she hoped to see when she visited there during the Thanksgiving holidays, 1979. Was that man Randy Woodfield? No one knows. The trail that might link Sylvia Durante to Randy ends there.

Again, is the Durante case simply a questionable combination of geographical locations and timing? Of fascinating circumstantial similarities? Without more evidence, it would be premature to link the three Washington State deaths to Randy Woodfield.

Woodfield certainly didn't need any more trouble. As it was, he faced so many trials that he might expect to spend the next several years going from court to court to court.

On August 28, 1981, The Municipal Court of Redding Judicial District, County of Shasta, State of California, officially charged Randall Brent Woodfield for a violation of Section 187 of the California Penal Code. In legalese, the criminal complaint read:

"Rick Burnett of Shasta County Sheriff's Office, in the county of Shasta, being first duly sworn, on information and belief, complains and accuses defendant Randall Brent Woodfield of the following crimes:

COUNT I:

The said defendant, Randall Brent Woodfield, on or about February 3, 1981, in the county of Shasta, state of California did willfully, unlawfully, and with malice aforethought murder Donna Lee Eckard, a human being.

It is further alleged that in the commission of the above offense, the said defendant personally used a firearm, to wit: a handgun, within the meaning of Penal Code Section 12022.5.

FIRST SPECIAL CIRCUMSTANCE

It is further alleged that the murder of Donna Lee Eckard was murder in the first degree and was committed by the defendant, Randall Brent Woodfield, and in addition to such murder, said defendant is now being charged with having murdered and has murdered Janell Charlotte Jarvis, on or about the same day, said murder being murder in the first or second degree, within the meaning of Penal Code 190.2(a) (3).

SECOND SPECIAL CIRCUMSTANCE

It is further alleged that the murder of Donna Lee Eckard was committed by Randall Brent Woodfield while the defendant was engaged in the commission of . . . the immediate flight after having committed and attempted to commit the crime of burglary in the first or second degree, in violation of Penal Code Section 460, within the meaning of Penal Code Section 190.2(a) (17).''

The document continued, repetitive and concise, dry as only legal documents can be, the horror and pain and ultimate tragedy of the victims buried somewhere within the tedious terminology.

COUNT II:

Violation of Section 187 of the California Penal Code, a felony. The said defendant . . . on or about February 3, 1981 . . . did willfully, unlawfully, and with malice aforethought murder Janell Charlotte Jarvis, a human being.

It is further alleged that . . . the said defendant personally used a firearm . . . a handgun.

COUNT III:

. . . The said defendant, Randall Brent Woodfield, on or about February 3, 1981, did willfully and unlawfully, then being a person over the age of twenty-one, participate in an act of sodomy with Janell Charlotte Jarvis, a person under the age of sixteen years.''

There were ten counts listed in the document naming Randy Woodfield: two counts of murder, one count of sodomy, two counts of robbery, three counts of burglary, one count of oral copulation, and one count of rape. All of the Shasta county victims, it was hoped, would one day have their turn in court. Two of them were dead, and physical evidence would have to speak for Donna Eckard and her daughter, Janell.

California wanted Randy Woodfield, and wanted him badly. But even though the arrest warrant was dated August 27, 1981, California would have to wait a long, long time to confront Randy.

Oregon Courts were far from finished with him.

The delay must have given Woodfield some comfort. There was, at the time of his crimes, no death penalty in Oregon. (The death penalty has been reinstated in the intervening years, but it is not retroactive.) In California, Woodfield would be walking into the long black shadow of the gas chamber.

Hard on the heels of the ten charges and the arrest warrant out of California, Shasta County District Attorney Steve Carlton announced that he would seek the death penalty if and when Woodfield was tried in his jurisdiction. California homicide trials are bifurcated. That is, the jury first decides if the defendant is innocent or guilty. If the defendant is found guilty of first-degree murder, the same jury is retained to dictate what the penalty will be. California law permits the death penalty in special circumstances. Among those special circumstances are multiple homicides and homicides committed during the commission of another felony crime. The Mountain Gate murders were committed during the course of a burglary—the theft of Steve Eckard's revolver.

With the specter of a cyanide "egg" dropping into a vat of sulfuric acid waiting for him down the line, Randy Woodfield's trial in Benton County, Oregon may have seemed a far lesser threat.

In September, 1981, the news about Woodfield dealt almost exclusively with the Benton County trial. A change of venue had been denied. Former District Attorney—and now Judge—Frank Knight reasoned that extensive pre-trial publicity could be expected almost anywhere in Oregon as much as in Corvallis. Knight stressed that the key to a fair trial depended more on careful jury selection.

As trials often are, this trial was delayed. Instead of beginning in September, the new date was set for November 2. The charges in Corvallis were sodomy, kidnapping, and being an ex-convict in possession of a firearm in the attack on the young waitress in the restaurant.

The second set of charges included sodomy, robbery, and sexual abuse in the attack on the eight- and ten-year-old Green sisters in Corvallis on January 14. And the third set of charges stemmed from the February 9 incident in the Corvallis fabric shop: robbery and sexual abuse.

But there were more—the charges in Linn County, resulting from the attack—also on February 9, in the Albany laundromat: attempted kidnapping, sodomy, and an ex-convict in possession of a firearm.

Jackson County, Oregon, and Washington State authorities would have to stand at the end of a long line to prosecute Woodfield.

The word "overkill" comes to mind when one considers the charges piled on charges against him, but then, the same word is chillingly apt when contemplating the crimes which resulted in those charges. Rarely in the Northwest, if ever, has there been a suspect whose alleged crimes occurred on an almost-daily basis.

*   *   *

On Monday, October 12, 1981, Marion County Circuit Judge Clarke Brown pronounced sentence on Randy Woodfield in his conviction in the shootings of Beth Wilmot and Shari Hull. Beth Wilmot sat quietly in the back of the courtroom as Brown asked her attacker if he had any remarks to make before sentence was pronounced.

He did. Randy Woodfield's incongruously high, soft voice sounded sincere. "I stand before you in complete innocence."

"Thank you, Mr. Woodfield," Judge Brown responded, polite as always, but he was hardly moved. He stared down at the prisoner in front of him, his face grim.

"Now, Mr. Woodfield, you have been found guilty by a jury of your peers of murder, attempted murder, sodomy in the first degree, and sodomy in the second degree. I sat there and listened to all of the evidence, although I was not the trier of the fact or of the credibility to be given the evidence, or to the witnesses who took the stand. I will assure you this—I agreed wholeheartedly with that verdict, with the verdicts that were handed down by the jury. I have found that you do have a severe personality disorder which indicates a propensity to criminal activity and this, of course, gives the power to the Court to enhance the sentences from twenty years maximum to thirty years.

"Basically speaking, there are four factors which this Court takes into consideration when it sentences a person. One of them is separation. Are you a danger to the community? Two is the deterrence. Will it deter you or will it deter anyone else in the future? Three is retribution, the old eye for an eye, tooth for a tooth idea. And number four is rehabilitation. Each case is different just the same as each individual person is a different person, and, as a result, the Court must put certain weights differently in each case on each of the four factors which are involved.

"Now, as to rehabilitation, although the law says that this was murder, the method in which this was accomplished was nothing more than execution. It reminded me of nothing more than the 'Godfather' coming to life. The execution of Miss Hull and the attempted execution of Miss Wilmot was, in my mind, the most cold-blooded type of execution which this Court has ever heard. The two acts of sodomy were vicious. Frankly, I do not think that rehabilitation is very much in the picture within this sentencing.

"Now, as to separation, Mr. Woodfield, I very definitely feel that you are a danger to the community and that the community has the right to be separated from *you* . . .

"And then we come into the third . . . deterrence. The sentence which I am going to impose, I think will deter you from any further ever (sic) committing any crime, and I sincerely hope that the sentence which I give to you will make other people think twice before they commit such a crime. . .

"As to Case Number 125,510, which is murder, it is the order of the Court that you be placed in the legal and physical custody of the Oregon Corrections Division for the period of the remainder of your life. As to Case Number 125,511, attempted murder, it is the order of the Court that you be placed in the legal and physical custody of the Oregon Corrections Division for an indeterminate period of time—not to exceed thirty years—which shall run *consecutively* with any other sentence imposed today. As to Case Number 125,512, it is the order of the Court that you be placed in the legal and physical custody of the Oregon Corrections Division for in indeterminate period of time not to exceed thirty years, which shall run *consecutively* to any other sentence imposed today.

"As to Case Number 125,513, it is the order of Court that you be placed in the legal and physical custody of the Oregon Corrections Division for an indeterminate period of time not to exceed thirty years, which shall run *consecutively* to any other sentence imposed today.

Judge Brown's eyes bored into Woodfield. "I have made the sentences consecutive because the Court has found that you are a menace to society. And the Court has the duty to protect the public by the use of consecutive sentences in order to protect the public from further criminal conduct by you. This Court is making the strongest possible recommendation to the Oregon State Board of Parole and Probation that you serve a *minimum* of fifty years before you are to be considered eligible for release.

". . . If the death penalty in Oregon had not been declared unconstitutional, I would have no hesitancy whatsoever to say, 'Mr. Woodfield, you are going to die . . .' "

Randy Woodfield fit within the parameters of the Oregon legal definition of a "dangerous offender." As such, the maximum sentences for each of the crimes he had been convicted of could be increased. And, indeed, Judge Clarke Brown gave Woodfield the maximum sentence.

Life in prison *plus* ninety years. "If you are released earlier, it will not be because the Court has failed in its duty."

24

The Benton County trial in Corvallis might seem superfluous. Why bring a man into trial when he has already been sentenced to life plus ninety years? There are many reasons. Chief among them was the chance that the Wilmot-Hull verdict might be reversed on appeal, an appeal whose wheels were already in motion. Not likely—but within the realm of possibility. Next, there was the victim's right to confront her attacker, a right that is just as important—if not *more* important than—the defendant's right to confront his accuser. Further, more and more judges, prosecutors, and detectives have become angry and frustrated at the number of criminals who commit two, or three, or *dozens* of crimes for the "price of one."

Since one of the Benton County victims was the daughter of a law enforcement officer, it was not surprising that she wanted her day in court. Jill Martin had been terrorized in the restaurant restroom on February 25 in Corvallis; she had heard all her life that unless victims are brave enough to testify, criminals go free. She was not about to let that happen.

Jury selection began on Monday, November 2, 1981. This time, the selection went rapidly and by day's end eight women and four men had been seated in the jury box.

Woodfield had a new defense attorney. Jim Hilborn of Corvallis had been court-appointed to defend him. He also had a new alibi.

Arden Bates, his former landlady—but mistakenly identified by the press as "Woodfield's girlfriend," had changed her story and was now prepared to swear that Randy had been home with her and her son in Springfield on the night of February 25. Perhaps Arden was suffering pangs of guilt; she had been the one who turned over her phone records to Captain Dave Bishop. Those phone records played a major role in tracing Randy's violent peregrinations along the I-5 freeway—and in convicting him in his first trial.

Arden, reversing herself, had flung herself into Randy's arms in the Salem courtroom, telling him how sorry she was. Randy's ultimate "forgiving nature," and barrage of letters had apparently softened Arden's heart.

Kenneth Osher, for the prosecution, would present his own witnesses—three of Randy's alleged victims. After a verbal tussle in court, Judge Knight granted Osher's motion to allow courtroom identification by the three victims: Jill Martin, and the two women who had been assaulted in the Corvallis fabric shop on February 9. Hilborn maintained for the defense, just as Charlie Burt had, that the victims' memory had been tainted by viewing a mug laydown and then the in-person line-up in Springfield in March.

Jill Martin took the stand on Wednesday, November 4. Chief Deputy D.A. Osher led her gently through the events of the night of February 25.

"Can you tell us what happened that night, Jill?"

"I left the kitchen of the restaurant about eight-thirty to use the restroom. I was just washing my hands and getting ready to go back to work when this man with a small silver gun forced his way in and told me that I couldn't leave."

"What did he say?"

" 'Do what I say and I won't hurt you.' He told me to sit on the toilet seat, and I said I wouldn't."

"And then what happened?"

"He cocked the hammer of the pistol, and I saw the cylinder move."

And then Jill had to tell the gallery and the jury the explicit details of the perverted sexual attack. In a steady voice, she said that the intruder had forced her to strip to the waist and perform oral sodomy on him while he fondled her. After he had ejaculated, he had bound her hand and foot with tape, and left her lying on the floor of the restroom.

"What did the man look like?" Osher asked.

"He wore a dark stocking cap on his head, and he had a full beard that looked fake. He had a white bandage over his nose. He was about five-feet-eight to five-feet-nine inches tall."

Jill had misjudged her attacker's height, and it was an error that Hilborn would attempt to blow up to major proportions.

"So you can be fairly certain that the man was five-eight or five-nine?" Hilborn asked Jill on cross-examination.

"Yes."

Randy Woodfield is, of course, six feet, two inches tall. But any expert on witness identification will agree that crime victims and witnesses are wrong about height more often than any other physical characteristic.

The jury wouldn't know that.

But the jury had watched, fascinated, as Jill selected Randy Woodfield out of all the males in the crowded courtroom, and said he was the man who had assaulted her sexually.

Tony Niri, Randy's ex-con, ex-friend, told the Benton County jury that he had watched Randy as he tried out disguises shortly before Thanksgiving, 1980.

"He put a piece of white tape across his nose, and then he put on a fake brown beard and a navy blue stocking cap."

"Where did that take place?" Osher asked.

"In my apartment in Portland. We were talking about pulling a job, and discussing what kind of disguises we might use."

Detective Neal Loper from the Beaverton Police Department testified to the search of Randy's room in Arden Bates's Springfield home. He had seized for evidence—with Randy's permission—a box of athletic adhesive tape and a small gun-cleaning kit.

Criminalist Michael Howard from the Oregon State Police Crime Detection Lab in Portland explained to the jury how something as seemingly prosaic and mass-produced as white adhesive tape can be reduced to its essential components—thereby making it unique. Howard had tested both the tape from Woodfield's bedroom and the tape used to bind Jill Martin's ankles and wrists.

"The elemental composition of the tape was the same," Howard explained. "That led me to believe that it was produced by the same manufacturer . . . and was probably from the same batch."

Perhaps the most intriguing testimony from forensic science experts came from Jim Pex of the Oregon State Police Crime Lab. Pex is one of America's definitive experts on blood components both in humans and in animals. He lectures frequently, and testifies often as an expert witness. Pex explained to the jury that Randy Woodfield was a "secretor," one of the majority of the human species whose blood type can be determined by analyzing body fluids—blood itself, saliva, semen . . .

A semen stain found on Jill Martin's clothing proved to have come from a type-B secretor. This is a relatively rare blood type which occurs in only nine percent of the population of the world.

And then Jim Pex moved into enzyme characteristics of blood, particularly Randy Woodfield's. "His enzyme genotype was one-two-plus—which narrows it down even further. That genotype is found in only 3.7 percent of the population. When you combine the three characteristics of that semen stain—that is, from a secretor, for someone with type B blood, and from someone with one-two-plus genotype, you are talking about *only .27 percent of the population of the world!* Randy Woodfield had all three characteristics in his body fluid . . .''

Would the jury even be able to understand the highly technical serology testimony Jim Pex had given, all those unfamiliar terms about what makes up a man's blood? Had they believed Jill Martin?

Apparently they had.

After only three hours' deliberation, the jury found Randy Woodfield guilty of sodomy and of being an ex-convict in possession of a weapon.

They had not believed Arden Bates. And they most assuredly had not believed Randy himself—not even when Jim Hilborn had asked him straight out if he had committed the crimes against Jill Martin, and Randy had answered earnestly, ''No, I sure didn't!''

On December 18, 1981, Randy Woodfield's Christmas season was blighted considerably when he was sentenced to thirty years on the sodomy charge and five years on the ex-convict in possession of a weapon. Judge Knight stipulated that this additional *thirty-five-year-sentence* was to run *consecutively* to the sentences handed down in the Shari Hull-Beth Wilmot attack.

Randy now faced life plus one hundred and sixty-five years in prison.

Merrisue and Megan Green were spared the ordeal of a trial, the fabric store victims' case was put on hold, as were the Linn County case, all the other Oregon cases, the Washington State cases, and the California murders of Donna Eckard and Janell Jarvis.

Randy Woodfield was transported once more to the Oregon State Penitentiary in Salem, where he would start doing his time as he awaited new trials through the appeal process. He had left that prison slightly more than two years earlier with promises about the Christian life he planned to lead, with dozens of people prepared to support him emotionally—and financially. Now the man deemed not to be a ''violence risk,'' was back in the ''joint,'' for the rest of his life.

UPDATE: 1988

Randy Woodfield was indigent; all of his attorneys were supplied by the taxpayers of Oregon. He was represented in his appeal by Gary D. Babcock, a public defender. Babcock cited thirty cases as precedents as he asked the Court of Appeals of the State of Oregon to reverse Randall Brent Woodfield's convictions for Murder, Attempted Murder, and Sodomy in the First Degree (two counts) in the death of Shari Hull and the near-death of Beth Wilmot.

Notice of Appeal had been filed November 13, 1981. How bizarre, really. Even as Randy Woodfield was being tried for sodomy in Benton County, his appeal had been filed in Salem.

Babcock's arguments were familiar; he hit at Beth Wilmot's identification of Randy Woodfield, suggesting her memory was flawed, that eyewitness testimony is fallible. He questioned the State's expert witnesses in ballistics and hair and fiber identification, and he argued that Judge Clarke Brown had not had the authority to invoke the dangerous offender statute when imposing Woodfield's minimum sentence: fifty years.

And, once again, an attempt was made to blame the shootings in the TransAmerica Building on Lawrence Moore, the loose cannon who had opened fire on patrons in the Oregon Museum Tavern. Moore's alleged crimes had a completely different M.O., and his resemblance to Woodfield was faint. Woodfield was dark and Moore was blonde. They were both young Caucasian males, and that was about all, but Randy Woodfield still clung tenaciously to his story that he was being persecuted for the crimes of another man. Appeals Attorney Babcock contended that Moore should have been brought into the courtroom for the jury to observe.

Babcock also took issue with Judge Brown's instructions to the jury that it was to presume that all witnesses speak the truth. Since the State had backed up its case with thirty-seven witnesses, and Randy Woodfield had had only twelve (including himself), Babcock felt the State had an unfair advantage, based on sheer numbers.

Perhaps. But the fact that Randy Woodfield had not *had* thirty-seven witnesses who could back him up in his protestations of innocence negated the argument.

Dave Frohnmayer, Oregon State Attorney General, William F. Gary, Oregon Solicitor General, and Stephen F. Peifer, Assistant Oregon Attorney General, responded to Babcock's arguments to overturn Randy's convictions. Speaking for the prosecution, they cited *forty-eight* cases for precedents to support *their* arguments.

The Attorney General's office deemed Lawrence Moore ". . . irrelevant to the case because defendant failed to demonstrate, beyond mere speculation and conjecture, that Moore was an alternate suspect. Other than by inflaming the jury, Moore's presence in the courtroom could not have exculpated the defendant."

It was a moot point anyway. Lawrence Moore's attorney had invoked *his* client's Fifth Amendment rights. Even if Brown had acceded to Woodfield's request that his designated suspect appear in the courtroom, Moore would not have come. Why on earth would he? He was Woodfield's red herring, a smoke screen, a "bushy-haired stranger" beloved of defense teams, and Moore's attorney was not about to bring him into Woodfield's trial to shoulder the blame.

Moreover, the State argued that Judge Brown was perfectly proper in his instructions to the jury that witnesses are presumed to speak the truth. "The instruction is well established in statutory and case law."

As to the five-decade length of Randy's minimum sentence, The State was succinct in their response," the trial Court properly ordered that defendant serve a minimum term totaling fifty years' imprisonment on the four counts. The law expressly permits a minimum sentence of up to fifteen years on each count when the defendant is found to be a dangerous offender."

The Oregon Court of Appeals sided with attorneys for the State; Randy Woodfield's appeal was denied.

Life in prison, despite the term, does not mean *life in prison*. It means whatever the minimum for life is set by statute in a particular state. In Oregon, life usually means somewhere between ten and twelve years. But the fifty-year minimum set by Judge Brown translates to a first parole hearing for Randy Woodfield in the year 2031, the year that will mark his 81st birthday . . . if he lives that long.

Back in 1981, as her hopes for a future with him faded in a barrage of arrests, Randy wrote to Shelly Janson, swearing his devotion. To underscore that, he signed his beloved gold Champagne Edition Volkswagen—albeit slightly crunched—over to his fiancée. Shelly wrote back for awhile, and then she faded out of his life. Randall was not the man she had thought he was; he was a stranger—he always had been, really. There could never be a marriage, or babies, or any of the things he had promised her. It had all turned to ashes.

Although the term is a misnomer in the accepted sense, there is a kind of "life in prison" that few outsiders know about—one that most laymen never even think or wonder about, a vast society of human beings captive inside walls. It is a society with its own language, mores, relationships, hierarchy. The majority of inmates are short-timers, men (and women) guilty of crimes against property—but who would no more think of doing physical harm to others than the average man on the street would. Those convicts who have hurt people, particularly those prisoners who have sexually attacked women and children, are relegated to the lowest social strata of prison society.

The thought of being locked up is horrific to free men, but seasoned cons explain, "You only do one year of hard time; after that, you adjust." It is somewhat harder for a sexual sadist to adjust inside the walls than for other prisoners.

A large part of adjusting to prison life involves fitting into one social group or another. Randy Woodfield has more time to do than almost any other prisoner in the Oregon State Penitentiary. He is a convicted woman killer, a child rapist. The only way Randy can hope to survive in prison is to excel in one of two areas: brains or brawn. He has consistently tested only average in intelligence—but Woodfield remains tremendously strong. He lifts weights, works out, concentrates on keeping the muscle tone that validates his masculinity.

As long as Randy can hold on to his strength, he will maintain his tenuous balance on the middle to lower-middle rungs of the prison's social ladder. He insists he has "earned the respect" of his fellow inmates, but that is doubtful. His crimes are anathema to prisoners who might consider robbing a liquor store, but who detest a man who rapes and sodomizes women. Randy's strength is his armor, and each passing year erodes it.

As this is written, Randy Woodfield has served seven years of his sentence. In July, 1983, The Oregon Supreme Court refused to review his final appeal. He will be thirty-eight years old on December 28, 1988, but, like Dorian Gray, he has scarcely aged externally. He keeps his "house" (cell) neat and perfect, and complains bitterly when he is sent to "the hole" for occasional infractions.

". . . I hate to fight and get 'D.R.'s cause they move all your stuff to the property room in bags, like a pile of junk. Things get lost, bent, broken and all dirty. They don't just lock up our cells and save it for us . . . We have cells and Isolation Building & "Black Box" for incorrables (sic). Crazy huh?" Randy wrote to a correspondent. "Sick place prisons are!!! Sick people run them too. And sick people live their lives saying other people are sick or weird. Everyone is equal—everyone has problems and will stand before God for Judging others . . ."

This is a common and continual theme for Randy Woodfield—that he is "equal." That all people are alike, and that he is no worse than anyone else, and thus should not be maligned.

For press interviews or on visitor's day, he strides into the room perfectly groomed, his jeans fashionably faded, ironed with knife-like creases. He wears his shirt open to show his muscular chest, and he is as tanned as the Oregon weather allows. Randy is a man totally obsessed with his physical perfection. Time seems to have suspended him in preservative gel; he has no responsibilities, no concerns about earning a living, or about where his next meal is coming from. He still looks like the man who was chosen to pose in the buff for a beefcake centerfold. He still talks and writes as if he were in high school.

There are more female guards in the Oregon State Penitentiary than there were during Woodfield's first incarceration there, and he continues to vent his rage that women are allowed in areas with male prisoners. And yet, he preens for his female captors, bragging that they sneak up on him to catch a glimpse of his nakedness. One guard laughs as she describes Woodfield's continuing exhibitionism. "I can walk past Randy's cell and he's fully clothed. Five minutes later, when I come back down the line, Randy's stripped and he's flexing his muscles—waiting for me."

Woodfield's need to expose himself seems as entrenched as it ever was—even if it is directed, of necessity, at female guards who are not even faintly impressed.

A quarter of his life has been spent in prison, and it would appear he has fashioned a world there—although he still writes and talks of appeals. Prison has given Randy Woodfield everything he needs—save the immediate proximity of young females.

He has worked his way around that. In a sense, Woodfield still uses women for both his sexual outlet and financial support. He has always been a prodigious letter-writer, and prison life has only increased this activity.

Randy Woodfield carries on a life through the mail. Women's names and addresses are gold to him. He writes to single women, married women, widows, divorcées, teenagers, gleaning his correspondents from other convicts, from the pen pal columns in tabloids, or in Christian magazines. He writes to women in the Oregon Women's Correctional Center, the facility next door to the prison where he is locked up, his correspondence part of the huge intra-facility mail—requiring no postage—a paper link between men and women. He writes to women held in other jails and prisons across America.

Some of his correspondents are aware that they are writing to a convict, but some are deluded, believing they are writing to "Randy Woodfield, student at the University of Oregon, 2605 State Street in Salem, Oregon." A handful of women who have journeyed to Salem to surprise their "fiancée" have found to their utter dismay that 2605 State Street is not the University of Oregon's address; the walls of the state prison loom there.

Randy Woodfield's letters move from friendship to intimacy to frank pornography very rapidly. Promises are made, proposals of marriage flow from his pen as easily as comments on the weather. He invariably encloses pictures of himself, and always includes the photograph he prizes most—Randy Woodfield in tiny blue bathing trunks, flexing his muscles, his tanned skin gleaming with oil. That man has a neatly clipped black beard, a trim moustache. That picture is almost ten years old; detectives found it displayed in his room in Arden Bates's house.

A picture—not of a woman—but of Randy himself placed where he could gaze at it from his bed. Now he uses it to lure pen-pals.

He has written to dozens, scores, *hundreds* of women, juggling his replies, explaining, soothing, cajoling and seducing. Many of them send him money, sometimes only a dollar or two. Sometimes thousands of dollars. The wife of a courthouse employee in a parish (county) in a southeastern state was so besotted in the early 1980's by the impact of Randy Woodfield's letters that she gladly sent him many thousand dollars. She also is alleged to have acquiesced to his request that she take a nude photo of her nine-year-old daughter and send it to him.

Charges are pending against Randy Woodfield in that case.

A young woman about to be paroled from the Washington

State Women's Facility at Purdy began to write to Randy, on a friend's recommendation, in 1983. As soon as she was released that fall, she traveled to Salem where she met Randy in person. She was entranced. Indeed, she was in love. She was even halfway convinced that Woodfield was the natural father of a child she had adopted in Portland a few years before she was arrested in Washington. She wanted to believe that, to think that her family was complete and miraculously reunited.

The recent parolee had found a mission during those last months of 1983; she vowed to win freedom for Randy. She believed devoutly he was innocent of all charges.

"I've just come back from visiting him for the first time," she said breathlessly in a phone call to the author. "And I know he's innocent. He's wonderful. Yes, I know he writes to other women—but *I'm* the only woman he really loves. I'm the one he wants to marry. He's going to introduce me to his family. I know the truth when I hear it."

She was—is—a nice woman, inexorably drawn to destructive men.

A few years later, it was a young married woman who began visiting Randy regularly in prison, and who called the author to announce that she was researching a book she would write—a book that would tell the truth. She visited Randy dozens of times, and she believed in him. "Anyone would believe him. He's innocent. He's the most sincere man I've ever met."

Some of Woodfield's "mail conquests" were pitiful. The mother of a dying child in Florida grew to count on Randy, to believe that he would be allowed out of prison to visit the little boy and to help her through the tragedy that lay ahead. He encouraged her to believe that there was a good chance Oregon authorities would grant him a "hardship furlough" so that he could rush to her side. Indeed, Woodfield may have actually thought he could parlay the child's fatal illness and emotional dependence on him into some time-out from prison.

There is bleak irony in how well Randy Woodfield understands women. For a male who has demonstrated over and over an almost visceral hatred for the opposite sex, he knows just which buttons to push, when to be forceful, when to offer tenderness. Nowhere is Randy's manipulation of women more evident than in the voluminous correspondence that began in the spring of 1984 between Randy and a female prisoner on trial for murder in Eugene, Oregon.

In a sense, their "affair" was a true "Battle of the Titans."

Each of them has had countless lovers; each is adept at manipulation and "games."

Diane Downs* had made headlines in the Northwest since she and her children were shot on a lonely country road outside Springfield, Oregon, in May, 1983. Cheryl Downs, seven, died, and Christie, eight, and Danny, three, had been left paralyzed. Diane, who had been wounded only in her lower left arm, was arrested on February 28, 1984, and charged with the shootings. The media said that Diane Downs had shot her own children—so that she might win back a married lover who "didn't want to be a daddy." That charge had yet to be proved, but Diane Downs's history indicated that she was a woman who predicated her whole existence upon being "in love," and on her sexual appeal to men.

Diane's image appeared almost daily in Oregon papers and on television, and Randy Woodfield was impressed by both her beauty and her notoriety, the latter perhaps more of an aphrodisiac to him. He craved publicity as much as he craved sex. The combination of Randy Woodfield and Diane Downs seemed, to him, to be a dynamite duo. No telling where they could go—together.

But first, Randy had to "meet" Diane.

In late spring of 1984, Diane was being held in the Lane County Jail, the same jail where Randy himself had been booked when he was arrested three years earlier.

He wrote to Diane, who, at twenty-eight, was seven months into her sixth pregnancy, and about to go on trial for murder. He felt it prudent, for the moment, to keep his true identity secret until she got to know him. He didn't want her to leap to hasty conclusions about his background. He used the name of another prisoner in the Oregon State Penitentiary, and signed his letters "Squirrely," or "Michael," or "Just me."

Mail from prison is almost always rife with unusual punctuation. A smiling or frowning cartoon-circle face at the end of a sentence is the most universal touch. Lower case "i's" dotted with a circle, fat exclamation points, "Ha-Ha's" XXXXs and OOOO's for kisses and hugs. Randy used all these—and more— in his letters. He favored a line drawing of a funny little man with pop eyes and his tongue sticking out of his mouth, the insouciant image appearing here and there to augment his words. Randy's style was staccato, spinning the reader and keeping her off balance. Randy peppered his letters with phrases and ques-

---

* Note: For complete coverage of the Diane Downs case, see *Small Sacrifices* by Ann Rule, Signet, July, 1988.

tions: "You smiling?" "How about it?" "You with me, Di?" and "Yowza!"

Even in letters, he demanded constant and immediate acceptance. And he had, perhaps unwittingly, chosen a woman whose whole life revolved around having a man. Diane was definitely looking—and the women's section of jail offers little choice. She was without a lover when Randy Woodfield came into her life.

Because Diane Downs was an escape risk, letters coming in to her were copied. Later, when "Squirrely" could not resist sending her the familiar blue-bikini picture of himself, jail censors recognized Woodfield as one of their former tenants. He too was considered an escape risk, and his letters were copied. Their fevered correspondence grew into thick stacks of letters.

Initially, when Diane knew her secret admirer only as "Squirrely," he bombarded her with supportive missives. He was fascinated with the gynecological details of her condition, and asked for an in-depth description of her pregnancy, what her pelvic exams were like, and how a baby was delivered. They made bets—these two total strangers—on when the infant would be born, and whether it would be a boy or a girl. If a boy, "Squirrely" suggested that Diane name the child, "Ian Randall."

When Diane Downs was informed of the true identity of her steamy correspondent, she questioned him about his murder and rape convictions. He evinced shock and hurt feelings at her lack of faith, and they were estranged for days. But they soon made up.

Randy's letters were gallant; Diane apologized for doubting him, and he apologized for being so angry. ". . . It's a crazy world here, and I try and do my own time. Well a little bit of yours too. (*Ha*) I may get into a fight (over her innocence) yet dear friend. But don't you worry about it none. I will be stubborn and stand up for what I believe in."

Diane Downs's future was up in the air, her trial lasting week after week. The letters coming down to Eugene from the Salem prison were encouraging. "Squirrely" and later Randy offered a strong shoulder to cry on.

"I want ya to live and work in Salem or Portland (if acquitted)," Randy wrote. "And get to know my family too. Me better for sure! Deal? *And* if you go to OWCC—SHAME—then I will want your promise to marry me and work with me on writing our own book about Justice in America, and how we can handle it all together. I know this is a shock to ya, but why not marry me and be able to visit me too? You could always divorce me later—(*Ha*). Well?

"Something to think on and dream about. You will need a dear friend next door to ya if you come here and I need you too. I'm sincere and want you to think about this. O.K. Di?"

She continued to write. He told her about run-ins he had with "dudes about my sex-crimes. I stood my ground to earn respect. I'm no woman killer, and I am angry as hell and will fight for my honor to exist."

Randy repeated to Diane Downs again and again that they were both paying the price for crimes they hadn't done, and vowing his sensitivity to her. "Smile now—I care. You're just too sweet . . ."

Beyond his emotional support, Randy's letters were stimulating. He was, apparently, in a constant state of priapism. He referred to his genitals continually, and went on for pages that sounded as if they'd come from reader write-ins to mens' magazines.

"I will be stroking 'Jr.' to your photo at exactly midnight on Saturday night (a.m.) Diane, so say 'Hi' and tell me you enjoy our time together. Will you remember to touch your body for me and say my name . . . Just a game to play together 'cause I feel you close to me and to climax my juices in memory of our togetherness like this. You brighten my life dear friend. So thank you and join me Saturday night if you want. I will be there for you. Totally in tho'ts of you . . ."

Through May, June, July, 1984, they wrote to each other almost every day. Curious letters, full of earthy sexual steam and tears. Diane wrote to a number of men in prison, and Randy, of course wrote to scores of women. Each promised absolute fidelity. He sent her pictures of himself and selected pages from magazines. She sent him pictures of herself and her paralyzed children and Bible tracts.

He wrote how he longed for children of his own. She wrote back her glowing thoughts on motherhood. Randy described his "eight-inch" penis, and Diane described her "D-cup" breasts. It seemed a long-distance coupling made somewhere other than heaven.

"Your life is in the balance for sure!!" Randy commented. "That damn jury better keep in mind 'Beyond a reasonable doubt' too! Let your attorney know *and* drive that home to their ears. I'm with you no matter what dear friend. So cry a happy tear for me too. I do too occasionally. Even for this grown man! (Ha.) Silly—huh? I wish you could *kiss* mine away. Will you on our visits? Not shy are ya? I will want to hold ya tight to me and show you that you're special people. Okay by you? A woman ought to be treated like a "Queen" in my book—maybe I'll write about it—being accused falsely of rape and murder (Sad face drawn). Your comments, Di?''

Randy wrote that he felt "Mothers are beautiful creations—like you, Di—(Smile?)''

Diane had little to smile about. She was convicted on June 17, 1984, of murder, two counts of attempted murder in the first degree, and two counts of first degree assault in the shootings of her three children. Ten days later, she gave birth—not to "Ian Randall" as Randy had hoped, but to a baby girl: Amy Elizabeth. The child was immediately placed out for adoption.

She would not be visiting Randy; Diane would be in the women's prison facility next door to the Oregon State Penitentiary with a sentence almost as long as his.

Randy still had plans for them.

As he had once urged Shelly Janson to get in shape, he now tried to inspire Diane Downs. He wrote of his daily work-outs, and his no-carbohydrate diet. He was stepping up the number of repetitions in his sets of weight lifting, preparing to pose for a "contest" photo. He did five-hundred sit-ups and five-hundred leg lifts each day. And there were the basketball games.

"Have a lot of work to do yet but at 33 years old, I'm doing okay. Heck—I can still run and bang with the best of the niggers on the basketball court now. So I'm doin' okay . . . And you'll be doing okay at 35 too! I want ya to start getting active and in good shape. We both have a long haul to do. So, let's get physical and make the best of it. Ya 'Game' Di?''

''. . . Our Warden is on vacation now, but when he returns I will discuss a way for us to visit . . .''

Randy explained a code that the two of them could use in future letters. It was not a code that would require a master cryptographer to decipher. Diane was to add an extra letter to each word in any paragraph in her letters after the term "Time to Close—'' spelling out her secret messages to him. He would do the same.

It was a code that might well have accompanied an Ovaltine premium.

But Randy Woodfield was working on a far more subtle game. Diane was a most worthy adversary, and he had to be cautious as he set her up for a tremendous fall. His letters had been so full of love and support that she apparently now trusted him completely. Diane had no way of knowing that Randy could never forgive her for doubting him. She was a female, treacherous like all females. He had come up with a plan that would not only make her look like a fool, but would probably bring him a great deal of publicity, a book contract, and a movie deal.

He had proposed marriage to Diane continually, and he soon promised her that marriage would allow them a private visit together. Not only did they have their wedding to plan for, he wrote, "I'm still serious about a book you and I could write," Randy added. "But I want to contact some Hollywood people . . ."

And still, both of them wrote "NO GAMES!" while the games accelerated on each side. Diane was writing to any number of men in prison, blissfully unaware that Randy was setting her up.

He wrote to an *Oregonian* reporter, to two Oregon women he had met when they did research on a book about sex offenders, and to Anne Bradley Jaeger, Anchor-person of KEZI-TV, the ABC affiliate in Eugene. Randy announced that he would soon be marrying a very, very, famous woman prisoner who was being transferred to the Oregon Women's Correctional Center from the Eugene area. He wasn't free to give her name, but—

Diane Downs was the *only* female prisoner in Eugene who was very, very, famous. When reporters questioned her about a romance with Randy Woodfield, she smiled slightly, reddened delicately, and refused to comment.

Randy had asked her to be discreet, and Diane, a woman known for her past indiscretions, followed his instructions to the letter. After all, Randy had been in the prison system for a long time—and she counted on him to plan their wedding, to protect her in the "joint" with his wisdom.

"Today I talked to . . . my caseworker," he wrote on July 19th, "And found out we can have a pre-marrital (sic) visit just once so ya wanna try for it soon as we can arrange it? Just let me know.

"Strange as it may seem Di—your fighting back to put me in my place, and say 'I love you too' touched me very much. I'm just amazed at how we've grown thru our letters. Ya happy to have me for a loving friend? NO GAMES is my motto too. Let's enjoy all we can together. Tomorrow may never come. Ya know my meaning? . . . Want you to think of me now. Smiling?

"Say Di—would your parents think about coming to your wedding? Just curious. We can have (10) people in our party. Then we only have 1 hour for the party to have pics & marry. Then guests have to leave with my counselor & yours and come back in if they are on the reg. visiting list. So—some Thur. (a.m.) we can marry at the far end (No smoking room) for privacy. The waiting list is 3-4 months now. But we will get to visit once behind (window) to talk it over some Tuesday (a.m.) at OWCC [Oregon

Women's Correctional Facility] Women visit on Tuesdays only. And married couples get every Tues. (a.m.) to visit. Nice—huh?

"And you'll be surprised at what kinds of 'fun & games' we'll be able to have and enjoy. Just be open and follow my lead? We'll have some very close and private visits one day . . ."

Diane Downs believed him. She believed Randy even more when he discussed the color scheme of their "wedding."

"Would you mind my asking you to wear the same colors as me in our ceremony?" he wrote. "You can't wear blue jeans but could tailor a blue shirt like ours. Comments? I think we'll make a very handsome couple too. Yes?

"I've written to some newspeople for responses about our story. Will you be open to an interview there or (OWCC)? Will you share your tho'ts on all this? And our own work on contacting an Agent and Writer to help us with a book and movie? Thanks.

"What kind of flowers do you like, Di? I will provide them for us—no problem. Rings we can talk more on . . ."

The letter was signed "Love and Kisses."

With that letter in her hand, Diane Downs admitted to newspapers, and to Anne Bradley Jaeger that yes, it was true, she was going to marry Randy Woodfield—they were in love! Yes, it was all a reality. The convicted murderess, admitted ex-mistress of a dozen or more men, blushed and ducked her head as she talked of her greatest love affair.

Just as soon as Diane Downs said she wanted to marry her pen-pal lover, Randy Woodfield pounced. He shook his head and appeared mystified by Diane's statements. When reporters questioned him, Randy suggested that Mrs. Downs was more confused and upset than he had realized. No, he had no idea where she might have gotten the idea that he wanted to marry her. He was sorry, and he knew it must be embarrassing for her—but the lady was mistaken.

It was a major "Gotcha!"

He wrote to Diane on July 27th, eight days after the letter he'd sent planning their wedding, knowing certainly that she must have been fuming with frustration and disbelief. The hot letters from his cell had cooled down to ice.

"Dear Di—

"My oh my—you sure have me shaking my head and holding news conferences all day long—Why did you say anything to anyone just now? I'm really confused, Di.

"I told you I was holding all the 'Aces' and was going to sell a story of some kind to a mag. & newspaper & T.V.—but now everyone thinks we're getting married and it's caused a lot of unnecessary problems . . . Hadn't I told you about my inquirey (sic) letter to (KEZI & The Oregonian Paper)? You were to just sit tight and be 'mum' and refer *them* to *me*. It may have taken a while to find a mag. or newspaper willing to pay for all this publicity—but it could have been done . . . But now I had to say our visit to meet was just misunderstood about 'marriage plans.'

". . . I'm not playing games, just covering my tracks right now. Let's try again. I hope & pray this publicity doesn't affect your sentencing. Write me & and ask all you wish. I care Di—Randy."

It was, for all intents and purposes, the end of the great romance. Randy had rejected Diane over all the wire services, and had had a day full of press conferences doing it. She would never really forgive him.

(Diane Downs served almost three years of her life sentence at the Oregon Women's Correctional Center in Salem, but there were no private visits with Randy Woodfield. On July 11, 1987, she escaped from prison, and was re-captured eleven days later. She is now imprisoned at the Clinton Correctional Institute for Women in New Jersey.)

Randy Woodfield received his Associate Degree through the prison educational system in June, 1987. He glowered at photographers and warned them convincingly that he did not want to have his picture taken. They moved on to other, more willing graduates.

Captain Dave Bishop is now Chief of Police in Newberg, Oregon. He teaches Criminal Justice classes at the college level, and often conducts seminars on the Woodfield case for other law enforcement personnel.

Detective Dave Kominek is now a Sergeant with the Keizer, Oregon, Police Department. He has investigated a number of difficult homicide cases since 1981, but none as challenging as the I-5 killing spree. His name and expertise are familiar to Northwest lawmen—forever connected to Randy Woodfield. His initiative in establishing a network of detectives working similar unsolved cases was a model for solving serial murder/rape cases in future investigations.

Beth Wilmot left Oregon and the tragic memories behind her after her testimony was no longer needed, and moved to a faraway state. Even so, she had a recurring nightmare that haunted her dreams. "I would dream about Randy—see him standing in the room, wearing the jacket with the hood, pointing the gun at me. It would seem as though he was really there . . . and then I'd wake up—and he wasn't there at all.''

The nightmare came less and less frequently. By 1983, Beth could go months without dreaming about the man with the gun.

"And then," she says, her voice incredulous as she tells it. "I was attacked again! I wasn't doing anything but minding my own business. I left work in broad daylight—I was wearing my uniform that I wore at the cleaners where I worked. It was just a plain smock and slacks, nothing enticing or sexy. I wasn't wearing makeup. And I walk like a boy. I'm skinny, and I walk like a boy, and you know I'm always aware of what's going on around me, but this day I just wanted to get home and take my shoes off.''

Beth noticed a large man standing across the street, and, although she didn't pause to look closely, she was afraid that he was exposing himself.

"I just walked faster, and then all of a sudden he ran after me and he jumped me. He knocked me flat on my face, and started tearing at my clothes. He weighed about two hundred fifty pounds, more than twice what I weigh, and I couldn't move. I started screaming and people kept driving by as though it was perfectly normal for some guy to be lying on top of a woman who was screaming her lungs out. Finally, a family stopped and they scared him away. I just felt like, you know, why me? Why me *again?*''

But Beth Wilmot reported the assault to the police in the city where she lives now, and her attacker was arrested and convicted.

She believes the bad days are behind her now; Beth is married and has a baby. She works at a job she loves. She keeps in touch with Shari Hull's family and with Dave Kominek and his wife, Gail.

"When do you think they'll give him a parole hearing?" she asks, wondering about Woodfield. Told he might possibly become eligible for parole by 1998—if Judge Brown's fifty-year minimum sentence is ignored, she is outraged, but adamant.

"I'll be there. I'll only be thirty-nine then. I'll be there if I'm one hundred. I'm going to be around for a long, long time and they'd better let me know if they start thinking about letting him out. 'Cause I'll be there to tell them again what he did to us. It doesn't matter where I live, I'll come back to Oregon and tell them.''

She means it.

As long as Randy Woodfield is in prison, there is a danger. He may escape. He may be in the Oregon State Penitentiary so long that the public forgets about his dangerousness, allowing him to convince some parole board in the future that he is a changed man. He has done it before; he might do it again.

In the meantime, Woodfield continues his correspondence with women. Hundreds of letters going out, slick with loving promises, seductive, conniving, and obscene. And the money comes in—a dollar, two dollars, more. Locked in prison, Randy Woodfield still "rapes" women.

If Woodfield is to be tried in Shasta County, California, he would face more than loss of freedom; he would face death.

Shasta County District Attorney Steve Carlton had an agonizing decision to make in the late summer of 1983. Randy had run out of appeals in Oregon; California could extradite him for trial in the murders of Donna Eckard, thirty-seven, and her fourteen-year-old daughter, Janell, if they chose. And, if Randy was convicted, he might well go to the gas chamber.

The decision was complicated by the fact that Randy had his Life-plus-165 year sentence in Oregon, and that a pending California Supreme Court decision might cripple Carlton's case. In 1982, the California Court concluded that statements obtained from a person under hypnosis could not be used as testimony in a trial. The court was presently deciding whether that initial decision would apply retroactively to other cases.

Dave Kominek had hypnotized Beth Wilmot to help her remember details about the man who had shot her in Salem. Beth's testimony would be crucial in Shasta County because ballistics tests showed that the bullets that killed Donna Eckard and Janell Jarvis were fired from the same .32 caliber pistol used to shoot Beth and Shari Hull. If the California Supreme Court should outlaw testimony elicited by hypnosis *retroactively*, Beth would not be able to testify in the Shasta County cases: two murders, and eight sex offenses.

"The overriding factor, and the only reason to bring Woodfield down here, is to execute him," said Carlton. "(I) must consider the prospects of being successful in that ultimate goal and the cost factor in attempting to achieve it."

"This is a monstrous case, we estimated that we're looking at probably one hundred fifty witnesses, and most of them are out-of-state witnesses (from Oregon.)"

Carlton felt that a trial for Randy Woodfield would last about six months, and that it was possible that it would have to be moved to another county because of extensive pre-trial publicity.

The cost to Shasta County, not a wealthy county, would be several million dollars.

There were so many "ifs." Even if Woodfield should be tried in California, and found guilty, Carlton doubted that he would be executed. The last legal execution in California had occurred in 1967. If the death penalty *were* handed down, Randy would be housed in San Quentin. California would pay for his upkeep, and Oregon would save thousands of dollars a year.

There was another option—an option that still exists. Carlton said that he could simply take no immediate action. In theory, because there is no statute of limitation on murder, Woodfield could be prosecuted many years down the road. However, with the passage of years, the likelihood of his facing a jury in California would grow dimmer.

Local attorneys tended to agree with Steve Carlton that it would be folly to try Woodfield in Shasta County. Shasta County Public Defender Frank O'Connor, a former deputy district attorney, said, "I wouldn't do it, period. He's never going to get out of prison, and it's a very expensive case."

Oregon State Assistant Attorney General Scott McAlister said he would be "mildly surprised" if Carlton should decide to prosecute Randy. "If I were in Carlton's position, I probably would not do it. But I'd like to encourage you (Shasta County) to do it anyway."

Shasta County Supervisor Don Maddox said he would support Carlton whatever he decided, but he admitted concern. "The thought of the fiscal impact of such a trial will undoubtedly keep me awake many nights. It could conceivably be devastating on top of other financial setbacks we are attempting to overcome . . ."

D.A. Steve Carlton met with family members of those who had been attacked or killed. What a dilemma it was. How do you tell a man whose wife and stepdaughter have been savaged by a trolling monster that there isn't enough money in the county to seek justice?

In essence, Randy Woodfield would be getting what so many detectives had feared—so many crimes for the price of a few if he never had to face a California trial.

On a Wednesday in September, 1983, Steve Carlton faced the press at a conference in the county courthouse in Redding. He would not be extraditing Randall Woodfield to stand trial for the murders of Donna Eckard and Janell Jarvis.

"I am satisfied after examining all material factors that this is the only responsible course of action. Public safety is not affected by this decision. I am convinced after meeting with the entire Oregon parole board that Woodfield will *never be released from prison*."

Carlton could not saddle Shasta County with a two-to three-million-dollar trial for a man who was serving life plus one hundred sixty-five years in another state.

Steve Carlton had the support of a vast number of people, but the decision was probably the most difficult he would ever have to make. Donna Eckard's widower, Redding Fire Department Lieutenant Steve Eckard, found no fault with Carlton. "I understand why he did it," Eckard said, adding that he was not displeased with the District Attorney.

Donna Eckard's father, Daryl Manville, concurred, "(He) made the decision for good reasons. I'm not dissatisfied. I have no quarrel with his decision, in other words."

Without Beth Wilmot's testimony, Shasta County might have lost the case, and the county might have gone bankrupt as well.

But, still . . .

The world goes on. Steve Eckard remains in Redding, serving the public in the city's fire department.

Beth Wilmot's nightmares rarely come now, but she still fears the dark.

There is one nightmare, however, that haunts anyone who ever met Randy Woodfield when he was in the grip of his compulsive deadly prowls. A nightmare that walks with the victims and the survivors and also with the detectives and the prosecutors and the judges.

What if the system should fail, as it has so many times before? What if Woodfield gets out—despite Judge Clarke Brown's efforts, despite D.A. Steve Carlton's assurances? What then?

One quote about Randy comes back at odd times, late at night, or on a winter Sunday evening in the rain. Dana Middleton, now co-host of her own ABC talk show in Seattle, was a young television reporter in Shasta County in 1981. She covered the murders of Donna Eckard and Janell Jarvis; she pored over police reports on similar cases in the Northwest. And Dana Middleton found herself, finally, in the same room with Woodfield. He was surrounded by detectives, but even so . . .

She controls an involuntary shiver as she recalls that night. "The first time I ever saw him, I noticed he was quite good-looking. But then he turned around and looked at me and I saw his eyes. They were flat. Dead eyes. Shark's eyes. It was exactly like looking into a shark's eyes. There was no emotion there at all, no compassion, just emptiness. I've never seen eyes like that in a human being, never before and never since."